Handbook of Business and Financial Ratios

Handbook of Business and Financial Ratios

Michael R. Tyran

Revised and adapted for publication in the United Kingdom
by Martin Ward

Woodhead-Faulkner

New York   London   Toronto   Sydney   Tokyo   Singapore

Original English language version published in 1986 by
Prentice-Hall Inc.
Englewood Cliffs, NJ, USA

First published in Great Britain 1992 by
Woodhead-Faulkner
Campus 400, Maylands Avenue
Hemel Hempstead
Hertfordshire, HP2 7EZ
A division of
Simon & Schuster International Group

Typeset in 10/12pt Times
by Hands Fotoset, Leicester

Printed and bound in Great Britain at the University Press, Cambridge

British Library Cataloguing in Publication Data

A catalogue record for this book is available from the British Library
ISBN 0-85941-890-1
ISBN 0-85941-795-6 pbk

2   3   4   5   96   95   94   93

Designed by Lesley Stewart

*To my daughter Trisha, her husband Stephen
and son, Seth Shrider*

CONTENTS

3   How to use direct cost and D&A expenditure ratios to avoid diluting profits   57

4   How to monitor and control those elusive overhead costs   82

WHAT THIS BOOK WILL DO FOR YOU

The Handbook of Business and Financial Ratios presents numerous ratios that represent useful and important guidelines in assessing, interpreting, and planning financial data to meet the objectives of managing a business entity more effectively.

There is no 'theory' in this book; it shows you, step by step, how to use ratios as a prime tool in isolating, identifying, and highlighting operating performance and financial position events. The ratios will enable you rapidly to troubleshoot specific areas that need special attention. With the help of this handbook, internal and external data are more quickly and accurately interpreted, enabling your management to make more discerning and profitable decisions.

This handbook is complete with fifty models that illustrate how ratios are used for analysis and comparison by period, data element, account description, item variance, and so on by management. It is full of formulae and examples showing you how to make calculations, and further outlines various types of ratios, showing their use, both in common and special situations.

Here are some of the many ways ratio analysis and this handbook will help you:

- It isolates abnormal or changing situations in operational and financial activities that require management's attention and action.
- It gives you a basis for investigating and interpreting specific changes in data relationships. These data could indicate possible problem situations or undesirable trends.
- It logically arranges data so that you can rapidly assimilate and interpret the information in terms of the organization's objectives and planning goals.
- It allows you to see how the company is perceived by outsiders influencing the cost of capital, price–earnings ratio, and bond ratings.
- It visually plots the analysis so that significant variations and data results are not obscured.
- It offers suggestions for improving management's decision making in the areas of profitability, financial stability, liquidity, return on investment, and solvency.
- It can help you quickly review quantitative and varied information in a manner that is easy to understand.

- It helps you interpret and define significant relationships that exist among relevant financial statements at a given point in time over varying time periods.
- It describes the significance of individual ratios as they apply to the control of direct and indirect costs, turnover rates of stock, debtors, cash and capital employed, and allows a realistic assessment and maintenance of an adequate capital structure for operational stability and growth.
- It is of specific interest to management who may be concerned with ratios relevant to efficient performance at competitive costs, profitability, growth patterns, managing assets and liabilities, and planning and achieving financial objectives.
- It can be of interest to creditors who have a major concern in an organization's ratios pertinent to their solvency or financial gearing, liquidity, and ability to pay debt obligations on schedule.
- It can serve as an important reference guide to investors who are concerned with management's operating performance, the organization's financial stability, and return on investment.

Each chapter in the book provides specific information needed to interpret the ratio, applications highlighting how and when to use these ratios, their advantages and disadvantages, and pitfalls to avoid in their utilization. Throughout the book, you will find:

- *Step-by-step illustrations and detailed procedures* that show how to calculate and more effectively use important ratios in analysing past performance results, making industry comparisons, and formulating valid future objectives.
- *Ratio guidelines* for isolating problem situations for immediate corrective action and precautionary indicators in establishing future goals.
- *Chapter highlights* as a preface to each chapter to acquaint you with its specific contents and objectives.
- *Illustrative ratio formulae* as examples of ratio calculations and use that can help save time when it comes to applying the ratios to a specific situation.
- *Graphic and numerical charts* to illustrate relevant statistical techniques and processes involved in ratio analysis.
- *Comparative worksheet data* for the statement of financial position indicating the relationship and importance of each line item to the relevant total assets and total liabilities and equity.
- *Ratio development worksheets* for calculating processes, their use and objectivity in ratio analysis.
- *System design-processing flow charts* that describe computerized procedures for ratio analysis. These flow charts present the logic for establishing relevant mechanical systems.
- *Variable budget scattergraph diagrams* for assessing operating performance and establishing control procedures.

- *Trend-line computations and graphics* for developing future operating/ financial prospects that are likely to occur in the business environment.

In review, this handbook segments financial ratio analysis into these critical areas:

tools for financial analysis to assess and plan an organization's financial and operational activities;

operational ratios to measure, plan, and control performance efficiency;

direct cost, distribution costs and administration expenses to assess, control and plan costs;

expense ratios to monitor, control, and budget overhead expenses;

profitability ratios to gauge a firm's operational success;

industry comparison ratios to assess and interpret data for planning, controlling and maintaining a competitive operational effectiveness;

financial position reporting to evaluate an organization's financial status and progress;

cash flow planning to support operational activities, minimize problem areas, and achieve a favourable cash flow position;

statistical techniques to analyse results from operating events and achieve realistic financial objectives;

investment analysis ratios to improve equity capital position for sustaining operational growth.

As a time saver, analytical tool, and troubleshooter the *Handbook of Business and Financial Ratios* will serve you well by helping you recognize changes and problem situations and highlight implications for management decisions and action.

Michael R. Tyran

The models throughout this book are provided to:

- *Illustrate* the calculation processes for using statistical tools and financial operations analysis and planning;
- *Express* data relationships among relevant reporting items for operating trend analysis, interpretation, and measurement;
- *Demonstrate* the use of significant ratios in making similar industry comparisons, sources of the information, and ratio objectives and assessment;
- *Compare* time periods and their vertical/horizontal ratio analysis in terms of profitability, liquidity, operating efficiency, working capital, and debt-paying capability;
- *Present* data correlation comparisons and displays among pertinent financial items such as purchases, creditors and payments and sales, debtors and receipts, and cash flow;
- *Highlight* the importance of stock and debtor turnover ratios as well as the ageing process in the planning cycle.
- *Illustrate visually* an assessment of changes to shareholders' equity between periods and describe the usefulness of this procedure in financial analysis and management actions;
- *Graphically display* computerized accounting system flow charts and the development of information for ratio and statistical analyses such as gross profit, overhead expenses, direct costs, manpower, indirect to direct labour, and performance results;
- *Provide* cost–volume–profit relationship charts and various aspects of break-even principles and analysis for operating and financial decisions;
- *Illustrate* the development and application of the profitgraph and capital-graph techniques as an aid to data assessment and financial projections;
- *Highlight* the evaluation of an organization's capital structure and provide analytical measurement ratios for loans and bonds, preference and ordinary shares.

MODELS

ADAPTER'S PREFACE

This book has been adapted for the UK market to take into account differences between US and UK taxation, terminology and accounting standards.

The main thrust of the book is to enable potential and existing financial directors, accountants and other executives to improve company performance through analysing available information, highlighting underperformance and then taking the appropriate action. If you are approaching ratio analysis for the first time it is important to realize the advantages that an internal analyst possesses over his external counterpart.

Internal information is either readily available or can be assembled if required. An external analyst of UK accounts has only published data to work with. Published data are regulated by the Government through the Companies Acts, by the Financial Reporting Council through the issue of Financial Reporting Standards, and by the London Stock Exchange where companies are listed thereon.

Under the provisions of the Companies Act 1989 small- and medium-sized companies (defined in the Act) are exempt from some of the accounting requirements and consequently may provide only the barest of information. Companies listed on the Stock Exchange provide more detail but, as the spate of company collapses in the early 1990s testifies, the information is often difficult to interpret and frequently criticized for 'creative accounting' techniques, designed for the most part to present a better picture than some would judge to be the case. I bring this to your attention so that you remain constantly on guard for new accounting standards and proposals (called exposure drafts) which may affect the way in which some of the ratios are calculated, and for media and academic comment on creative activities. New regulations are frequently issued which aim to bring about uniformity in the presentation of information and deal with 'innovative' financial instruments designed for the flexibility required by today's businesses.

I Tools for financial analysis and planning operations

Chapter highlights

Financial reports are of interest to users both internal and external to a business organization. Without adequate analysis, however, these reports may not be fully useful to their recipients. Statistical analysis therefore plays a vital role in the financial and business environments.

After explaining the vital role of statistical analysis, this chapter presents a step-by-step method for the collection, preparation, analysis, interpretation, and presentation of statistical data.

Most of the chapter takes you through the definitions and formulae that you need to calculate the various types of arithmetic averages, deviation analyses, and time series trends. You will find simple definitions, clear examples, and listings of advantages and disadvantages.

The chapter concludes by focusing on the uses and potential misuses of statistical ratios in financial analysis. You will also be made aware of the cautions necessary for making your presentation and interpretation of the data validity and usefulness.

For periodic and summary reporting, the primary tools of a business entity are its financial statements. Outside the business, financial information is made available to shareholders, creditors, credit agencies, government, the Stock Exchange and other users who are involved in the firm's financial status and progress. Reports for external use typically include a profit and loss statement, balance sheet, cash flow statement and possible statements of retained earnings and capitalization. Half-yearly or yearly periods are generally compared in these reports.

By comparison, the reports for use within an organization contain much more detailed and varied data on specific performance results, organizational progress, financial position, and problem situations. This information is used for in-depth analysis, interpretation, control, decision making, and planning.

The vital role of statistical analysis in the business environment

The statistical analysis approach plays a vital role in the everyday financial environment. This important technique enables a business to:

- Handle its growth, operational complexities, and information needs.
- Compete in the marketplace to achieve its sales goals, control costs, generate sources of capital, and increase profitability.
- Lay down reliable guidelines for decision making.
- Aggressively pursue operational growth and financial stability.
- Establish the basic criteria for sound and achievable operational objectives – and control performance within the plan's limits.
- Evaluate and interpret the accomplishment of performance goals.
- Cope with the increasing intervention of government in the business economy, with its attendant influence on operations.
- Introduce more and better scientific methods into the operation and administration of the business.

For the business to enjoy these benefits, you the financial manager must use statistical analysis selectively to assemble, analyse, interpret, and present the relevant quantitative data. Specifically, you must:

- Collect, assemble, and collate the data.
- Classify the data appropriately and condense them into a related data series.
- Present the resultant information in a comprehensive form – text, tables, graphics, or some combination of the three – to meet the user's particular requirements.
- Analyse and interpret the reported data.

As you can see, the statistical approach is normally characterized as objective in nature. As a scientific tool, it falls into the realm of classification. The technique applies not only to data that can be reduced to quantitative form, but it can accommodate large masses of specific data items. Reliable data, therefore, must always be utilized.

This is not to say that your subjective interpretation will not affect results. To understand, interpret, and assess the quantitative results properly, you often have to supplement reports with qualitative data.

What to do with the primary data

Before all else, you must have reliable data to work with. Most businesses, in their transaction documentation, collect the data needed for use in the statistical approach. remember, however, that the technique assumes that the data are reliable.

One the data are on hand and shown to be reliable, you must take the following steps:

Steps in handling primary data

1. Classify the data.
2. Condense and summarize them.
3. Correlate them.

Classification

First, categorize the data into expense, cost, and general ledger accounts as delineated in your firm's chart of accounts. This step ensures reliability and consistency in classification and summation. Initially, some of the data may have been collected, classified, and reported by subaccounts that are subservient to the prime or control accounts.

Condensation and summation

Total the pertinent subaccount data for prime or control account summations that are reported in the appropriate registers or ledgers. Data from these summary sources are then used to prepare a *trial balance*, which represents an aggregate debit and credit summation of all transactions during a given period. Prior-period ending balances are considered, if appropriate, in the development of balance sheet values. Operation data (sales, costs, and the like) are reported for both the current period and year to date.

Correlation

After summarizing the financial data into the trial balance from the updated general ledger, structure the information to meet the reporting requirements of the financial statements.

When analysing data over time periods, your objective is to isolate, wherever possible, recurring downward trends. In other words, concern yourself with such influencing factors as seasonal trading irregularities (fluctuations in sales volume and cost, along with their possible long-term tendencies), the need for borrowing due to cash flow problems, delays in debt collection, changes in work flow scheduling, and so on.

Applying statistical analysis to financial data

Inasmuch as the statistical approach is concerned with data relationships and variations, it entails a familiarity with various statistical applications. The objectives and reasoning of the technique are expressed in terms of 'averages', 'estimates', and 'probabilities'. In this chapter, we will look at some of the common statistical applications to financial data analysis and assessment. In particular, you will see how to use

- averaging;
- deviation analyses;
- time series trends (including the least squares method);
- ratios.

How to employ data series averaging

An average represents a measure for 'central tendency' – that is, a typical value around which other figures congregate or which divides their number in half. An average describes a whole series of figures involving magnitudes of the same data set; it represents an overall value. This data measurement permits you to compare either individual items in the grouping or different series of figures with regard to the central tendencies.

There are different types of averages, each with its own particular characteristics. The four most common averages include the

- arithmetic mean;
- median;
- mode;
- geometric mean.

Calculating the arithmetic mean ($\overline{X}$)

The *mean* is the resultant quotient when the sum of all the items in the series is divided by the number of items. This process is algebraically expressed as:

The mean formula

$$\overline{X} = \frac{\Sigma X}{N}$$

where $\overline{X}$ = the mean
ΣX = the total of the item values
N = number of items in the series

EXAMPLE
Here is how an arithmetic mean is developed for sales volume:

Period	Period sales (in £000s)
1	520
2	530
3	525
4	535
	2110

$$\overline{X} = \frac{2110}{4}$$
$$= 527.50$$

Another approach to finding the mean is the *deviation method*, which is based on the selection of an arbitrary midpoint value. This method yields what is called an *estimated mean*, and the formula is as follows:

The estimated mean formula

$$\overline{X} = X_0 + \frac{\Sigma(fd)}{N} \cdot c$$

where X_0 = the assumed mean.
$\Sigma(fd)$ = the sum of the frequency deviations.
N = the frequency.

The average can then be calculated by means of the above formula.

EXAMPLE

What is the average ratio of current assets to current liabilities, given the following information? The estimated mean, in this case, is 3.00. Since the combined sum of the deviations equals zero, the average ratio is a determinable value.

Ratios (class interval)	Midpoint (MP)	Number of organizations' frequency	Deviation*	Frequency deviation
0–1.99	1	20	− 2	− 40
2–3.99	2	50	− 1	− 50
3–4.99 →	3	40	0	0
4–5.99	4	30	+ 1	30
Totals		140		− 60

*Midpoint differences from an estimated mean of 3 (arbitrary starting point).

$$\overline{Z} = \frac{\Sigma(fd)}{N}$$

$$\frac{-60}{140} = -0.43$$

$$\overline{X} = \overline{Z} + \frac{\Sigma(fd)}{N}$$

$$\overline{X} = 3.00 - 0.43 = 2.57 \text{ (average ratio)}$$

The *advantages* of this method are as follows:

1. It is the most commonly used and recognized.
2. It is easily understood.

3. The computation is simple.
4. Only the total values and number of items are necessary for the computation.
5. The procedure may be treated algebraically.

The *prime disadvantage* is that the arithmetic mean is determined by every item included in the distribution series and is affected by extreme values in the series. The resultant value may therefore be distorted and not representative.

This method can be used in analysing sales, overhead expenses, cash, debtors, and creditors, among other types of accounting data.

Calculating the median

Whereas the arithmetic mean is a *calculated* average, the median is a *position* average. It refers to the location of a value in a series. The median represents the value of the middle item when the items are arranged according to their relative sizes or magnitudes. As the average of position, the median average is referred to as *probable value* because the selected value may be located above or below the median value. The sum of the deviations about the median will be less than the total about any other point.

While the median divides the distribution into two parts, quartiles divide it into four parts and deciles divide it into ten parts. These position averages make possible a more detailed analysis of a distribution.

To determine the median for *ungrouped data* with an *odd number* of data sets:

1. Make an array of the primary data arranged by magnitude.
2. Count the items and select the middle one.
3. Evaluate the middle item or *median*.

If the array has an *even number* of items, there is no actual value in the middle of the series. For example, if a series contains 12 items, the median position is 6.5, or the value between items 6 and 7.

The median formula
The median formula is:

$$\overline{X} = l_1 + \left(\frac{\frac{N}{2} - \Sigma f_1}{f\,\text{med}} \right) i$$

where $\overline{X}$ = median

l_1 = lower limit of median class

Σf_1 = sum of all frequency cumulations before entering the median class

$f\,\text{med}$ = frequency in median class

i = size of class interval

N = number of organizations

EXAMPLE

Calculate the sales median for the following organizations:

Sales (in £000s)	Number of organizations involved	Cumulative frequencies
0–199.0	40	40
200.0–299.0	60	100
300.0–399.0	100	200
400.0–499.0 ←	100	300
500.0–599.0	100	400
600.0 and over	80	480
Median class	480	

To solve the equation:

$$\overline{X} = 400 + \left(\frac{\frac{480 - 200}{2}}{100} \right) \times 100$$

$$= 400 + \left(\frac{40}{100} \right) \times 100$$

$$= 400 + 40 \text{ or } 440.0 \text{ median sales}$$

where N = 480 organizations
l_1 = 400.0
Σf = 200
f med = 100
i = 100

The *advantages* of the median average are:

1. It is easily calculated.
2. It is not distorted in value by unusual items.
3. The calculation is possible even when distribution is open-ended.
4. It is more typical of a data series due to its independence of unusual values.

The *disadvantages* of the median approach are:

1. It is not as common or as familiar as the arithmetic mean.
2. Items must be arranged according to magnitude before the median can be computed.
3. It has larger standard and probable errors than the arithmetic mean.
4. It cannot be manipulated algebraically.

Using the mode

The *mode* represents the value that occurs most frequently in a data series; it assumes that enough data items are available for a smooth distribution. If a frequency distribution is smooth or *ideal*, the *modal value* corresponds to the valiue of the maximum point of the distribution; it is the value in a series that is most likely to occur. The *midpoint* of a modal class may not be used as the value of the mode since its value will change if the size of the class interval is changed.

The modal formula
The modal can be calculated as follows:

$$\overline{X} = l_1 + \frac{\Delta_1}{\Delta_1 + \Delta_2} \, i$$

where $\overline{X}$ = the modal value
   l_1 = the lower limit of class
   Δ_1 = difference between frequencies in modal class
   Δ_2 = the difference between frequencies in the modal class and the *postmodal* class
   i = the size of the class interval

EXAMPLE
Calculate the mode for profit versus sales:

Period profit £ (class)	Sales volume (in £000s)
2000–2500	100.0
3000–3500	120.0
3000–3500	150.0
2500–3000	130.0
2200–2700	100.0

$$\text{Modal value} = 3000 + \left(\frac{30.0}{30.0 + 20.0} \right) 500$$
$$= 300 + (3/5 \times 500)$$
$$= 3000 + 300 = 3300$$
$$\text{pounds profit average}$$

where l_1 = £3000
   Δ_1 = 150.0 − 120.0 = 30.0
   Δ_2 = 150.0 − 130.0 = 20.0
   i = 500

The *advantages* of mode are that:

1. As an average of position, its value is entirely independent of extreme values.
2. It is the most typical and therefore the most descriptive of averages.
3. The mode is simple to approximate by observation with a small number of data items.

The *disadvantages* include:

1. The mode can only be approximated when limited data are available.
2. Its significance is limited with a large number of values.

Using the geometric mean

This type of mean is used primarily for *averaging ratios* and computing average rates of increase or decrease among data sets. The logarithm of the geometric mean is equal to the average of the data items' logarithms. The geometric mean is a calculated value that depends on the sizes of all the values. It is therefore less affected by extreme items than the arithmetic mean. The formula is:

The geometric mean formula

$$Gm = \sqrt{x_1.x_2.x_3...x_n} \text{ (product of } x)$$

EXAMPLE

In 19X3, one plant increased its sales volume by 40 per cent as compared to another plant's increase during the same period. Estimate the *average percentage increase* in 19X3 as compared to 19X2. For the first plant, sales in 19X3 over 19X2 are 140 per cent; for the second plant, they are 150 per cent. If equal importance is give to each plant irrespective of the absolute sales volume figures, then the geometric mean is used.

$$Gm = \sqrt{140\% \cdot 150\%}$$
$$= \sqrt{21,000\%}$$
$$= 144.9\% \text{ or an average increase of } 44.9\%$$

The *advantages* of the geometric mean are:

1. It is a more typical average than the arithmetic mean.
2. It can be manipulated algebraically.

The prime *disadvantages* are:

1. It is not widely known or used.
2. It is relatively more difficult to compute.
3. The average layperson does not easily understand the principles involved.

Applying the various types of averaging

Let us summarize what we know about averages:

- Whereas the arithmetic mean is a computed average, the median and the mode are positional averages.
- As a computed average, the mean cannot be determined graphically.
- In a symmetrical frequency distribution, the mean, median, and mode are located at the same point.

- Extreme values in a data series affect the usefulness of the mean average but not that of the median or mode.
- Varying class intervals usually make the mean unreliable but do not affect the median.
- The mean average can be combined, but not the median or mode.
- The mean average can be obtained from primary data, but the median and mode cannot be determined without an array or frequency distribution.

Each averaging method has its own usefulness in statistical analysis. Your selection of the appropriate method depends on:

- the quality of data you have and how they are distributed;
- how the data are classified;
- the type of problem you are trying to solve.

How to use deviation analysis

Calculating mean deviation

Graphically, the data points in a series are scattered, or dispersed, around the arithmetic mean or median. The measure of dispersion – how far a point is from that point – is the *mean deviation*, or the average of the deviations of the points from the mean or median. The mean deviation (dispersion) range can be computed about either the arithmetic mean or the median because it depends on every value in the series.

To determine the mean deviation of a data series, take the average of data points and divide it into the total deviation value: the smaller the average deviation about the point, then the smaller the scatter, or dispersion, of the values. Since the sum of the deviations about the arithmetic mean is zero, ignore signs in determining the average.

EXAMPLE
Compute the mean deviation from monthly sales volume.

Monthly periods	Sales volume (in £000s)	Deviation from monthly average (£000s)
January	500.0	7.25
February	496.0	11.25
March	508.0	0.75
April	510.0	2.75
May	512.0	4.75
June	507.0	0.25
July	515.0	7.75
August	510.0	2.75
Totals	4058.0	37.50

Calculation of average volume:

$$\frac{£4058}{8 \text{ months}} = £507.25 \text{ average volume}$$

Each entry in the right-hand column reflects the difference between the actual volume for the month and the average for eight months. For example:

7.25 → 500.0 and 507.25
11.25 → 496.0 and 507.25

Remember, signs are ignored.

Calculation of mean deviation:

$$\frac{£37.50}{£507.25} = 0.074 \text{ or } £74 \text{ mean deviation}$$

The deviation of sales by period averaged £74, a very small dispersion or scatter among periods.

The same process of analysis can be applied to cash flow, debtors, creditors, costs, and the like.

Determining standard deviation

The *standard deviation* is a special kind of average deviation from the mean. It is computed by taking the quadratic mean of deviations from arithmetic mean of the values (root mean square of the deviations from the arithmetic mean). The computation (long method) formula is:

The standard deviation formula

$$\sigma = \sqrt{\frac{\Sigma(x^2)}{N}}$$

σ = the standard deviation
x = the deviations from the arithmetic mean
N = the total number of data sets or items

A more convenient (short method) calculation formula for ungrouped data is:

The short method formula

$$\sigma = \sqrt{\frac{\Sigma X^2}{N} - \left(\frac{\Sigma X}{N}\right)^2}$$

By the long method, the computation for ungrouped data is as follows:

- Compute the difference between each actual value and the arithmetic mean.
- Square the resultant values and calculate the average of the squares.
- Find the square root of the resultant value or total.

EXAMPLE

Let us illustrate the short and long methods for calculating the standard deviation for period net income.

Period	Net income (in £000s)	Deviations from average	Net income (squared in £000s)	Deviations squared
	X	x	X^2	x^2
1	25	−3	625	9
2	28	—	784	—
3	29	+1	841	1
4	26	−2	676	4
5	29	+1	841	1
6	31	+3	961	9
	$168 \div 6 = 28$		4728	24

Long method formula:

$$\sigma = \sqrt{\frac{\Sigma x^2}{N}}$$

$$= \sqrt{\frac{24}{6}}$$

$$= \sqrt{4}$$

$= 2$ or £2000 standard deviation

Short method formula:

$$\sigma = \sqrt{\frac{\Sigma X^2}{N} - \left(\frac{\Sigma X}{N}\right)^2}$$

$$= \sqrt{\frac{4728}{6} - \left(\frac{168}{6}\right)^2}$$

$$= \sqrt{788 - (28)^2}$$

$$= \sqrt{788 - 784}$$

$$= \sqrt{4}$$

$= 2$ or £2000 standard deviation

The uses of mean and standard deviations

Deviations, or variations, indicate how well an average represents the data. Measures of variation therefore supplement your description of the data. Variations can be measured on an absolute basis (mean deviation) or on a relative basis (standard deviation). Both methods, however, are based on the deviation of each item in a data series from an average. In the average or mean deviation, the mean of the deviation is taken irrespective of sign (+ or −), but in the standard deviation the square root of the mean of the squared deviations is used.

The standard deviation is the more important measure in absolute variation or dispersion. You can analyse the normal curve in terms of standard deviation and apply these findings to data series tending towards normality. This method is usually employed in sampling and correlation techniques. Inasmuch as the value of every item in the data series affects the standard deviation, this method places greater emphasis on extremes than does mean deviation. The reason is that, in the calculation of the standard deviation, all values are squared.

How to put time series trend analysis to work

A *time series* is a sequential arrangement of selected statistical data according to their occurrence in time. The objective of time series trend analysis is to measure the variation of a data set about the measures of central tendency, typically for the purpose of data comparisons. Comparisons may be made with comparable organizations in the same industry or related overall industrial averages. Current data may be compared with past data in the same series, such as sales volume or product costs. Using this approach, you can generally project what can be expected in the future.

Projecting the time series can be classified as *statistical forecasting*. Time series analysis is therefore very important to analysts who apply statistics to business activity and economics. An economy's dynamic nature makes the time factor a vital element in analysing sales, product costs, income, production, and so on. A time series represents economic data moving through time, and its analysis provides the basis for reviewing the statistics in motion.

The factors to be taken into account in time series analysis are:

- trend;
- seasonal variation;
- cyclical changes;
- irregular data series fluctuations.

Things to watch for in the series analysis

A *trend* is a long-term movement, either upward or downward. It may develop in production, sales, costs, and other areas of a business. Time series trends can be attributed to a number of factors, such as the introduction of mass production, technological changes, variations in population growth, development of new products, revisions in product production mix, war, inflation, and so on.

Seasonal variations represent period movements that occur at regular time intervals, particularly during the calendar year. For example, consumer expenditures in retail stores increase at Christmas and Easter, and costs for utilities go up during the winter season. Similarly, employment fluctuates during the year in certain industries, such as agriculture. In essence, the two major causes for seasonal variations are: weather changes (winter, summer) and customs (holidays, personal habits).

Cyclical variations are usually influenced by prosperity, recession, and depression. In periods of prosperity, sales, production, income, and employment are accelerated, whereas the opposite effect is predominant in periods of depression. The cycles of economic activity show no regularity with respect to their occurrence or duration. History has shown that predicting future cycles with any degree of accepted accuracy is extremely difficult, if not impossible.

Irregular variations represent movements with no apparent pattern or regularity. Unlike cyclical economic conditions, irregular variations, such as strikes, floods, fires, wars, and the like, may occur once or a number of times. Their effects may last for a day, two weeks, two months, or much longer. Both the occurrence and the duration of this type of variation are very difficult to predict.

Steps in the preliminary data series review

For the sake of *realistic measurement*, you must take certain preliminary steps to ensure the relative comparability of the time series data. The point of preliminary review is to put data on a comparable basis before the actual analysis. Adjustments may be required due to

- variations in the time periods;
- price changes or units sold;
- product mix;
- industrial comparisons.

Important adjustments in data for realistic assessment

Time period. Production and sales volume may vary among periods due to the different number of working days in a given period (February or 'vacation' months versus months with no holidays). To eliminate this problem, divide production and sales volumes by the number of working days, so that the data are comparable for activity analysis purposes. Do the same for debtor and creditor balances, as well as for other financial data to be analysed and measured.

In some organizations, a quarter consists of two four-week periods and one five-week period for accumulating and reporting purposes. In such cases, the four- and five-week periods are segregated and separately analysed. Other organizations split the year into thirteen equal periods.

Price and unit changes. The sales price is generally calculated by multiplying product sales quantities by price per unit. In the case of services, the sales value may be a lump sum or a cost rate per hour. Because units and prices change from time to time, you cannot make valid sales comparisons unless you make adjustments for price changes. To do so, divide the sales by the relevant unit price for the period(s). This gives you the actual units sold, because the unit quantities must be equal to the relevant sales divided by the appropriate price. If more than one product is involved, perform a separate calculation for each.

Product mix. A product mix entails different prices, quantities, and marginal or gross profits. To analyse the individual contribution and progress status of specific product data in the organization's overall operations, you have to segregate them. Further, this information must be known for future planning purposes.

Related industry comparisons. When making reliable and related inter-industry comparisons, you must know the composition and objective of what you are comparing. Ratios can play a significant role in these comparisons. For example, who is to say that stocks should always be maintained at an industry average? For some organizations, the average may be too high or too low, depending on their requirements. The same logic applies to comparing days of sales in debtors, bad debt average, capital asset requirements, working capital, extent of liability commitments, and the like with industrial averages.

These comparisons are often healthy and productive because they indicate that a problem might exist. You have an indication that a situation should be thoroughly reviewed and evaluated, perhaps with some sort of corrective action taken.

Making your analysis easy to grasp

To make your time series analysis easy for others to understand, plot the comparable data on a graph, a technique utilized by many organizations. A graph makes trends and developments in a data series immediately visible. Arithmetic or semilogarithmic plotting may be appropriate. A graphic display may also present the basis and method for the actual conducting of a time series analysis.

Why trend analysis is used

If you were to graph primary unanalysed data, your presentation would be at best superficial. With trend analysis, you can determine the direction of a specific data series – growth or decline. You can further establish the

- intensity of the growth or decline
- consistency of the trend
- basic causes for the directional trend or data fluctuations.

In assessing trends, you can also make meaningful comparisons with organizations in the same industry, the general industrial economy, gross national product, population, and so on.

Comparing trend determination methods

Because trend determination methods are predicated on estimates rather than on absolute precision, a trend is more realistically determined over a long time span. The short-term analysis may not be significant.

The continuation of past trends may provide an invaluable insight into future expectations, which aids in assessing and planning an organization's operations. The process of *forecasting*, or extending the trend into the future, is generally known as *extrapolation* (the projection of known values). This process can be accomplished by

- inspection or estimate (the freehand method)
- calculation (semi-averaging, moving average, and least-squares methods).

Inspection or freehand method. After plotting the data points on a graph, you can draw a line indicating the trend of data. This line reflects a very subjective decision since its direction depends on what the analyst perceives as the trend. In some instances, the line can be accurate if the data series trend is reasonably constant or the statistician is experienced and knowledgeable in the background of the data series. Model 1.1 presents a simplified illustration of this method.

MODEL 1.1. A simple example of a sales trend line by inspection (in £000s)

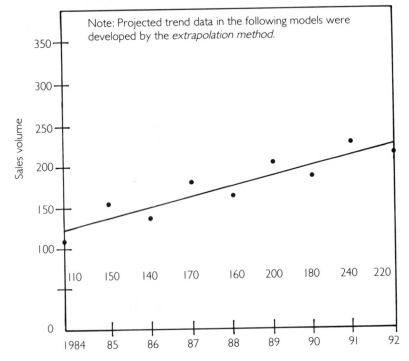

Note: Projected trend data in the following models were developed by the *extrapolation method.*

The *advantages* of this method are:

1. It is simple to accomplish.
2. It may be more representative and logical than a line drawn based on a mathematical equation.

The *disadvantages* include the fact that the results may vary among statisticians. Considerable practice and experience are required to make a realistic and representative trend line fit.

Semi-averaging process. In this method, you segregate the time series data into two equal parts and calculate the arithmetic mean for each part of the series. Plot two points and draw a connecting line that represents the trend.

The *advantages* of this method are its simplicity and its totally objective results.

The *disadvantages* are:

1. The arithmetic mean, which is strongly influenced by extreme values, is used to locate the trend line.
2. This approach is limited primarily to fitting straight line trends.

Moving average procedure. You can use this procedure not only for establishing a trend line but also in connection with seasonal, cyclical, and irregular variations. This method tends to eliminate any type of fluctuations by smoothing them out and removing their influence.

To calculate the moving average, take a series of successive periods in which the first item in each group averaged is dropped and the next item in the series is included in the averaging process.

As shown in Model 1.2, no trend moving average (the dashed line) is reflected for the first and last periods. As viewed on the graph, the trend line is smoothed out in comparison to the line for the original plotted data.

The *advantages* of the moving average are:

1. Only simple computations are involved.
2. It may adequately replace the fitting of complex mathematical curves.

The *disadvantages* of the method are:

1. It cannot be brought up to date because the last point in the trend must occur several years (or periods) before the end of the data series. For example, a five-year moving average ends three years before the end of the data.
2. The moving average is computed by the use of the arithmetic mean, which is affected by extreme values.
3. The trend concept involves the presumption of a smooth growth or decline – the moving average is generally irregular in appearance.

MODEL 1.2. Demonstration of the moving average procedure

Sales volume trend computation using a 3-year moving average

Year	Sales volume (in £000s)	3-year moving total	3-year moving average
1985	150	—	—
1986	160	480	160
1987	170	490	163
1988	160	510	170
1989	180	530	177
1990	190	570	190
1991	200	580	193
1992	190	590	196
1993	200	—	—

Trend line graphic display (in £000s)

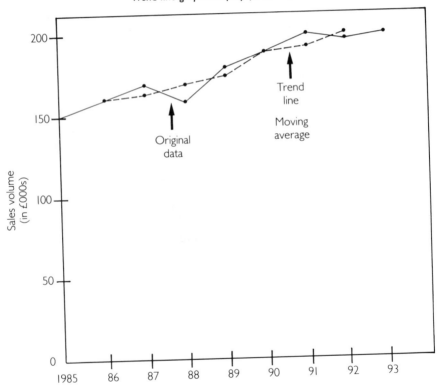

Least squares approach. This method aids in determining the *line of best fit* to a series of values that describes the trend of the data sets. This method can also be employed in fitting curvilinear trends. If the trend is assumed to be a straight line, the trend line will be represented by the formula $Y = a + bX$. In this formula, the a and b values must be determined.

The prime logic of least squares is that the line of best fit is a line about which the sum of the squares of the deviations will be minimal. The deviations represent the differences or variances between the trend line (or theoretical) data and the actual values.

To determine the least squares line for a given data series, you must use a set of normal equations:

The least squares method equations

(1) $\quad \Sigma Y = Na + b\,\Sigma X$
(2) $\Sigma XY = a\Sigma X + b\Sigma(X^2)$

where Na = the number of data sets.
$\quad\quad \Sigma Y$ = dependent variable (Y).
$\quad\quad b\Sigma X$ = independent variable (X).

The coefficient of the second unknown (b) is X. Multiplying the equation $Y = a + bX$ by X, the result is $XY = aX + bX^2$. In summarizing the second equation, the result is:

$$\Sigma XY = a\,\Sigma\,X + b\,\Sigma\,(X^2)$$

Using these two equations, you can determine the values of the two unknowns and fit the line. Note that the sum of all the squared deviations of Y values from the Yc values must be at a minimum to be representative of a least squares trend. The result is a *dynamic average* path through the original data. (See Model 1.3.)

MODEL 1.3. An illustration of deviations of original values (Y) from trend values (Yc)

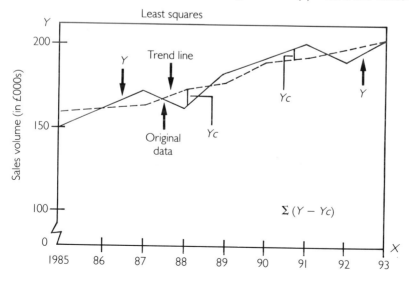

Applying the least squares method. The upper part of Model 1.4 shows how to determine the least squares trend line for annual sales volume, as well as how the equation values are computed. The year of origin is 1982, and the unit of measurement is sales volume in thousands of pounds. The sum (Σ) of X, or 55, is obtained by adding the numbers of each year. N represents the number of years, 11. In substituting the computed values in the equations, the trend line formula is:

$$Y \text{ (Sales)} = 109.5 + 3.95X$$

Displaying a mathematical trend line graphically. At the bottom of Model 1.4 is a graphic presentation of the trend line reflected in the analysis formula. To obtain the trend values, the various values of X by year are substituted in the equation. For 1984, for example, the X value is 2. The computation is:

$$Y = 109.5 + 3.95 \times 2$$
$$= 109.5 + 7.9$$
$$= 117.4 \text{ for } 1984$$

The points located on the graph are for 1982, 1987, and 1991. In actual practice, two points are sufficient to draw a straight line trend.

Using the short method with an odd number of periods. For odd numbers of time periods, the mean of the X values coincides with one of the periods. The short method for computing trends can therefore be *simplified* with an odd number of years. Take the middle year as the origin year and assign it an X value which is equal to 0. A minus sign is given to the X values for the years previous to the origin year and a plus sign to the years following the origin year. The sum of the X values will therefore be zero since the values comprised two similar arithmetic progressions that are equal in amount but opposite in sign. The *normal* equations have to be modified since ΣX is zero. Here is a comparison of the two sets of equations before and after the simplification:

The short method equations

Normal equations	*Simplified equations*
(1) $\Sigma Y = Na + b\Sigma X$	$\Sigma Y = Na$
(2) $\Sigma XY = a\Sigma X + b\Sigma(X^2)$	$\Sigma XY = b\Sigma(X^2)$

Model 1.5 presents the computations involved in the least squares trend line using the *short method* and an odd number of years. Compare it to Model 1.4, noting that the total values for ΣX, ΣXY, and $\Sigma (X^2)$ have changed using the short method. In Model 1.5, the resultant equation for the sales volume trend is calculated to be: $Y = 129.27 + 3.95\,X$. Note that b retains the same value (3.95) as in the long method since the slope of a straight line *does not vary*.

Using the short method with an even number of periods. If the time series has an even number of years, the mean falls between two years, thereby necessitating the use of decimals or fractions to measure the distance of any year from the original.

MODEL 1.4. A demonstration of the least squares method

Computation of least squares trend line annual sales volume (in £000s for 1982–1992)

Year	X	Annual sales volume (in £000s)		
		Y	XY	X²
1982	0	112.0	0	0
1983	1	115.0	115.0	1
1984	2	120.0	240.0	4
1985	3	125.0	375.0	9
1986	4	120.0	480.0	16
1987	5	130.0	650.0	25
1988	6	130.0	780.0	36
1989	7	125.0	875.0	49
1990	8	135.0	1080.0	64
1991	9	150.0	1350.0	81
1992	10	160.0	1600.0	100
	$\Sigma X = 55$	$\Sigma Y = 1442.0$	$\Sigma(XY) = 7545.0$	$\Sigma(X^2) = 385$

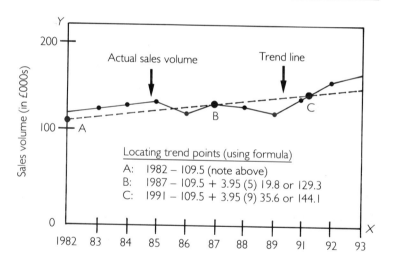

Locating trend points (using formula)

A: 1982 – 109.5 (note above)
B: 1987 – 109.5 + 3.95 (5) 19.8 or 129.3
C: 1991 – 109.5 + 3.95 (9) 35.6 or 144.1

To simplify the calculations, use half-year units instead of annual units. For the years 1982–1991 in Model 1.5, the origin is between the years 1986 and 1987. The X value of 1986 in half-year units is −1; in 1985, it is −3 and so on. The X value for 1987 is +1; in 1988, it is +3 and so on. Under these circumstances, the sum of the X values for even-numbered years (time periods) also equals zero.

Example of the short method with an even number of periods.
Here is an illustration of the least squares short method for finding the trend using an even number of years.

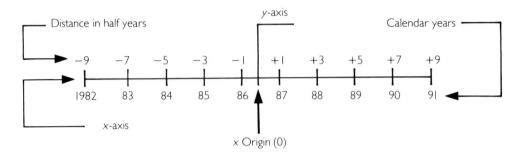

MODEL 1.5. A demonstration of the short method

Computation of least squares trend line annual sales volume (in £000s for 1982–1992)

		Annual sales volume (in £000s)		
Year	*X*	*Y*	*XY*	*X²*
1982	−5	112.0	−560.0	25
1983	−4	115.0	−460.0	16
1984	−3	120.0	−360.0	9
1985	−2	125.0	−250.0	4
1986	−1	120.0	−120.0	1
1987	0	130.0	0	0
1988	1	130.0	130.0	1
1989	2	125.0	250.0	4
1990	3	135.0	405.0	9
1991	4	150.0	600.0	16
1992	5	160.0	800.0	25
	$\Sigma X = 0$ ·	$\Sigma Y = 1422.0$	$\Sigma XY = 435.0$	$\Sigma(X^2) = 110$

Simplified equations   *Substituting values*
(1) $\Sigma Y = Na$ $1442.0 = 11a;$ $a = 129.27$
(2) $XY = b\Sigma(X^2)$ $435.0 = 110b;$ $b = 3.95$

Sales volume trend equation:
$Y = 129.27 + 3.95X$

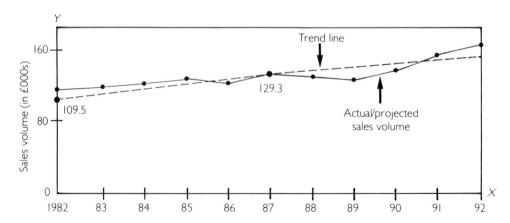

The following table shows you how to use the least squares short method (with an even number of years) to find the straight line trend for annual sales. The data are from Model 1.5, except only the years 1982–1991 are used:

Least squares short method with even number of years

	Annual sales			
Year	Annual sales (in £000s) Y	X	XY	X^2
1982	112.0	−9	−1008.0	81
1983	115.0	−7	−805.0	49
1984	120.0	−5	−600.0	25
1985	125.0	−3	−375.0	9
1986	120.0	−1	−120.0	1
1987	130.0	+1	+130.0	1
1988	130.0	+3	+390.0	9
1989	125.0	+5	+625.0	25
1990	135.0	+7	+945.0	49
1991	150.0	+9	+1350.0	81
	1262.0	0	532.0	330

$$\Sigma Y = 1262.0 \quad \Sigma X = 0 \quad \Sigma XY = 532.0 \quad \Sigma X^2 = 330$$

$$a = \frac{\Sigma Y}{N}$$

$$= \frac{1262}{10} = 126.2$$

$$b = \frac{\Sigma XY}{\Sigma X^2}$$

$$= \frac{532}{330} = 1.61$$

Trend line: $Yc = 126.2 + 1.61X$

Note: In this method, the slope increases or decreases by semi-annual increments, and b therefore is one-half of what it would be in annual units. However, since the movement from one year to the next is $2x$ (half-year units), the trend values obtained from the trend equation are annual values. The trend value for year 1991 is:

$$Yc = 126.2 + 1.61 \times 9 = 140.69$$

How to use the trend equation

With the trend equation, you can obtain any trend value either *within* the range of time covered or analysed or *beyond* the range in either direction. The latter capability permits you to project a time series into the future. In determining a trend value for a given time period, substitute the X value for a particular time period in the trend equation.

The trend line can be plotted by means of the following steps:

Steps in plotting a straight line trend

1. Substitute for any two X values in the trend equation.
2. Plot the two trend values calculated for their respective time periods.
3. Connect a straight line through the two points.

It is preferable to use two time periods that are *some distance* from each other on the graph, such as the first and last periods. The wide spread lessens the possibility of inaccuracy in drawing the trend line.

Shift the origin (or starting point). You can shift the data origin of a trend value. A shift in the origin does not affect the b value (the measure of the slope) because the trend line always has the same slope no matter where the starting point is taken. In both the long and short methods, the b value was 3.95.

The a value, however, does change, because it reflects the value of Y when X equals zero. Suppose you want to change the origin from 1982 to 1986. In Model 1.4, the derived equation was $Y = 109.5 + 3.95X$. By substituting 4 for X, the value for Y becomes 125.3, and therefore $Yc = 125.3 + 3.95X$.

Why shift the origin? For refined data series analysis, especially for cycles, you may need to obtain cyclical turning points during a year; these would not be noticeable in annual data. Shifting the origin enables you to convert a trend equation from an annual to a monthly basis. To fit the trend line to original monthly data, you could use the same procedure as for annual data, but this method may be time-consuming. An alternative approach is to obtain the trend equation for the corresponding annual data, and then convert the equation to the monthly level by dividing b by 12; a remains unchanged.

Benefits of the trend method

The *advantages* of this method are:

1. It expresses trend in the form of a mathematical formula that is easily interpreted.
2. The results are definite and independent of any subjective estimate.
3. The form of the equation is convenient for extrapolation (projection into the future or past).

As for *disadvantages*, the technique assumes that the data follow a trend and that the trend can be expressed by a mathematical equation.

How to use ratios in data analysis

Ratios compare one magnitude (a relative size) with another in the form of a multiple, such as 200:100. The multiple may also be a fraction, a percentage, or a rate. This is the basic principle of ratios.

Ratios simplify the numbers used in certain comparisons and analysis. With ratio analysis, a common financial technique, you can evaluate an organization's performance in terms of established or recognized standards based on historical experience.

Ratios highlight significant, abnormal, and changing trends as variations in the data being assessed. They involve the interpretation and explanation of the relationships between data sets at a given point in time or over a certain number of time periods.

Various types of ratios are used in business:

1. Ratios can compare a part or segment to its whole. In a given organization, for example, Product A sales are calculated to be 40 per cent of total sales. Product B represents 35 per cent and Product C represents 25 per cent. Expressed as percentages their total equals 100 per cent:

Product A	40%
Product B	35%
Product C	25%
Total	100%

2. One part or segment can be compared to another within the whole. For example, Product A amounted to £8 million as compared to Product B sales of £5 million. Expressed as a ratio, Product B sales are said to be 62.5 per cent of Product A sales.

3. Another type of ratio compares one whole to another. For example, the sales volume of one organization can be compared to that of another organization. Sales for Organization A are 60 per cent of the total sales in Organization B. This type of ratio reflects the relation of one magnitude to a similar magnitude at a comparable and compatible period in time.

Which type of ratio comparison you use depends on your purpose. Are you going to measure sales volume, profitability, an investment return, or a similar industry assessment?

What financial ratios do

Financial ratios are important tools that are directly and indirectly useful in *managing* a business. Ratio indicators and comparisons provide relevant and important information, which becomes the basis for a sound decision-making process. Ratios help you to analyse an organization's operations, performance, and financial position – past and present. They serve as a planning basis to predict future trends, which provide management with a comparative means for assessing 'what happened' when variances occur. Standard ratios are used to measure an organization's performance relative to other representative organizations in a particular industry. Although you have to be very cautious about the reliability of ratios, historical experience plays a significant role in validating the usefulness of ratio statistics, analysis, and measurement.

Whereas management is concerned with efficient performance, profitability, stability, and successful planning of future operations, ratio analysis is also important to investors who are concerned with an organization's operating and management performance and its financial stability. Creditors have a strong interest (the protection of their investment) in an organization's solvency and ability to meet its debts on schedule.

In financial reporting, the primary objective of ratio analysis is to *measure* an organization's return on sales, profitability relative to shareholders' equity, liquidity, operations efficiency, and so on. These applications are explained in detail in subsequent chapters. For now, attention is called to a few things in general about ratios.

How you can misuse ratios

Certain percentage ratios can be misleading or uninformative if not used properly.

Magnitude too large
As a rule, the magnitude to be measured should not be *much* larger than the base – perhaps you should question whether the base is too small for the intended comparison. In such cases, the high percentage factor obtained may be meaningless. For example, if an analyst were to state that an organization's profits increased by 1000 per cent in the past five years, the comparison would be difficult to comprehend and its implication hard to assess.

Magnitude too small
Conversely, the comparative magnitude should not be *too small* in relation to the base. For example, take the following statement: 1/40 per cent of the consumers in Sales Territory A are prospective buyers of a product, as compared to 1/20 per cent in Sales Territory B. This comparison is difficult to assess and understand realistically. Undoubtedly, the absolute comparative values would make more sense. Specifically, 1 person out of 20 in a sales territory population of 100,000 is a prospective product consumer. This comparison provides a magnitude that can be understood and evaluated.

Ratios or numbers

This brings us to an important question: when should the management analyst report changes in data magnitude in terms of ratios or absolute numbers? The answer generally depends on the situation. Suppose that sales increased 50 per cent over two years from £50 million to £75 million. That is a significant increase, and the percentage factor dramatically expresses its magnitude. What if an organization were to report that its profits increased 500 per cent over the prior year's profits? The information appears to be significant. Yet the prior year's profits – let's say – were £1000 on a £50,000 sales volume, and the 500 per cent increase amounted to only £5000. The '500 per cent' increase is misleading.

Exercise caution when using ratio percentages for analysing or reporting purposes. They may communicate an ambiguous and misleading message.

The caution in using standard ratios

A number of average ratios may serve as measuring tools of an organization's specific operations and performance. Yet to be useful and informative for data analysis, standard ratios should represent normal and comparable relationships among compatible items in the financial reporting of a business enterprise. Over the years, ratios have been developed that are common evaluation indicators, particularly among related organizations. The extreme precaution is this: for comparison to be relevant, ratios must use only data that are representative in context and composition. At best, average ratios provide only guidelines to existing proportions that are representative in a given industry. They permit an organization to compare its financial results with the averages in other organizations, thus ascertaining its relative standing or providing benchmarks for planning and attainment.

Taxation is one area where significant differences can occur between ratios in different organizations and within organizations on a year-to-year basis. The differences arise as a result of complex tax legislation dealing with items such as capital allowances, trading losses brought forward, overseas taxation, etc. Taxation ratios are not emphasized in this book because of the difficulty in recommending what action should be taken when there is a change. For example the recent share stake by Hanson Trust PLC in ICI PLC resulted in speculation that Hanson might bid for ICI. As the media began detailed discussion on the merits of a bid attention focused on Hanson's low ratio of tax to profits. Some analysts took the view that one of management's obligations is to minimize tax, thus leaving more cash in the company for the benefit of shareholders. Thus for them a low ratio was desirable. Others felt that a company has an obligation to pay its taxes for the greater good of the UK as a whole and so favoured a higher ratio.

The issue was complicated further because no one outside the company appeared to be fully aware of how the tax bill had been kept low, except that numerous subsidiaries registered in Panama seemed to be involved. This problem is perhaps unique in considering what ratio a company should seek but serves as a useful reminder of how ratios require the analyst to give thought to the objectives.

The caution in calculating standard ratios

The data elements used in the development of standard ratios should be homogeneous in terms of their degree and dimension. In other words, they should be comparable in nature and in the type of business being assessed. Yet sometimes specifically defining a similar industry and/or type of business is difficult, because many facets and subdivisions are involved. Comparisons can be misleading. Comparative questions have to be resolved regarding similarities in product(s), operational environment, relative size, financial structure, sales volume, and the type and number of customers. Major differences in these factors can influence the financial performance of the organization, as well as the character or composition of the data being assessed.

The growth of global conglomerates in the past decade has made external comparisons more onerous. An analyst has to wrestle with the possible future effects of:

● currency exchange rates;
● overseas taxation;
● political and economic factors.

Influences on compatibility

Product. In a similar industry, one organization may be producing one product, whereas a comparable organization may be manufacturing a diversified line of products. Each product in the line can have its own gross margin, investment resource requirement and sales outlets, and each of these in turn can influence the financial performance and results of the organization.

Type of operation. Mass-production techniques versus manual operations have a significant bearing on product price, profitability, manpower requirements, and investment in advanced machinery and equipment. Each of these factors can affect the comparative value of financial data and specific ratios.

Changes in organization. Major internal changes or restructuring will often render past information obsolete. For instance changes arising from new technology may result in machines replacing employees as a result of which ratios of labour costs to sales will change. Similarly, as companies look for increased efficiency and control they may well decide to contract out some of their existing activities. Previous ratios of sales per employee will then be affected. Any ratios involving the number of employees should be treated with caution particularly if you are analysing industry averages. Additionally, advances in the use of information technology may lead a company to change the whole basis on which it prepares its management information. It may decide to switch measurement from a regional to product basis. Thus a regional salesman's costs may be booked directly to product costs in the future, thus making comparisons with previous data worthless. Consider a construction or housebuilding company that has in the past allocated the costs of production managers directly to sites. These costs are deducted from sales in arriving at gross profit ratios. If the company suddenly decides that this allocation of costs has no merit and switches the charge to general administrative or establishment overheads, then the gross profit ratio increases at a stroke.

Size of the organization. A business's asset investment value and/or sales volume can have an important effect on its data relationships. Net profit to working capital and shareholders' equity may vary disproportionately. Stock to working capital may have major variances, current ratio (current assets/current liabilities) may be distorted, and debtor turnover may not be realistically comparable.

Customers, the type and number. Customers can have an impact on developing and assessing average ratio results. In one instance, credit policies may be too liberal, whereas in related organizations the extension of credit may be a very conservative approach. This factor could easily affect the collection time period, cash inflow, debtor turnover, occurrence of bad debts, the acid test (debtors + cash/current liabilities), product price, profitability, loan requirements, and so on.

Uniformity of data. In computing average ratios for comparative purposes, the uniformity of accounting procedures is relevant and important. The guidelines for uniform financial reporting have been issued by the Financial Reporting Council. In the audit of an organization's financial statements, the auditing firm will always include a statement to the effect that, in its opinion, the financial statements are 'in accordance with Auditing Standards and have been properly prepared in accordance with the Companies Act 1985'. This is an assurance to the reader that 'accepted principles and practices have been followed'. Uniformity in accounting principles ensures that the composition of the reported data is comparable in nature and conducive to average ratio development and analysis.

Uniformity of accounting periods. Organizations included in standard ratio development and assessment should have compatible accounting periods. Some organizations use a calendar month, while others employ four weeks or a four-four-five week quarter. On an annual basis, this disparity in period length poses no problem unless the month of closing is different. For example, some UK banks' financial year ends in October, others' in December. The difference in the annual closing date has an important impact on the validity of the data to be used in establishing reliable standard ratios.

The need for a standard of measurement

When making comparisons and analysing results in terms of *variances*, you need an adequate standard of measurement. In the financial environment, quantitative measurement takes the form of relative pound sterling values at points in time, measured increases or decreases over time periods, and the use of percentages and ratios. The profit and loss statement reflects period and year-to-date operating result values, while the balance sheet measures the assets, liabilities, and capital at a point in time.

Two primary comparative tools in data measurement are categorized as 'horizontal' and 'vertical'. Both approaches use pounds and percentages as the units of measurement.

Applying horizontal analysis

In the profit and loss account analysis, the horizontal approach reveals the rate of change in the factors affecting profit. In balance sheet analysis, it provides a dynamic approach to reviewing the increases and decreases that occurred over time periods.

Applying vertical analysis

For the profit and loss account, the vertical method indicates how sales income is distributed among the factors involved in producing it, such as the relationships of cost of sales, and distribution and administration expenses. For the balance sheet, the vertical approach indicates the quantitative relationships among the data items at a particular point in time. For example, debtors may be expressed as a percentage of current or total assets, or creditors as a percentage of current or total liabilities. This type of analysis can also be used in comparing one relevant organization against another.

Common mistakes in collecting, analysing, and interpreting data

Collection

The *collection of statistical data* must be complete. The data must be consistent and comparable if they are to be representative and valid for analysis and measurement. It must coincide with the objectives for its accumulation and collection. As a data collector, you must thoroughly review the data and eliminate anything that is extraneous or irrelevant. The careful selection and collection of data goes a long way towards precluding the misuse and misinterpretation of the resultant ratio analyses.

Analysis

In the *analysis of the data*, using absolute values rather than percentages may be more practical, enlightening, and valid. Percentages can be misleading if relative weight is not applied. Improper or invalid analyses can result from the misuse of correlations, from the irrelevant or noncomparable use of ratios, from faulty interpretation of trends, from the inappropriate use of the arithmetic mean, and so on.

Interpretation

The *interpretation* of statistical data entails problems. Misuses include a superficial assessment of one or two related facts as opposed to the presentation of the underlying total background of the data (appropriate basics must be understood). Seasonal variations, when interpreted as cyclical, have a valid bearing in decision making; if interpreted as future trends, these variations may not reflect the actual situation. Assumptions may be misleading when they are based on averages rather than on individual cases, and vice versa. Data interpretation is extremely vital to successful data analysis and understanding.

Presentation

The *presentation of statistical data* must be suited to the communication objective. In presenting comparative data highlighting variances allows for rapid assimilation of pertinent facts for further investigation. Excessive detail – such as a large array of data with irrelevant data included – tends to confuse rather than enlighten. Exercise extreme care when presenting statistical data so that worthwhile assessments can be achieved.

These are only some of the misuses of statistics. If you establish appropriate procedural guidelines in the use, analysis, and presentation of statistics, you can prevent the improper use and interpretation of statistical presentations.

2 How to measure operational effectiveness and control in resource utilization

Chapter highlights

Debtors, stock, and creditors all play a vital role in an organization's operational performance and in capital utilization planning and control. Management can use data from each of
these areas to measure, plan, and control performance efficiency.

The primary sources of such data are two major financial reports: the profit and loss
account and the balance sheet. This chapter discusses pertinent data from both reports as
they apply to performance measurement and control. Covered are ratios for:

- Measuring and interpreting the debtors position for the purpose of estimating
  collections, cash flow planning, and assessing an organization's credit policy.
- Analysing the relationship among purchases, creditors, and payments as an aid to
  business planning. This chapter explains how to measure an organization's debt-
  paying ability and determine whether trade creditor commitments can be met.
- Assessing stock controls to measure their effectiveness, projecting stock levels, and
  implementing stock classification to cut costs and release working capital.
- Manpower planning for projecting costs and sales forecasts. Also, indirect-to-direct
  personnel ratios are developed to measure and control the effectiveness of
  manpower utilization and cost.

Model 2.1 provides the basic information that will be used to develop ratios and trend
analyses.

How to interpret and measure the debtors position

To analyse, plan, and control a desirable debtors position thoroughly, you should
consider a number of factors. The more important factors involve data relationship
ratios, trends, and assessment of certain variables.

MODEL 2.1. Basic information for developing ratios and trend analyses

Financial statement data for analysis 31 December 19X4 (in £000,000s)

Profit and loss statement	First quarter Values	%	Second quarter Values	%	Third quarter Values	%	Fourth quarter Values	%	Annual period Values	%
Sales	252.8	100.0	274.9	100.0	276.2	100.0	273.1	100.0	1077.0	100.0
Cost of sales	223.9	88.6	243.3	88.5	248.1	89.8	247.7	90.7	963.0	89.4
Gross profit	28.9	11.4	31.6	11.5	28.1	10.2	25.4	9.3	114.0	10.6
Distribution & administration	11.8	4.7	12.0	4.4	11.6	4.2	12.6	4.6	48.0	4.5
Trading/operating profit	17.1	6.7	19.6	7.1	16.5	6.0	12.8	4.7	66.0	6.1
Interest (42.6M × 8%)	(0.8)	(0.3)	(0.8)	(0.3)	(0.9)	(0.3)	(0.9)	(0.3)	(3.4)	(0.3)
Net other income/deductions	(1.3)	(0.5)	(1.5)	(0.5)	(1.2)	(0.5)	(1.1)	(0.4)	(5.1)	(0.5)
Profit on ordinary activities before taxation	15.0	5.9	17.3	6.3	14.4	5.2	10.8	4.0	57.5	5.3
Taxation	7.5	2.9	8.6	3.1	7.2	2.6	5.4	2.0	28.7	2.6
Net profit	7.5	3.0	8.7	3.2	7.2	2.6	5.4	2.0	28.8	2.7
Relevant balance sheet data										
Fixed assets										
Tangible assets	64.9		66.3		67.0		68.2		66.6	
Investments	11.7		11.5		12.4		12.5		12.0	
Current assets										
Stocks	260.0		268.5		256.9		243.4		257.2	
Debtors	110.4		111.5		102.3		105.1		107.3	
Cash in hand and at bank	38.0		32.9		36.6		35.5		35.8	
Other investments	22.1		21.3		27.4		21.1		23.0	
	430.5		434.2		423.2		405.1		423.3	
Creditors due within one year										
Trade creditors	(310.5)		(308.7)		(294.1)		(273.9)		(296.8)	
Net current assets/liabilities	120.0		125.5		129.1		131.2		126.5	
Total assets less current liabilities	196.6		203.3		208.5		211.9		205.1	
Creditors due after one year										
Borrowings	(42.6)		(42.6)		(42.6)		(42.6)		(42.6)	
Net assets	154.0		160.7		165.9		169.3		162.5	
Capital and reserves										
Called up share capital	154.0		160.7		165.9		169.3		162.5	
Annualized sales	1011.2		1099.6		1104.8		1092.4		1077.0	
Indirect manpower (no.)	16,522		16,608		16,595		16,910		16,634	
Direct personnel	34,737		34,550		34,824		35,779		34,972	

Using the ratio of sales to debtors to assess the debtors position

Making the calculation

EXAMPLE

The following *quarterly ratios* were developed from the information in Model 2.1. (Although the more precise procedure is to use annualized sales and average debtor balances for comparative purposes, monthly values may also be used.)

Sales and debtor balances (in £000,000s)

	First quarter	Second quarter	Third quarter	Fourth quarter	Annual
Sales	252.8	274.9	276.2	273.1	1077.0
Debtor balances	110.4	111.5	102.3	105.1	107.3
Debtor turnover	2.29	2.47	2.70	2.60	10.04
	(or 229%)	(or 247%)	(or 270%)	(or 260%)	(or 1004%)
Annualized turnover	9.16	9.86	10.80	10.39	

These data results indicate that the relationship was more favourable in the last two quarters compared to the first two periods. In the last two periods, the debtors were below the average of £107.3 million, whereas the sales were above the quarterly average of £269.2 million.

Interpreting the results

Generally, changes in the sales ratios can be attributed to disproportionate increases and decreases in sales volume or in debtors, which cause fluctuations in the ratio values. When measuring the proportions among various related items in the financial statements, note the data variations that may indicate problem areas requiring further investigative analysis. You may find that the variations are due to circumstances that do not require any action. Instead, they may be the result of situations either common to all business entities or characteristic of the operating environment.

Using trend ratios to measure the sales/debtor position

Making the calculation

You can also measure the sales/debtor position by means of trend ratios over periods of time. This approach is more effectively employed by annual periods.

EXAMPLE

Quarterly data from Model 2.1 is used.

Sales and debtors (in £000,000s)

Quarters	Sales values	Sales trend ratio	Debtor values	Debtors trend ratio	Sales/debtor ratio
1	252.8	100%	110.4	100%	229%
2	274.9	109	111.5	101	247
3	276.2	109	102.3	93	270
4	273.1	108	105.1	95	260

The sales volume clearly increased in the last three quarters compared to the first-quarter base. Conversely, the debtors decreased in the last two quarters but slightly increased in the second quarter (101 per cent). The ratio trend is favourable in the example because the increases in sales did not result in higher debtors, which would have involved an increase in working capital.

Sales trend ratios: two key factors that affect the sales position

Interpreting the results

The next step is specifically to assess the cause(s) for the variations in the sales and debtor values. Although the sales data in the example do not appear to be of major significance – since the last quarter's sterling amounts are fairly comparable – the factors affecting sales values should be ascertained as a basis for analytical assessment of more extreme situations.

Generally, the two major factors affecting the sales position are sales volume and price. Behind these factors are other relevant considerations, such as the general economy (rising, falling, static), seasonal situations associated with particular industries, and factors affecting specific organizations in their operating environment.

Sales volume. Situations that affect product and service sales volume involve such common circumstances as

- product/service demands by the customer
- product/service quality
- the efficiency and aggressiveness of the marketing organization
- favourable markets due to a rising/recovering economy
- an organization's reputation with regard to the products or services it markets.

Business cycles definitely influence an organization's marketing results. The upswings create demand, whereas the downswings make customers cautious and conservative in their buying activities.

Prices. The factors governing sales prices include the

- scope and aggressiveness of the competition;
- unique features and quality of the product or service;
- organization's ability to meet customer requirements on schedule;

- efficiency of the organization in controlling costs effectively;
- 'state of the art' progress an organization reflects in enhancing its product usefulness and capabilities.

Factors that influence the debtor position

The extent and collection of outstanding debt are primarily contingent on the customers' ability to pay their obligations. In turn, their ability depends much on the same factors as those discussed for sales above: prevailing market conditions, business cycles, and the problems associated with specific industries and individual customers.

Customers' inability to pay can result from such circumstances as

- sellers' overextension of credit
- inadequate investigation and verification of a customer's credit ratings (past and current)
- generous concessions in the form of liberal terms to favourite customers to increase their purchases.

Certain customers may also be experiencing internal problems, such as operational inefficiencies and costs, poor sales volume, labour relations and elemental catastrophes (flooding, fires, snow storms, and the like).

The collection of debts may therefore be delayed or impaired. The selling organization may be forced to bank borrowing with its attendant interest costs (drain on profits), and/or it may have to depend more on greater creditor financing to meet its own obligations. Neither alternative is conducive to sound financial operations.

Solution

The solution may be to exercise constant supervision, analysis, and control of debtors. The goal would be to take corrective action when customer account balances increase too rapidly in relation to sales. This may mean a thorough review of the organization's collection policy, more stringent control of customer credit, and a discerning assessment of the prevailing policies on credit terms.

Using the debtors to sales ratio to measure financial performance

How to make the calculation

When measuring the financial stability and performance of an organization relative to its debtor position, determine the average age or level of its customer accounts outstanding at given points in time. To do so, calculate the *debtors to sales ratio*. Divide the average debtors by the total credit sales. For example, the average debtors on an annual basis would be the sum of the beginning and ending balances divided by two.

EXAMPLE

Quarterly end balances for debtors and relevant periods for sales were used to calculate the trends in the following table. The annual ending balance and total sales are also provided.

(in £000,000s)

	First quarter	Second quarter	Third quarter	Fourth quarter	Annual values
Sales	252.8	274.9	276.2	273.1	1077.0
Annualized sales	1011.2	1099.6	1104.8	1092.4	—
Debtors	110.4	111.5	102.3	105.1	107.3
Debtors to sales ratio	43.7%	40.6%	37.0%	38.5%	10.0%
using annualized sales and quarterly debtors balances					
Debtors to sales ratio	10.9%	10.1%	9.3%	9.6%	10.0%

Debtor turnover ratio

This ratio measures the average number of times that debtors *turned over* during a reported time period. In general, it reflects the relationship between operating results (in this case, sales) and the capital employed (debtors). These ratios, quarterly and annual, were presented under 'Using the ratio of sales to debtors to assess debtors position'. The ratio is calculated as follows:

$$\text{Debtor turnover ratio} = \frac{\text{Total credit sales}}{\text{Average debtors}}$$

Average collection period: one way to size up an organization's credit policy

How to make the calculation

The collection period represents the average number of days between the day that the invoice is sent out and the day the customer pays the bill. The formula for calculating this average is:

$$\text{Average collection period} = \text{Sales ratio} \times \text{number of days in period}$$

EXAMPLE

Calculate the average collection period using the debtors to sales ratio from the preceding example:

$$\text{Average collection period} = 10\% \times 365 \text{ (days in year)} = 36.5 \text{ days}$$

Alternative approach

Another approach is to

1. Divide the *annual credit sales* by 365 to obtain the average daily credit sales.
2. Divide the average debtors (include bills of exchange if appropriate) by the average daily credit sales.

EXAMPLE
(in £000,000s)
Step 1:
$$\frac{1077.0 \text{ (credit sales)}}{365} = 2.95$$
Step 2:
$$\frac{107.3 \text{ (average debtors)}}{2.95 \text{ (sales/day)}} = 36.4 \text{ days}$$

Interpreting the ratio

The collection period measures an organization's efficiency in enforcing its credit policy in terms of controlling the debtors position within desirable limits. Directly related to the credit terms, the collection period generally can be readily compared to related industry average ratios. If a thirty-day payment cycle is used, then the collection period should not exceed 1⅓ times the established payment period. (This is the situation in the preceding example – 36.4 days.)

Usually, changes in the collection ratio (particularly if significant) result from revisions in the organization's credit policy (more or less liberal terms) or from inability to collect its debts on the scheduled due dates.

Using an aged debts analysis to estimate collections and cash flow

Another method of assessing the debtor position is to analyse the individual debtor balances at the period end. This can be done on a monthly or quarterly basis, particularly if the system is computerized. If significant collection changes are occurring from one time period to another, then the ageing process can assist in highlighting specific problem areas.

Making the calculation

In the ageing procedure, the debtor accounts are classified according to their invoice dates. Generally, the time periods are under 30 days, 30–60 days, and 61–90 days. Accounts may be over 90 days in some situations.

EXAMPLE
The annual periods in the following table end on 31 December of 19X3 and 19X4.

		Ageing procedure (in £000,000s)			
Age of invoices	*Invoiced 31 Dec. X3*	*% of total*	*Invoiced 31 Dec. X4*	*% of total*	*% variance*
Under 30 days	77.7	80	89.3	85	+5
30–60 days	14.6	15	12.6	12	−3
61–90 days	4.9	5	3.2	3	−2
Totals	97.2	100	105.1	100	

Interpreting the ratio

The invoice age of the debtors seems to indicate a favourable trend in the collection activity. Outstanding debts, as of 31 December 19X4, show a 5 per cent increase in the invoice category under 30 days, in spite of a 15 per cent increase ((89.3 − 77.7)/ 77.7 = 15 per cent) in customer invoices. In the 30–60 days classification, the invoices outstanding decreased 3 per cent in 19X4, and 2 per cent lower uncollected invoices were scheduled in the 61–90 days category. The trends are basically favourable relative to the anticipated collection process.

The aged debts analysis approach can be very useful in cash flow planning as well as in estimating possible doubtful debts. If unfavourable trends occur, then it may be necessary to produce a detailed report of the specific overdue accounts for investigation and corrective action with the customer.

Days of sales in debtors ratio

Making the calculation

To ascertain the trend of days of uncollected sales in debtors:

1. Convert the quarterly sales to a sales per day factor.
2. Divide the resultant value into the ending debtor balance.

This process can be performed on a monthly basis (which is more precise for trends) or annually (for comparative purposes).

EXAMPLE

A 90-day factor is used for the quarterly periods and 360 days on an annual basis for purposes of consistency. The debtor balance annual average is £107.3 million.

	First quarter	*Second quarter*	*Third quarter*	*Fourth quarter*	*Annual period*
			(in £000,000s)		
Sales/period	252.8	274.9	276.2	273.1	1077.0
Debtor balances	110.4	111.5	102.3	105.1	107.3
Days/period	90	90	90	90	360
Sales/day	2.81	3.05	3.07	3.03	2.99
Days sales in debtors	39.3	36.5	33.3	34.7	35.9

The first two quarters had the highest days of sales in debtors primarily because of the higher-than-average debtor balances. First-quarter sales were the lowest of the periods, which accounted for the high 39.3 days factor of sales in that period.

How to estimate period-end debtor balances

These results, if proven consistent over time periods, can provide at least a preliminary basis for *estimating period-end balances* predicated on sales projections. The calculating process is as follows:

$$(1) \quad \text{Daily sales} = \frac{\text{Credit sales}}{\text{Days/period}}$$

$$(2) \quad \text{Period-end debtor balance} = \text{Days of sales factor} \times \text{Sales/day}$$

Further, days of sales in debtors provides *trends among periods* for analysis and assessment relative to future projections.

A word of caution

Different industries will have different debtor positions as a result of custom and practice and therefore there is no 'ideal' ratio. For example in the housebuilding industry it is customary, except perhaps in a recession, for there to be a chain of buyers all anxiously awaiting a move-in date. As a result the housebuilder usually finds he is pressed for a completion date to enable the chain to move together. The housebuilder will also demand payment before releasing the keys to the property and so he tends to issue an invoice a few days prior to completion and receives payment almost immediately. Clearly his trade debtor ratio in days is likely to be very low. Mail-order companies present different possibilities. If cash is sent with order and well before delivery of goods you can have a very impressive ratio.

Calculating days of sales in orders outstanding to measure the effectiveness of orders outstanding

The success and growth of any organization depends upon its ability to sustain its current business volume and acquire new business. This task is accomplished by zealous sales promotion, in connection with the development of new products and/or services. Therefore, sales bookings (new business) clearly represent one of the most sensitive areas that command management's attention when evaluating operational trends. Management must continually monitor progress because of its importance in operating and planning decisions.

To compute the orders outstanding balance:

1. Combine the period's opening balance with new orders booked.
2. Deduct period sales/deliveries.

Also consider adjustments for cancelled or additional quantities, price changes, and possible errors in data entry or computations.

How to measure the effectiveness of the orders outstanding

Management and their planning/marketing staffs spend considerable time and effort developing realistic sales goal plans. Their projections are based on:

1. past performance
2. market intelligence
3. anticipated sales predicated on customer objectives and feedback
4. production capability
5. adequate and skilled manpower
6. facility/equipment requirements
7. availability of financial resources.

Making the calculation

To measure orders outstanding effectiveness, you must analyse the historical performance of the *days of sales factor in orders outstanding*. To do so, convert period sales into days of sales, and divide this factor into the orders outstanding balance. The equation is as follows:

$$\text{Days of sales in orders outstanding} = \frac{\text{Balance of orders outstanding}}{\text{Sales volume} \div \text{Days in period}}$$

EXAMPLE

The following data are for the years 19X3 and 19X4:

	*(in £000s)**				
	Orders outstanding balance	*Total sales*	*Days in period*	*Sales/ day*	*Days sales in orders outstanding*
19X3	130.0	1070.0	360	2.972	43.7
19X4	160.0	1250.0	360	3.472	46.1

*Excluding sales/day

A word of caution when interpreting the results

Note that the orders outstanding position may be misleading because some sales may be for long-range delivery. These may not help in the current period's operational activity, where the objective is to maintain a stabilized work force on a scheduled plan of operations. Therefore, a detailed analysis must be made of the orders outstanding position to ensure a continuing level of activity on a sustained and scheduled basis. The volume of orders outstanding affects all organizations' operations either directly or indirectly and has a decided effect on financial resources, profitability, and return on investment.

How to analyse the relationship among purchases, creditors, and payments as an aid in business planning

A definite and constant relationship exists among the purchasing activity, trade creditor commitments, and their payment. Model 2.2 illustrates an assessment of the 19X4 quarterly and annual actuals, along with the *resultant statistics and ratios* that evolved from the analysis of the data.

The information presented in Model 2.2 has no major or significant implications. Among quarterly periods, the sterling values were fairly consistent, indicating that seasonal fluctuations were minimal and that there were no radical changes in the operating environment. The opening and closing creditor balances were practically identical (£42.0 million versus £41.9 million). The same holds true for both the annual purchases and payments.

How to interpret the data

Applications

The *days purchases in creditors* averaged 48.1 days or approximately 1½ months of purchases in the creditor balance. This factor, if proven valid over future periods, would be of importance in the projection of creditor balances based on the purchasing activity. If nothing else, the days factor can be used as a guideline in verifying creditors' integrity developed by more detailed conventional methods.

Average daily purchases versus daily payments were practically on a *one-to-one* basis for the year. On a quarterly assessment review, the average days purchases in payments were approximately 90 days. This factor may be used for planning material/supplies creditor payments based on their purchase values.

The *creditor turnover ratio* was approximately 1.8–1.9 times per quarterly period, with the annual rate being 7.5. This ratio indicates the number of times the creditors turned over within a time period (quarterly and annual periods were used). Multiplying the quarterly factor by four will yield the annual turnover, indicating payment cycle results.

This ratio can be used not only for comparative purposes among periods but also for estimating purchases based on a given account's *period-end creditor balance*. Generally, however, purchases are estimated before creditor balances are projected. Yet the factor approach may be useful in projecting period-end creditor balances by dividing the estimated purchases by the turnover rate.

Payments as a percentage of opening creditor balance plus purchases averaged 65 per cent per quarter. This statistic can be used for comparative purposes among time periods. It might also be used for estimating payments based on the combined total of the opening creditor balance plus the period's purchases.

MODEL 2.2. Analysing purchases, payments, and creditors: quarterly assessment of relationships

(in £000,000s)

	First quarter	*Second quarter*	*Third quarter*	*Fourth quarter*	*Annual period*
Creditors, OB	42.0	40.7	41.8	43.3	42.0
Period purchases	78.3	79.2	78.9	77.1	313.5
Total	120.3	119.9	120.7	120.4	355.5
Cash payments	79.6	78.1	77.4	78.5	313.6
Creditors, CB	40.7	41.8	43.3	41.9	41.9
Averages per day (90 days in quarter; 360 annual)					
Purchases (£000s)	870	880	877	856	871 avg.
Payments (£000s)	884	868	860	872	871 avg.
Days purchases in creditors (40,700 ÷ 870)	46.8	47.5	49.4	48.9	48.1
Days purchases in payments (79,600 ÷ 870)	91.5	88.8	88.3	91.7	90.1
Ratios					
Creditor turnover	1.9	1.9	1.8	1.8	7.5
Payments to purchases + opening balance (79.6 ÷ 120.3)	66%	65%	64%	65%	—
Trends in % using first quarter as base period					
Purchases	100	101	101	98.5	—
Payments	100	98.1	97.2	98.6	—
Period-end creditors	100	103	106	103	—

How to use financial data trend ratios

At the bottom of Model 2.2 are the *calculated trends* for purchases, payments, and period-end creditor balances. They were developed by dividing the first-quarter values into the other three quarter amounts. The trend variations among periods were minor, except the third-quarter creditor payments balance of 106 per cent. This figure resulted from a decrease in cash payments compared to payments in the other periods.

A series of *trend ratios* is designed to show an increase or decrease in an item, as well as the rate of increase or decrease. The trend ratios do not in themselves indicate whether movement is favourable or unfavourable but rather reveal the behaviour of the items as time passes. Further, they provide a horizontal analysis of comparable data among periods.

How to employ the velocity procedure to assess an organization's debt-paying capability

Historically, this method of analysing an organization's debt-paying ability was used primarily for liquidation assessment – that is, for determining whether a business could pay its debts in the extreme event that it liquidated its operations. However, an organization can also use this procedure to analyse its ongoing operations relative to its financial position in terms of its debt-paying ability.

This method compares the *velocity* (the rapidity of debt-paying status change) of the current assets and current liabilities. The data involve the *maturity and ageing* primarily of the debtors, creditors, and stock. Further, they present the current position on an estimated time-cash-realizable (timing of cash availability inflow versus outflow) basis.

Analysing the current financial position

Model 2.3 illustrates the computation process and results, using basic and generalized data. The estimated results indicate that the debtors represents 41.5 per cent of the total current asset collections and that the stock is 51.6 per cent. The aged creditor commitments represent 85.5 per cent of the total current liabilities listed.

With respect to the *maturity of the debtors*, 69.5 per cent are anticipated to be collected within 30 days with the balance due in 31 to 90 days. Relative to stock, 15.5 per cent of the cash sales will be collected within 30 days, and the balance is to be received in 31–60 days. Credit sales, representing 72.3 per cent of the stock sales, will be collected in 90 days.

In the *creditors* section, 52.1 per cent of the creditors are scheduled for payment within 30 days, and the balance is due in 31–90 days.

The current position (the ratio of current assets to current liabilities) reflects a 2.6 rate, which appears to be adequate in light of industry averages. The *working capital ratio* (that is, working capital to liabilities) is calculated to be 1.6, indicating that the owners' equity in the current assets is 1.6 times the current creditors' contribution to capital.

Interpreting the results
The sum of the estimated cash receipts within 30 days and the cash balance exceeds (£62.9 million − £28.0 = £34.9 ÷ 28) creditors due in 30 days by 125 per cent. These estimates indicate that the organization is in a favourable position to meet its immediate debt commitments. The data in Model 2.3 do not represent a cash budget because they do not reflect estimated expenses, tax provisions, and miscellaneous commitments.

MODEL 2.3. Current position of debt-paying ability: velocity method

(£000s)

Current assets		% of AR	Current liabilities		% of AP
Cash	10,000		Bills payable in 30 days	8,000	
Aged debtors (estimated)			*Aged creditors (estimated)*		
Due in 30 days	41,400	69.5	Due in 30 days	28,000	58.1
31–60 days	15,000	25.1	31–60 days	14,700	30.5
61–90 days	3,200	5.4	61–90 days	5,500	11.4
	59,600			48,200	
		% of inv.			
Aged stock (estimated)					
Cash sales					
In 30 days	11,500	15.5			
31–60 days	9,000	12.2			
Credit sales in 90 days	53,600	72.3			
	74,100				
Totals	143,700			56,200	

Application

This type of current position assessment affords management an opportunity to review its debt-paying ability. It can also be used as a basis to support future debt commitments and creditor confidence in the organization's ability to pay its debts on schedule.

How to use the days purchases outstanding ratio to determine whether you are meeting your trade creditor commitments

Making the calculation

The primary objective of this ratio is to review an organization's trade creditor commitments and to determine whether it is meeting them on schedule. The equation for the calculation is as follows:

$$\text{Days purchases outstanding} = \frac{\text{Trade creditors}}{\text{Period purchases} \div \text{Days in period}}$$

EXAMPLE

Using the following data, calculate the days purchases outstanding. Although the information is on an annual basis, the same calculation can be used for monthly and quarterly periods.

		(£000s)		
	Average trade creditors	*Total purchases*	*Days in period*	*Days purchases outstanding*
19X3	10,150	90,100	360	40.6
19X4	12,400	113,500	360	39.3

Calculations:

$$\frac{£10,150}{£90,100 \div 360 = 250.3} = 40.6 \text{ days} \qquad \frac{£12,400}{£113,500 \div 360 = 315.3} = 39.3 \text{ days}$$

Interpreting the results

As you can see, the fewer the number of days of purchases in the creditor balance, the more favourable the debt-paying ability. Further, from a supplier viewpoint, the ratio is one measure of an organization's ability to pay its debts on schedule.

This illustration indicates that there were 1.3 days fewer purchases in the 19X4 creditor balance as compared to 19X3. In 19X4, purchases increased by 26 per cent (£113,500 − £90,100 = £23,400 ÷ £90,100), whereas the creditor balance increased by only 22 per cent, which accounts for the fewer days purchases outstanding.

Using the number of times interest earned to assess debt paying

Another ratio that focuses on debt-paying ability is the *number of times* interest is covered by operating profits.

Making the calculation

EXAMPLE

The following computations are based on the data in Model 2.1 by quarterly periods. The equation is:

$$\text{Times interest earned} = \frac{\text{Profit from operations}}{\text{Interest expense}}$$

(£000s)

	First quarter	Second quarter	Third quarter	Fourth quarter	Annual period
Profit from operations	17,100	19,600	16,500	12,800	66,000
Interest earned	800	800	900	900	3,400
Times interest earned	21.4	24.5	18.3	14.2	19.4

Profit from operations represents the amount of earnings available to meet the fixed interest obligations on the loan capital of £42.6 million. The times interest earned ratio ranged from 14.2 times in the fourth quarter to a high of 24.5 times in the second quarter, with an annual average of 19.4 times.

The primary cause for the fluctuations in the times interest earned ratio is due to the changes in the profit from operations (from a high of £19.6 million to a low of £12.8). Interest expense remained relatively stable. This radio *signifies* that there is an average of £19.40 of operating profit earned for each pound of interest expense.

Interpreting the results

The high ratios in the example are favourable to the organization's financial position. Conversely, the lower ratios may indicate a weakening financial position particularly if the operating profit were to decline substantially, since interest expense is a basic commitment that must be paid on schedule.

In the example, the low times interest earned ratio of 14.2 is due primarily to the reduced profit from operations of £12.8 million. This figure was 34.7 per cent below the second-quarter high of £19.6 million operating profit. As shown in Model 2.1, the operating profit decline was due to reduced gross profit and higher distribution and administration expenses.

Application

This ratio is used to measure the level to which operating profit can decline without adversely affecting the organization's ability to meet interest payments on its fixed loan capital. Note that the profit from operations values is used because, if profit decreased, corporation taxes would decline proportionately. Note too that an organization may have fixed commitments other than interest expense in the form of rental obligations on leased property. In such situations, the fixed costs are added to the interest expense, and the *ratio* would properly be classified as the *number of time fixed costs earned*. The addition of other significant fixed charges to interest expense may have a decided impact on operating income results.

A word of caution
An external analyst must be on the lookout for 'innovative' financial instruments. Convertible bonds may or may not result in holders converting into equity. If the share price is depressed at the time of conversion then the company may have to find a large amount of cash. Either way the effect on the ratios has to be considered. Bonds, options, futures and swaps come in a variety of sophisticated combinations. The International Accounting Standards Committee has published an exposure draft (E40) dealing with financial instruments.

How to assess stock controls

General management policy is to carry enough stock to support the actual and/or anticipated sales volume. In addition to the stock investment, management must consider the expense incurred to support activities related to stock management, such as purchasing, inspection, handling, storage, and record keeping (a computerized process).

Control of stock is probably one of the most difficult management problems. The dilemma is that stock must be large enough to meet customer demands and, at the same time, conservative enough to minimize

- support expenses;
- possible interest on borrowed funds;
- deterioration or obsolescence losses;
- the negative impact on cash flow from holding too much stock.

To measure stock efficiency and monitor significant changes, you must employ some form of performance measurement and planning. Three approaches used by most organizations are the

1. ratio of stock to cost of sales
2. turnover factor
3. average age of inventories in terms of days.

Using the ratio of stock to cost of sales to assess and project stock levels

Making the calculation
To calculate this ratio, divide the average stock by the cost of sales.

EXAMPLE

In the following table, the annual stock average was derived by combining the quarterly balances and dividing the total by four. Normally, the average would be obtained by combining the opening and closing balances and dividing by two.

	(in £000,000s)				
Stock values	260.0	268.5	256.9	243.4	257.2
Cost of sales	223.9	243.3	248.1	247.7	963.0
Ratio of stock					
to cost of sales	116%	110%	104%	98%	27%
Annual basis	29%	28%	26%	25%	

Interpreting the results

Note that the stock ratio to cost of sales declined from 116 per cent to 98 per cent in the fourth quarter. This is a favourable trend in that the stock balances on hand were decreasing whereas the cost of sales by period was increasing. The situation indicates that the stock levels were being used more effectively over the course of the year. The *annual average* of 29 per cent means that the stock balance represents just over a quarter of the cost of sales.

Application

If these ratios are proven to be valid historically, they can be used to estimate (at least, preliminarily) stock levels based on cost of sales projections. They may also be useful in checking projected stock levels that have been developed by more conventional methods.

Using turnover of average stock to measure stock effectiveness

Turnover ratios express the relationship between operating results and the capital resources employed. Stock turnover can be expressed on the basis of sales or cost of sales. A number of organizations use sales because this element is commonly employed for other types of turnover calculations, such as expense and profit margins. The consensus, however, among professionals is that the most appropriate basis is *cost of sales*. The more acceptable turnover ratio is therefore the *cost of sales relationship to average stock*.

Generally, the sales ratios reflect similar trends to cost of sales, but they are *less accurate* due to the variations in profit margin. Sales can be used as a substitute when cost of sales data are unavailable. Note that, in the retail environment, the ratio of sales to stock at *sales prices* provides the same turnover ratio as cost of sales to stock at *cost prices*.

Making the calculation

EXAMPLE

Quarterly turnover ratios and annual average (in £000s)

	First quarter	Second quarter	Third quarter	Fourth quarter	Annual period
Cost of sales (C/S)	223.9	243.3	248.1	247.7	963.0
Average stock	260.0	268.5	256.9	243.4	257.2
Annual C/S	895.6	973.2	992.4	990.8	
Turnover ratios					
Number of times	0.86	0.91	0.96	1.0	3.7
Annual	3.4	3.6	3.9	4.1	3.7

Interpreting the results

The aggregate average annual turnover rate is 3.7. Quarterly period ratios varied from 0.86 to 1.0, which signifies an improved stock utilization – indicating more stock is being absorbed into the cost of sales.

The preferred approach: turnover of stocks by classification

The turnover ratios in the preceding example represent the aggregate stock. Another approach is to ascertain the turnover ratios by stock categories. This approach is more informative because you can more thoroughly assess capital resource efficiency and highlight specific problems or stock management achievements.

Making the calculation

The ratio classifications are as follows:

Turnover of	*Calculating equations*
1. Finished goods	= *Cost of sales ÷ average finished products stock
2. Work in progress	= *Cost of products manufactured ÷ work in progress average stock
3. Raw materials	= *Cost of materials used ÷ raw material average stock

*Costs could be annual.

Application

Determining the turnover ratios by stock classifications gives an indication of excessive or depleted stock levels; it also highlights the slow-moving and/or potentially obsolete stock. Further, this process permits the assessment of (1) the degree of coordination between the production and sales of the various products and (2) the balance maintained in the raw materials used in production. You can also ascertain which materials are overstocked and which are insufficient.

A word of caution
Advantageous purchasing resulting in surplus stock may be justified under certain circumstances. Yet you should carefully consider the disadvantages of possible obsolescence, increased carrying costs, expenditure of resources, and future price falls.

Drawbacks to physical turnover ratios

To determine the turnover of stock, compare the average monthly volume in units of stock with the volume of units sold or issued. The results represent a *physical turnover ratio*, which is often used as a *measure of operating performance*.

Certain negative features are associated with the use of the physical turnover ratios:

The assumption that all units of stock are homogeneous is generally not valid. You therefore have no means for comparing the experience of one period with another.

The available stock units fluctuate between minimum and maximum. As a result, the ratio improves as the minimum is approached and becomes more negative when receipts increase the available stock.

The selection of the base affects the turnover ratio – namely, opening, closing, and average balances. Business cycles and seasonal fluctuations will further complicate the selection of a basis.

Implementing stock classification ratios to cut costs and release working capital

Stocks provide material items for various product/function activities. Some items are used immediately and others turn over slowly. Items that you consider inactive or obsolete only increase costs and absorb working capital needlessly. This type of stock should be minimized.

Since material-handling costs can be expensive, their impact can affect net profit – especially in the case of slow-moving stock. Storage costs can be reduced and control simplified if such stock is handled and moved less often. Rapidly moving items can then be stored for immediate accessibility and movement at minimal effort and cost.

With stock classified into activity (or usage) categories, you can establish periodic stock cycles so that slow-moving and inactive stock items will be counted less frequently. The segregation of stock offers a number of advantages, particularly in organizations with a substantial working capital investment in stocks. Adopting this procedure will result in a reduction of materials handling, storage, and obsolescence costs; it also makes more working capital available for priority operational requirements.

Stock segregation has another distinct advantage as a decision-making tool because it gives management an index of associated activity for each item carried in stock. This index should substantially improve the purchasing and stock control functions. For the purchasing cycle system, you can use a series of *control ratios* to classify the stock and provide realistic stock balances.

Computing the average age of stock in days to measure stock utilization

Making the calculation

The average days of stocks is computed by using the following equation:

$$\text{Average days} \atop \text{of stocks} = {\text{Number of days} \atop \text{in period}} \times \frac{\text{Period-end stock balances}}{\text{Total cost of sales}}$$

EXAMPLE

For simplicity, a 90-day quarter and a 360-day annual calculation were used in the following table:

	(in £000,000s)				
	First quarter	*Second quarter*	*Third quarter*	*Fourth quarter*	*Annual period*
Stock balances	260.0	268.5	256.9	243.4	243.4
Cost of sales	223.9	243.3	248.1	247.7	963.0
Days in period	90	90	90	90	360
Stock divided by cost of sales	1.16	1.10	1.04	0.98	0.253
Average age of stocks (in days)	104	99	94	88	91

Interpreting the results

The average age of stocks declined in each quarter, with an annual average of 91 days. This result indicates a favourable trend, particularly if it continues. The reason for the declining trend is a decreasing stock balance, whereas the cost of sales was increasing, apparently as the result of a more effective utilization of stock.

How to estimate stock balances based on projected cost of sales

Making the calculation

If your age factors and trends prove to be valid over time, you may be able, at least on a preliminary basis, to estimate stock balances based on projected cost of sales. The following procedure assumes an annual basis, but it can apply to other time periods:

Steps	Refer to preceding example	Annual basis
1.	Select average age of stock factor to be used.	91 days
2.	Indicate number of days in period.	360 days
3.	Divide results in Step 1 by Step 2 (91 ÷ 360).	0.253
4.	Multiply projected cost of sales by factor in Step 3.	£963.0 million × 0.253
5.	Result is an estimated stock balance.	£243.6 million

Using the sales-to-stock ratio to measure sales efficiency

This ratio measures the relationship of stock to sales volume, indicating whether there is too much or too little stock to support a given level of sales. (Again, cost of sales is generally used for this ratio, but sales can substitute for it.)

The relation of stock to sales volume is a general measure of sales efficiency. The major objective is to have the smallest possible stock to meet sales requirements efficiently. As a rule, an organization that conducts a large volume of business on a comparatively small stock has a high degree of sales efficiency.

When you compare the sterling amount of sales with the sterling value of the stock, note that these two amounts are on different bases. The stock is valued conventionally at cost or net realizable value, whichever is lower. On the other hand, sales are valued at selling price (cost plus gross margin). Further, to compare two or more periods, you must know the prevailing business conditions. For example, a change in the price level at which new stock is acquired would change the relationship between sales and stock. The monetary relationship could vary markedly without any actual change in the physical volume of sales or stock.

A word of caution

The ratio of sales to stock is generally considered to be a very rough measure of performance. Moreover, most businesses have seasonal fluctuations, and the stock on a balance sheet date may therefore represent a very high or a very low point.

Making the computation

To compute this ratio, divide sales by the stock balance (preferably an averaged value).

EXAMPLE

(in £000,000s)

	First quarter	Second quarter	Third quarter	Fourth quarter	Annual period
Sales volume	252.8	274.9	276.2	273.1	1077.0
Annual sales	1011.2	1099.6	1104.8	1092.4	1077.0
Stock balances	260.0	268.5	256.9	243.4	257.2 avg.
Sales-to-stock ratio	0.97	1.0	1.1	1.1	4.2
Annual sales to stock	3.9	4.1	4.3	4.5	4.2

Interpreting the results

On a quarterly basis, the sales-to-stock ratio ranged from 0.97 to 1.1, with an annual average of 4.2. Based on annual sales, the ratios ranged from a low of 3.9 to a high of 4.5; in essence, sales were approximately four times stock. The variations among periods are primarily attributed to an increasing sales base. The decline in stock, on the other hand, represents a favourable situation if it does not hinder operational objectives.

How to use indirect-to-direct-personnel ratios for manpower planning and control

One of the essentials in all organizations regardless of size is a pool of competent human resources, both direct and indirect, to perform the tasks and services necessary to achieve operational goals and objectives. Manpower planning and control are vital functions to all levels of supervision in order to produce a competitive product or to perform services that can be sold profitably. Management should give indirect personnel requirements particularly close scrutiny because of their impact on profitable operations and overhead costs.

Making the calculation

To monitor indirect manpower planning and control, you can use the *indirect-to-direct-personnel ratio*. To calculate this ratio, *divide the indirect personnel level by the direct*.

EXAMPLE

The following quarter-end ratios were developed using the data from Model 2.1.

19X4

	March	June	September	December	Annual
Indirect-to-direct ratio	47.6%	47.8%	47.7%	47.3%	47.6%
	(16,522 ÷ 34,737)				

Interpreting the results
The ratios are relatively consistent throughout the year with an average of 47.6 per cent. Between the end of March and the end of December, direct personnel increased 3.0 per cent and the indirect manpower increased by 388 or 2.3 per cent. This represents a favourable trend, indicating that management has maintained a desirable relationship between direct and indirect personnel.

How to project indirect manpower

As part of the organization's preliminary operating plan, indirect manpower projections can be made in two ways: (1) by multiplying direct manpower requirements by the average ratio (such as 47.6 per cent) or (2) by a management-controlled objective ratio if historical experience supports the validity of this approach. However, indirect manpower – like direct – is planned in the final analysis by individual organizational units according to their variable activities and needs. Justification of the forecast must be based on the overall operating plan's objectives.

Using the sales-to-direct-personnel ratio to project sales

Making the calculation
Projecting preliminary sales data, if properly validated, may be appropriate, based on a direct manpower forecast. You can use the relationship of sales to direct manpower to check the reasonableness not only of sales projections based on historical experience but also of future expectations developed by more conventional procedures. The factors are developed using the following equation:

$$\text{Sales to direct manpower} = \frac{\text{Sales volume}}{\text{Direct manpower}}$$

EXAMPLE
Based on the data in Model 2.1, these quarterly period and annual average factors were developed:

					Quarterly
	March	*June*	*September*	*December*	*average*
Sales to direct manpower (per direct person)	£7278	£7957	£7931	£7633	£7698

19X8

For the period ending March, sales of £252.8 million were divided by the average direct manpower of 34,737 to obtain the £7278 figure. The quarterly average was obtained by using the period average sales of £269.2 million divided by the quarterly direct manpower average of 34,972. The total sales for the year per direct headcount are approximately £30,796 (£1077.0 million sales divided by the average direct manpower of 34,972).

Interpreting the results

The primary cause for the low sales factor in March is below-average quarterly sales. The higher factors for June and September resulted from a larger sales volume, while the direct manpower strength remained below the annual quarterly average.

Sales-to-total-manpower factor: one approach to sales assessment and planning

Making the calculation

Although this relationship is not usually helpful to most organizations, it is a possible approach to sales assessment and planning. The equation for its development follows:

$$\text{Sales to total manpower} = \frac{\text{Sales volume}}{\text{Total manpower}}$$

EXAMPLE

Using the data in Model 2.1, the following factors were calculated:

	March	June	September	December	Quarterly average
Sales to total manpower	£4932 (per employee)	£5384	£5372	£5183	£5218

Interpreting the results

The below-average ratio in March is primarily attributed to below-average quarterly sales. The above-average factors for the June and September quarters resulted from higher sales without an attendant increase in total manpower.

A word of caution

The drawback to this ratio is that indirect headcount is included in the factor. Indirect manpower is not, of course, directly involved in producing or performing customer services. The ratio may be skewed as a result. An organization may be top heavy in administrative, clerical, and support activities due to either inadequate controls or the nature of the business. Only historical experience can verify the usefulness of this factor for performance assessment and planning. In using historical experience beware of utilizing data no longer relevant due to changes in operating practice, for example, sub-contracting of functions, mentioned earlier.

3 How to use direct cost and D&A expenditure ratios to avoid diluting profits

Chapter highlights

Cost ratios are commonly employed in analysing operational cost activity. With these ratios in hand, the analyst is well equipped to control and plan costs with the object of establishing a competitive yet profitable product price.

To supply the data for analysis, objective setting, and program control, an effective cost accumulation system is indispensable. The requirements and phases of such a system make up the first section of the chapter.

Next you will become acquainted with what you must consider when making use of cost ratio analyses, specifically the relative merits of cost of sales versus sales data.

Overhead is then the focus of the discussion, particularly how to allocate equitably factory overhead expense to direct labour expenditure and hours, prime cost, sales and cost of sales, machine hour rates, product units, and weighting factors.

Unit cost rates, in relation to product cost methods, are described and explained, with special attention given to D&A* and selling expense ratios to product units, sales, and total costs.

You will then see how a manpower plan is put together and how direct manpower is converted to labour hours by means of a computer program or manual calculations. The final section deals with the reporting of actual manpower for assessment and planning.

Direct cost expenditures are costs directly associated with and identifiable to a tangible product, service, and/or project. Direct costs involve direct labour, direct material, plant (factory) overhead, and other direct costs such as computer usage, direct travel, production outside the plant, and possibly consultants. Costs are considered 'direct' if they meet the following major criteria:

1. *Authorization to expend* resources comes through approved product/project work under guidelines.
2. Costs are properly *identified* as direct within the scope of the labour and organizational classification codes.
3. There must be appropriate *consistency in cost classification* and application throughout the organization.

*Distribution and administrative expenses

4. *Cost measurement must be in terms of specific units* (direct hours, pounds sterling or other quantities) that are both practical and economical to use.
5. *Direct costs must fulfil product/project requirements* for production, service, and/or end item needs through one or more of the following:
   - R&D, engineering, or other related technical effort;
   - material contribution to the product or the physical alteration to material;
   - direct manpower utilization and performance;
   - preparation of end item or services rendered documentation.

How to establish a cost accumulation system

Applications

A cost accumulation system enables you to identify the direct elements of cost in accordance with the established organizational procedures and specifically relate them to a product, service, project, contract, or sales order as required. Indirect costs are generally identified to organizational levels and/or through an overhead rate application.

Costs are charged to the organization performing the task or to the responsible organization for which the work is being performed. The cost charging justification is based on an approved budget authorization notice. The cost charge assignment is resolved by the responsible management before the work activity actually commences and resources (in the form of labour, material, etc.) are expended. This is a cost control procedure for ensuring appropriate organization identification and responsibility for proper and specific cost charging and accumulation before effort is initiated.

The collected information must be accurate and timely for all organizational levels of reporting as required, such as cost centre, section, department, project budget centre, functional (manufacturing, engineering) and division summaries.

In most organizations, particularly those dealing with high volume transactions and diversified activities, the cost accumulation process is computerized for ease of extensive record keeping, additions and multiple-user reports on a timely basis for analysis, corrective task direction, and planning.

Requirements

To establish a rewarding and efficient cost accumulation system, you must be certain of the following prerequisites:

1. Approved work authorization documents.
2. Integrity in, and disciplined adherence to, cost system processing requirements.
3. To the extent possible, all relevant direct cost elements should be related to the basic labour charge, machine hour rate or activity.
4. Supervision incurring the cost expenditure must be responsible for cost assignment.

5. The appropriate and responsible financial operations organization should provide the users with the account structure, the system for cost accumulation, and supervisory guidelines at pre-established control points.

The cost accumulation process, step by step

Control points are linked to the phases of the cost accumulation process. The pertinent steps are as follows:

- *Project*. To initiate a project, there must be a request (with cost justification) for management approval and authorization, which would include overhead expenditure requirements.
- *Budget assignment and control responsibility*. The approved project authorization is forwarded to the concerned budgeting organization, which assigns the expenditure budget and the responsibility for control.
- *Authority to expend resources*. The budget expenditure authorization requires that source documents (such as time cards or requests to purchase materials and supplies) be properly approved during the progress of the work activity.
- *Cost expenditures*. Expenditures are to comply with the governing organizational policies and procedures so that they can be identified and classified as either direct or indirect.
- *Cost classification*. The assigned cost classifications are validated in the mechanical master file through a matching process of input data versus data established in the file. If incorrect or non-existent in the file, they are returned to the responsible organization for correction and re-entry.
- *Industrial or cost accounting responsibilities*. The responsibility for maintaining the master audit file includes its composition and updating. Their task is to develop, maintain, and monitor the cost accumulation system with respect to the following:
  - validating the work order and work authorization;
  - verifying the responsible source of cost incurred;
  - comparing relevant estimates and budgets;
  - monitoring project stocks and open commitments;
  - accepting responsibility for required cost distributions;
  - maintaining such system supervisory activities as verifying direct/indirect cost classification, proper account distribution, labour charging by organization, request-to-purchase documentation and compatibility of labour charges with travel expenses, computer utilization audits, material payment documentation, and so on.
- *System reporting*. This system produces various reports both for management review and for reasonable budget and cost control organizational units.

The primary reports include cost data ledgers by contract/sales order, accounting work order, cost elements, and the work in progress trial balance, which includes the cost of sales and expense information by contract. Special analytical reports are provided to meet organizational needs in terms of cost data assessment.

The cost accumulation system is the source for estimating, pricing, and other accounting statistics required for analysis and reporting. System mechanization enables you to capture such information at its basic source. Further, it permits you to update simultaneously more than one file to meet varied organization reporting requirements. Most important, the cost accumulation system provides the actual cost information needed to develop, use, and interpret direct cost expenditure *ratios* as well as their relationship to

- cost of sales;
- sales;
- direct labour;
- cost per product unit.

What to consider when using cost ratio analyses

Caution

Before looking at specific ratios, remember one thing about them: Although ratios are used as indexes of performance measurement, data analysis, and planning guidelines, your utilization of them must be tempered with discretion and judgement. Because most ratios attempt to reflect a great deal of information in a single figure, they can be misleading if you do not consider additional assessed data, such as

- ratio trends in successive periods of activity
- a detailed analysis of events that affected an organization's operations during the year
- ascertaining and evaluating the behaviour of the related industry as a whole as it pertains to the organization.

Comparing the cost of sales to sales

Model 3.1 displays the relationship of cost of sales to sales for a six-month period plus the average of 88.0 per cent for the combined periods. The lowest ratios of 86.5 per cent and 86.8 per cent in February and March are attributed to the relatively lower accumulated direct costs. The highest ratio of 90.2 per cent in the month of June reflects the largest cost by element, which was 43.8 per cent greater than the lowest month. The increase was partially offset by a 37.8 per cent higher sales volume for the same comparable periods.

MODEL 3.1. Sales and cost of sales ratio analyses

(in £000,000s)

Description	Jan.	Feb.	Mar.	Apr.	May	Jun.	Six-month period
Sales	44.0	37.0	38.0	41.0	45.0	51.0	256.0
Direct labour	9.6	8.0	8.1	10.0	11.1	12.2	59.0
Overhead	13.0	10.9	11.0	13.5	14.8	16.4	79.6
Material and other direct costs (ODC)	15.8	13.1	13.9	12.6	14.1	17.4	86.9
Cost of sales	38.4	32.0	33.0	36.1	40.0	46.0	225.5
Gross profit	5.6	5.0	5.0	4.9	5.0	5.0	30.5
D&A/selling expenses	2.7	2.1	2.2	2.7	2.1	2.0	13.8
Profit from operations	2.9	2.9	2.8	2.2	2.9	3.0	16.7
Operating profit to sales ratio	6.6	7.8	7.4	5.4	6.4	5.9	6.5
Direct cost ratios to sales	%	%	%	%	%	%	%
Labour	21.8	21.6	21.3	24.4	24.7	23.9	23.1
Overhead expense	29.6	29.5	28.9	32.9	32.9	32.2	31.1
Material and ODC	35.9	35.4	36.6	30.7	31.3	34.1	33.9
Cost of sales	87.3	86.5	86.8	88.0	88.9	90.2	88.1
D&A selling/expense ratios	6.1	5.7	5.8	6.6	4.7	3.9	5.4
Total cost ratios	93.4	92.2	92.6	94.6	93.6	94.1	93.5
Direct cost ratios to cost of sales							
Labour	25.0	25.0	24.6	27.7	27.8	26.5	26.2
Overhead expenses	33.9	34.1	33.3	37.4	37.0	35.7	35.3
Material and ODC	41.1	40.9	42.1	34.9	35.2	37.8	38.5
Total	100.0	100.0	100.0	100.0	100.0	100.0	100.0

When the cost of sales is compared to sales, the lowest ratio is only 1.8 per cent below the average, and the highest monthly period ratio is 2.4 per cent above the average. The average cost of sales ratio indicates a fairly reliable planning statistic to project a total cost of sales value based on sales volume.

Comparing individual cost elements to the cost of sales

Note in Model 3.1 the period ratios by direct cost element, as well as the six-month averages.

Direct labour. The ratio of direct labour cost to cost of sales averaged 26.2 per cent for the six-month period. The *lowest ratio* of 24.6 per cent occurred in the month of March, while labour costs increased 1.3 per cent over February, yet the cost of sales was 3.1 per cent higher, and thus reduced the ratio. The *highest ratio* of 27.8 per cent occurred in May. While direct labour cost exceeded April's by 11.0 per cent, the total cost of sales increased by 10.8 per cent, thereby accounting for the higher ratio.

Let us analyse the direct labour cost ratio further. If the lowest ratio of 24.6 per cent were applied to the six-month total of cost of sales (£225.5 million), the direct labour cost estimate would be £55.5 million, instead of an actual of £59 million, with a negative difference of £3.5 million, or a 5.9 per cent lower direct labour figure.

If we were to apply the largest ratio of 27.8 per cent to the total cost of sales, the result would be £62.7 million, which is plus £3.7 million or 6.3 per cent over the actual cost of sales of £59 million. This indicates that the lowest estimated ratio would be under 5.9 per cent and the highest ratio would result in an increase of 6.3 per cent in the cost of sales. These factors represent the maximum margin of difference in using the calculated ratios in the estimating/planning process based on the presented data.

Overhead expenses. As shown in Model 3.1, the average overhead expense ratio to cost of sales was 35.3 per cent for the six-month period. The lowest period ratio of 33.3 per cent, occurring in March, is primarily attributed to a 3.1 per cent increase in cost of sales over February, whereas the overhead was only 0.9 per cent higher for the same period.

The highest period ratio of 37.4 per cent occurred in the month of April. The primary cause is that overhead increased 22.7 per cent over March, whereas the cost of sales was only 9.4 per cent greater for the same period.

The lowest ratio was 2.0 per cent under the six-month average, and the highest ratio was 2.1 per cent over the average. Based on these factors, the maximum range of error of the calculated period ratios approximates a ±2.0 per cent. Note that the overhead costs fluctuate by period with direct labour cost but not in the same relative proportion.

Implications of the overhead expense ratios to cost of sales. In the above discussion, an analysis was made of the relationship of overhead expense incurred for a six-month period to the relevant time-period total cost of sales. This information provides management with a basis to project overhead expense as (1) a percentage of cost of sales if that value is preliminarily forecast in total as a *percentage of sales*; (2) if overhead expenses are budgeted in detail (which they are before the budget is finalized), then the total overhead budget can be compared to historical experience as a percentage of cost of sales to determine reasonableness based on the past. Predicated on the above two points, an *overhead rate* can be developed that will indicate to management:

- rate is too high in the competitive market (or possibly too low);
- usefulness in product/contract estimating and pricing;

- highlights of revisions required to the overhead budget plan;
- controls are necessary for specific overhead expenses;
- overhead projections valid within the scope of operational objectives.

The objectives in developing overhead expense ratios are to establish their usefulness in expense data analysis, determine and assess variations from the planned overhead budget and their cause, and to provide a realistic basis for planning future overhead expenses. The potential usage and value of overhead expense ratios are emphasized throughout this chapter.

Material and other direct costs. The six-month average ratio of material and other direct costs to cost of sales is 38.5 per cent. The lowest ratio of 34.9 per cent occurred in April. The primary reason for the low ratio is a 9.4 per cent increase in cost of sales over the March period, whereas the direct material costs were 10.4 per cent lower.

The highest material cost ratio of 42.1 per cent occurred in March. This situation resulted from a 6.1 per cent increase in material and other costs over February, whereas the cost of sales increased only 3.1 per cent over the comparable period.

The low April ratio of 34.9 per cent was 3.6 per cent under the six-month average of 38.5 per cent, and the high ratio of 42.1 per cent was 3.6 per cent greater than the average. This indicates that the maximum error in estimating material costs based on cost of sales would be a ±3.6 per cent for the high and low ratio periods.

Putting cost ratio analyses to work. Let us assume that your organization bases its preliminary cost planning data on the historical relationship of cost of sales to sales. To obtain the direct cost element values, simply apply the past exerience ratios (if proven valid over time periods) to the cost of sales, as discussed. If this approach serves no other purpose you can use it to compare and assess planning data that are developed by more detailed and conventional procedures in the planning process. The approach represents an expedient means for finalizing the organization's operating plan relative to direct costs.

Comparing individual cost elements to sales

As shown in Model 3.1, the six-month average of direct labour costs to sales was 23 per cent. On that basis, £1.00 in direct labour costs represents £4.34 (£256 million sales ÷ £59.0 million labour) in sales. If, however, you were to apply this factor to direct labour cost from period to period, it would not truly represent the specific sales results. The differences ranged from 4 per cent to 7 per cent in sales values, both pluses and minuses, but the monetary value variances are not considered to be of major significance.

The overhead costs to sales ratio averaged 31.1 per cent for the six-month period. The ratio fluctuated between 28.9 per cent in March and 32.9 per cent in both April and May. The higher overhead ratios are attributed to the greater percentage increases in overhead costs for April and May (22.7 per cent and 24.4 per cent, respectively, over March), as compared to the higher sales volumes of 7.9 per cent and 18.4 per cent for the same periods.

The ratio of material and other direct costs to sales averaged 33.9 per cent for the six-month period. The differences between periods ranged from 30.7 per cent in April to 36.6 per cent in March. The low ratio is attributed to a 2.7 per cent increase in sales over February, whereas overhead increased only 0.6 per cent for the same comparable periods.

Caution

Any major fluctuations in the ratios of cost elements to sales from one period to another require further analysis. You must determine the specific causes for the fluctuations before you can realistically use them for estimating and planning guidelines. As a form of performance measurement and analysis, the ratio approach is appropriate only if proven to be valid based on historical experience.

Allocating overhead expenses equitably

Direct labour costs, material costs, and other direct costs associated with manufacturing, either in total or per unit of production, are accumulated from basic source documentation. Timecards/reports, computer terminal input, bills of material, stores requisitions, work orders, and sales invoices are all examples of such documentation. Manufacturing overhead, however, cannot be related specifically to any particular item of output. Yet burden or overhead application for overhead costing is essential to pricing policies, estimating, budgeting, stock valuation, cost of sales determination, and so on. So you need methods to spread overhead over the production activity on an equitable basis.

Comparing actual versus predetermined overhead rates

Overhead may be applied to the product on the basis of rates or ratios, either before or after you actually ascertain the expenditures. If the overhead rate is based on actual costs for the period, then the *application rate* is obtained by dividing the overhead expenses by the *actual* production in terms of units, direct labour hours, or pounds sterling:

Making the calculation

$$\text{Application rate} = \frac{\text{Overhead expenses}}{\text{Production}}$$

To calculate a *predetermined rate*, divide the estimated overhead by the estimated production in units, direct labour hours, or pounds sterling:

$$\text{Predetermined rate} = \frac{\text{Estimated overhead}}{\text{Estimated production}}$$

Pros and cons

When you use the actual overhead, however, you cannot complete the costing procedure until the close of the accounting period. This delay is often disadvantageous because you do not know the final costs on completed work until some time after the production order is filled, thereby delaying the accounting function also. When the overhead expenses are realistically *estimated in advance*, you can determine product costs immediately and smooth seasonal fluctuating activity. On the other hand, using estimates can lead to under- or overabsorbed overhead variances that must be adjusted periodically through accounting journals.

How to apply overhead to products

Some of the common overhead applications are as follows:

- ratio of overhead expenses to direct labour cost;
- rate per direct labour hour;
- ratio of overhead expenses to prime costs (direct labour + material and ODC);
- percentage of sales and cost of sales;
- rate per machine hour;
- product unit cost rate;
- overhead related to activity.

Ratio of overhead expenses to direct labour cost. As shown in Model 3.2, the average ratio for the six-month period is 1.349. To obtain this value, the overhead costs of £79 million were divided by the direct labour costs of £59 million. The ratio indicates that every £1.00 of direct labour activity generates an average of £1.349 of overhead expense.

The lowest ratio of 1.333 is primarily attributed to the direct labour costs being 12.9 per cent above the six-month average, whereas the overhead expenses were only 11.3 per cent higher than the average. The highest ratio of 1.363 in February represents a 1.0 per cent increase over the six-month average.

Applications

As long as the overhead ratio factors developed in Model 3.2 are reasonably consistent from one period to another, you can use the ratios to estimate the overhead expenses based on direct labour cost projections.

The *advantages* of the direct labour cost method are:

1. It is simple to use.
2. It is economical in that the information is readily available. Direct labour

MODEL 3.2. Miscellaneous ratios and rates

Costs, hours/pounds, and product units (hours, units, and cost values in £000s)

Data description	Jan.	Feb.	Mar.	Apr.	May	Jun.	Six-month period
Direct hour rates							
Direct labour hours	3,500	3,000	3,000	3,600	3,300	3,700	20,100
Rates							
Direct labour costs	2.743	2.667	2.700	2.778	3.364	3.297	2.935
Overhead expense	3.714	3.633	3.667	3.750	4.485	4.432	3.960
Material and ODC	4.514	4.367	4.633	3.500	4.273	4.703	4.323
Cost of sales	10.971	10.667	11.000	10.028	12.122	12.432	11.218
Cost ratios							
Prime costs (DL + DM + ODC)	25,400	21,100	22,000	22,600	25,200	29,600	145,900
Overhead to prime costs	51.2	51.7	50.0	59.7	58.7	55.4	54.6
Overhead to DL cost	1.354	1.363	1.358	1.350	1.333	1.344	1.349
Material to DL cost	1.646	1.638	1.716	1.260	1.210	1.426	1.473
D&A/selling expense ratio							
To sales	0.061	0.057	0.058	0.066	0.047	0.039	0.054
To total costs	0.066	0.062	0.063	0.070	0.050	0.042	0.058
Total labour cost rate							
Cost of sales	38,400	32,000	33,000	36,100	40,000	46,000	225,500
D&A/selling	2,700	2,100	2,200	2,700	2,100	2,000	13,800
Total costs	41,100	34,100	35,200	38,800	42,100	48,000	239,300
Labour cost rate	11.743	11.367	11.733	10.778	12.758	12.973	11.806
Cost rates per unit							
Production units	8,800	7,400	7,600	8,200	9,000	10,200	51,200
Rates							
Direct labour costs	1.091	1.081	1.066	1.220	1.233	1.196	1.152
Overhead	1.477	1.473	1.447	1.646	1.644	1.608	1.555
Material/ODC	1.795	1.770	1.829	1.536	1.567	1.706	1.697
Sales costs to units	4.363	4.324	4.342	4.402	4.444	4.510	4.404
D&A/selling	0.307	0.284	0.289	0.329	0.233	0.196	0.269
Total cost ratio to units	4.670	4.608	4.631	4.731	4.677	4.706	4.673

costs are derived from the labour distribution system and/or payroll summary, and the actual overhead expenses can be obtained from the expense ledger by organization, account, and total.

The *disadvantages* include:

1. The labour cost expenditure bases are not necessarily adequate measures of the expense value contribution, as many overhead expenses (such as taxes, depreciation, and the like) do not depend on fluctuations of labour costs.
2. The application ignores other factors in the cost of production, such as the use of expensive machinery that can exceed straight labour costs in some departments.
3. The method charges operations performed by high rate operators with proportionately more overhead than those performed by low rate operators.

Direct labour hour formula. To obtain the rate per direct labour hour, divide the overhead expense in pounds by direct labour hours. Before applying overhead, you must determine the relationship (or ratio) between the amount of overhead expenses to be applied and the number of direct labour hours involved. The expense application can be by cost centre, department, product, service, or total plant, as appropriate and required by the organization.

In Model 3.2 the six-month average direct labour hour rate is £3.96 per hour. The *lowest* expense rate of £3.63 occurred in February. This rate is attributed to a 16.2 per cent reduction in overhead expenses, as compared to January, while direct labour hours were 14.3 per cent lower in comparison.

The *highest* expense rate per hour of £4.485 occurred in May. The primary cause is that the May overhead increased by 9.6 per cent over April, whereas the direct labour hours decreased by 8.3 per cent for the same period. The simultaneous increase in expenses and decrease in labour hours accounted for the higher rate.

The *advantages* of the direct labour hour procedure are:

1. It is simple to use.
2. It represents a realistic application base when labour operations are the central factor in production.
3. By employing a time factor, the method overcomes a major objection to the direct labour cost application because time is costed at the same overhead rate in spite of varying pay scales.

The *disadvantage* of the direct labour hour procedure is similar to that of direct labour costs: it ignores the value contribution to the product by factors (expense) other than direct labour. For example, suppose that a machine shop is composed of drill presses, lathes, automatic screw machines, and the like. It is unrealistic and inaccurate to apply overhead on a departmental direct labour hour basis for such a department.

Overhead expense ratio to prime costs. Some organizations use a ratio of overhead to prime costs, if proven valid, as a factor for planning and performance measurement. Model 3.2 displays the ratios developed for the six-month period with a resultant average of 54.6 per cent. The lowest ratio of 50.0 per cent occurred in March (although January and February were close seconds). This ratio is primarily attributed to a relatively greater fluctuation in prime costs as compared to the overhead cost values.

The highest ratio was in April, when the prime costs were 2.7 per cent higher than March but the overhead expenses were 22.7 per cent greater. The result of the higher overhead expenses was an increased ratio.

Applications
To use the ratio of overhead to prime costs effectively, you have to make a detailed analysis of the specific causes for cost data changes. You must also determine if this type of situation will continue to occur or if unusual circumstances caused the fluctuations.

Pros and cons
The *advantages* of the prime cost method are:

1. It is simple to use.
2. All the required data values are immediately available from the accounting records.

The *disadvantages* include:

1. It does not make use of the time factor in applying overhead.
2. There is no logical relationship between the major part of overhead costs and the monetary value of raw materials.
3. It is unlikely that accurate overhead costing can result from using both direct labour (due to varying direct labour calculation methods) and potential errors in time-projected material costs. These prime cost values are on a gross estimated value basis that would distort a valid relationship or ratio of overhead expense to prime costs for application purposes.
4. Use of this ratio is restricted to situations in which there are no extreme variations in product processing.
5. This method may prove to be more useful in certain departments rather than in the overall plant operations.

Percentage of sales and cost of sales. The ratio of overhead to sales and to cost of sales is displayed in Model 3.1. The analytical implications were discussed earlier in this chapter.

Machine hour rate method. To apply overhead as a rate per machine hour, first determine the *ratio* between the amount of overhead expense to be applied and the number of machine hours. Overhead is then allocated to the job or process by multiplying the machine hours involved in a specific operation by your rate. To derive the machine hour rate, divide the overhead expenses for a specific machine (or for a group of machines if they are identical in operation and cost) by the relevant machine hours:

$$\text{Machine hour rate} = \frac{\text{Overhead expenses}}{\text{Machine hours}}$$

Generally, the machine hour rate represents an estimate of the actual overhead cost per hour for operating each machine.

Computing machine hour rates

The three steps in calculating machine hour rates are as follows:

1. The affected departments project the estimated overhead expenses for the period in the form of a budget plan.
2. You regroup expense items into three classifications, such as: (a) specific charges to each machine relative to power, maintenance, and depreciation; (b) heat, light, and building costs; and (c) all other general and service costs, including indirect supplies and miscellaneous labour, supervision, and engineering support.
3. Combine the direct and pro rata machine costs to determine the total projected overhead expenses to operate each machine during the year. The machine rate would be the result of dividing this total by the number of operational hours. The estimated machine hours may include either setup time or separate rates developed for operating and setup time.

Pros and cons

When machinery is the major factor in production, the machine hour application has undoubtedly the greatest number of *advantages* in allocating overhead:

1. *Cost accounting.* It provides the most accurate means for applying overhead expense to each task or job. Since the machine hour rate application uses time as a base in allocating overhead expenses, the rate is realistic even when one operator has to operate several machines or when several operators are required for each machine. The procedure also combines the operator's pay rate with the machine's overhead to obtain the total cost centre rate for labour and overhead.
2. *Marketing.* Machine hour rates permit the sales group to quote definitively the estimated selling prices for each specific job.
3. *Engineering.* It provides a realistic procedure for estimating the job cost on a product specification basis with a great degree of accuracy.
4. *Management.* The overhead costing method involved in this rate is both logical and scientific. Management can therefore depend on accurate cost reports and be secure in price quotations to the customer. With such assurance, management can avoid either operating losses or the failure to obtain jobs. Further, the machine rate method provides a sound basis for the measurement of the monthly cost of idle machines.

The primary disadvantages of the machine hour rate include:

1. The cost accounting procedure increases costs since additional records, which ordinarily would not be required, have to be generated and maintained for each operation's machine time.
2. The method may not be universally applicable because it can be used only for costing machine operations.
3. It increases the detailed cost accounting workload because a blanket rate cannot be used if individual or group machine rates are utilized.
4. As relatively few organizations can use only machine rates, other types of rates must be employed in conjunction with the machine hour method. On the other hand, a number of affected organizations can use direct labour rates more uniformly throughout the plant, thereby applying the procedure more widely.

Product unit cost method. The simplest and most direct method of overhead application is on the basis of the product unit quantities produced. To develop the rate, divide the overhead expense costs by the product units produced. The calculations may involve actuals, estimated actuals, or normal activity data. Further, the rates may be for the total plant, department or cost centre.

Model 3.2 displays the rates for a six-month period with an average of £1.555. The results were obtained by *dividing the period overhead costs* by the *related units produced* in that period (see Model 3.1 for the overhead cost values). In January, for example, the overhead costs were £13,000 and the unit quantities produced were 8800 (Model 3.2). These values produced a rate of £1.477 per unit (£13,000 ÷ 8800 units).

Rate analysis for six-month period

The average rate for the first three months was calculated to be £1.466 versus £1.633 for the second three months or an 11.4 per cent increase. The difference in average rates for the two three-month periods seems to be that overhead expenses increased by 28 per cent in the second three-month period, whereas the units produced were only 15 per cent greater. This situation accounted for the higher average rate.

This is one of the basic approaches to the analysis of rate differences between periods. A more detailed analysis of the circumstances relating to the reported figures may uncover other factors to be considered.

Pros and cons

The product unit method has its advantages and disadvantages. The product rate application is the simplest to use in applying overhead. Yet its usefulness is limited to situations involving only one product or a few closely related products characterized by a common denominator, such as weight. If no common denominator exists, you must determine some other pertinent and reasonable weighting factor, such as the *relevant point or factor basis*.

Weighting factors for overhead applications

You must adapt relative weighting factors per unit for a given period to the character of the specific industry. For example, units can be expressed in terms of pounds weight, gallons, feet, or whatever. Overhead is then applied on the basis of the factors you decide on.

EXAMPLE

The following data are on a *unit weight basis* (£):

Unit quantity produced	500	400	600	—
Product per unit	3 lbs.	5 lbs.	2 lbs.	—
Total weight produced	1500	2000	1200	4700
Cost per pound	0.4567	0.4567	0.4567	0.4567
Overhead cost applied	685.05	913.40	548.04	2146.49
Cost per unit	1.37	1.52	0.91	—

Applying direct cost rates per product unit

Model 3.2 displays the ratios of direct cost of sales and total cost to the number of product units produced. The cost rate per unit in each type of ratio was developed by dividing the elements of cost by the number of units.

Comparing the cost of sales to product units

In Model 3.2, the ratio of total cost of sales to product units ranges from a low of £4.324 (February) to a high of £4.51 (June), with a six-month average of £4.404. The percentage difference between the low and high rates is 4.3 per cent. When February's cost of sales data is compared to June's, note the 43.8 per cent increase (£32,000 to £42,000) in June. At the same time, the product units increased only 37.8 per cent (7400 to 10,200), thus accounting for the increase in the June rate.

The *total cost ratio* to product units averages £4.673 for the six-month period. The highest rate, April, is primarily attributed to the higher D&A and selling rate (0.329), which was 22.3 per cent greater than the six-month average of 0.269.

Applying the direct labour rate to product units

The direct labour rate (or ratio) per product unit averaged £1.152 for the six-month period. The highest rate of £1.233 occurred in May, and it was 7.0 per cent above the six-month average. The cause is principally the relatively greater increase in direct labour costs as compared to the increase in units produced.

The lowest rate of £1.066 for the six-month period occurred in March; it was 7.5 per cent below the six-month average. This low resulted from a relatively greater increase in units produced as compared to the increase in direct labour costs.

Using the overhead expense rate

These rates have already been discussed (see 'Product Unit Cost Method'). In Model 3.2, the overhead costs for the second three months exceeded costs for the first three months by 30.9 per cent (£34,900 to £45,700), whereas the units produced (23,800 to 27,400) were only 15.5 per cent higher for the period. This situation resulted in the higher rate for the second quarter.

Calculating the material and other direct cost (ODC) rate

The material and ODC cost rate per product unit averaged £1.697 for the six-month period as displayed in Model 3.2. The lowest rate of £1.5677 occurred in April. April's rate was 9.5 per cent below the six-month average, primarily due to a reduction in material/ODC costs versus an increase in the number of units produced.

March saw the highest material rate per production unit (£1.829), which was 7.2 per cent below the six-month average. The reason was a relatively greater increase in material costs as compared to the increase in units produced.

Note that the product units increased 15.1 per cent in the second quarter over the first quarter, whereas material costs were only 3.0 per cent higher, thereby accounting for the increased material cost rates.

Applying D&A/selling expense to product units

The six-month average for the D&A/selling expense rate is £0.269 per production unit. April had the highest expense rate of £0.329, which is 22.3 per cent above the average. Compared to those of March, expenses were 22.7 per cent higher but the production units increased by only 7.9 per cent. A detailed analysis is required to determine the cause(s) for the higher expenses.

In June the expense rate dropped to a low of £0.196, which was 27.1 per cent below the six-month average. This situation resulted from the lowest expenses in the six-month period in tandem with the highest units of production.

Application
These period rates per unit help you rapidly to assess product unit costs and highlight unusual variances.

Calculating the labour hour rate for total costs

To obtain the labour rates, divide the total costs by the direct labour hours. The rates in Model 3.2 vary from a low of £10.78 in April to a high of £12.97 in June, with a six-month average of £11.81. The lowest rate is 0.2 per cent below average and the highest is 1.4 per cent greater. In the low rate situation, the April direct labour hours increased 20 per cent over March, whereas the total costs were only 10.2 per cent higher, thus creating the low cost rate.

Compared to the low rate in April, the high June rate of £12.97 is 20.4 per cent greater. In reviewing the two periods' basic data, observe the cause for the high cost rate: The total costs in June were 23.7 per cent higher, whereas the direct hours increased by only 2.8 per cent (3,600 to 3,700).

The labour hour rate approach is a rapid means for estimating total costs based on the labour rate – assuming that historical experience proved to be both reasonable and reliable.

Determining cost units in relation to product costs

A major objective of cost accounting is to determine product unit costs. Yet the product unit is not always used as a cost unit. Unit costs are considered to be average costs, which are accumulated by jobs and processes or by operations, and spread out over the units produced.

Cost accumulation by the job method

In the job method, the production cost for a job or lot is collected on a job order and posted to a cost sheet. Labour and material are charged directly to the job. Factory overhead is added to these costs according to rates predetermined by organizational practices and procedures. The total job cost is then divided by the number of units produced to obtain the *average cost per product unit*.

Cost accumulation by process costing

Under the *process costing* procedure, all the costs for a process function (week, month, and so on) are accumulated on a process cost sheet. These costs are then divided by the period production to obtain unit costs. All the units produced from a particular process during a period have the same average cost.

Putting unit costs to work

Application
The ratio of cost elements to product units helps you to estimate costs, price products, and measure cost performance based on historical experience (if proven to be reliable). The component cost element ratios enable you to analyse cost data in detail. Further, you can use the cost ratios for budget development and planning. Period-to-period production cost results can be compared, readily assessed, and variances derived for corrective action and future planning changes. (See Model 3.2.)

Comparing D&A/selling expense to sales

Although the D&A and selling expense ratios to sales are generally computed separately, Model 3.2 presents them as a composite total, with a six-month average of 5.4 per cent.

During the six-month period, the lowest ratio of 3.9 per cent occurred in June. The principal cause for this low was the large sales volume of £51,000, compared to the lowest expense results in June.

The largest percentage of 6.6 per cent came about in April. The cause was that April's sales of £41,000 were 16.9 per cent less than June's but D&A/selling expenses were 35 per cent greater.

In view of these high and low ratios, you have to analyse the detail to determine the specific causes for the fluctuations in the expense values. The investigation may provide the clues for their behaviour that can be very important in estimating more realistically and in planning for the future.

With the expense ratio to sales, you can derive the estimated costs for product pricing and customer quotations based on the sales and cost projections. Direct cost ratios to sales can be useful in developing reasonable cost of sales, and, together with D&A/selling expenses, they provide the total cost projections and estimated income from operations.

Comparing D&A/selling expense to total costs

Model 3.2 displays the subject ratios for six periods plus the average of 5.8 per cent. The lowest percentage of 4.2 per cent occurred in June, and the highest ratio of 7.0 per cent materialized in April.

When the April data are compared to those of March, the D&A/selling expenses increased 22.7 per cent, whereas the total costs were only 7.4 per cent greater (£35,200 versus £38,800). The changes in the April results were the contributing cause to the high percentage experienced.

In comparing April's high rate of 7.0 per cent to June's low of 4.2 per cent, observe that June's total costs *increased* 23.7 per cent (£38,800 to £48,000), while the D&A/selling expenses *decreased* 25.9 per cent (£2,700 to £2,000). This situation accounts for the decline in the rate to 4.2 per cent, which was 27.6 per cent below the six-month average of 5.8 per cent.

Application
The D&A/selling expense ratio to total costs can be used to estimate these expenses by applying the developed monthly percentages shown in Model 3.2 or on an estimated half-year average (5.8 per cent) basis to the appropriate time-projected costs. Total costs may have been estimated on the basis of a labour rate per direct labour hour (see Model 3.2) or as a total cost ratio to projected sales volume.

Planning, controlling, and analysing manpower

To be successful, a business entity must plan and control its manpower. Manpower projections are based not only on current and anticipated sales volume, but also on the number of employees and the skills required to generate the product. In the planning process, you must also consider indirect support needs for managing, administering, maintaining records, and otherwise assisting the direct production effort.

Each organizational unit develops a manpower operating plan on which labour costs and various payroll expenses are based. Manpower, generally the major cost in operating a business, involves all types of personnel in research, engineering, manufacturing, administration and other activities.

Preparing the division manpower plan

The division manpower projections represent a summary of the departments, wherein direct personnel planning may be at the cost or budget centre levels. Labour needs are developed in detail by job classification, payroll category (direct or indirect), and unit functional organizations. Justification of the required headcount is based on current and anticipated workloads by job classification.

Major functional manpower projections are based on the following relevant considerations:

Engineering departments plan their manpower needs within the framework of their current authorized and projected engineering projects. The manpower plan also includes the requirements for general research and development programmes, as well as for specific customer engineering applications.

Manufacturing or production departments base their planning on the product unit sales requirements and projections, which reflect stock levels and a time-phased schedule of needs. The manufacturing schedule generally includes product quality assurance and inspection, packing, receiving, and delivery. The functional structure may vary among organizations depending on their needs and organizational practices.

Administrative functions (accounting, budgeting, estimating, marketing) plan their manpower needs and departmental expenses according to management-approved headcount projections and unit budgets.

The approved manpower forecasts become a part of the operating plan, which is the basic blueprint for the organization's operation. Actual performance is analysed and measured on the basis of this plan of operation.

Converting direct manpower to labour hours by computer

Model 3.3 presents an overview of the conversion of direct manpower projections to hours and pounds. A brief description of the computerized process follows.

Primary input. The direct *manpower projections* are approved by the responsible members of management. The input is by cost centre (if applicable) and identified to a department showing the projected headcount by period. The manpower is segregated into hourly, salaried, and possibly job classifications. The computer process summarizes the cost centre's planned headcounts to functional department and division totals.

A planned *overtime cost percentage limit* is input. The percentage constraint is at the designated cost centre or department levels.

A planned overtime *premium rate* is provided by the budgeting group in accordance with organizational policy. The rates consist of time and a half, double time, or a flat rate per hour over 40 hours per week.

The *straight time hours per day factor*, generally eight hours, is entered into the computerized system. Some organizations may use ten hours per day for a four-day week. The factor depends on the organization's policy and practices.

A *productive hours per day* factor may be entered into the system depending on an organization's needs. The objective is to let non-productive time have its effect on the overhead expense budget. The factor of 0.925 is shown in Model 3.3, which represents the historical relationship (or ratio) of productive hours to straight time. To get the 0.925 factor, divide the productive hours of 7.4/day by the straight time hours of 8.0. The 0.6 hours' difference represents the estimated time for sickness, training, meetings, idle time, and so on.

The *work days per accounting period* are provided as a direct input. This factor may vary among periods depending on their established accounting month periods, which take into consideration holidays, calendar month workdays, or cycles of five, four, and four weeks in a quarter.

Direct and indirect *labour rates* are direct input. The labour rates may be on an hourly basis by job classification, by average organizational rate, or possibly by cluster rates (more than one organization's average rate). The rates are based on actual historical experience. The projected rates usually anticipate merit increases within the next twelve months.

Depending on the objectives of the computerized labour system, other relevant input may include:
    direct hour projections by contract, project, product and/or work order;
    direct manpower, direct hour, and monetary actuals;
    actual direct labour rates and averages by job classification.
This type of input permits mechanical comparisons (actuals versus projections), varied variance analyses, and highlights problem situations.

Computer processing functions

Direct manpower projections are converted into straight time labour hours per day and per period by organization and/or project.

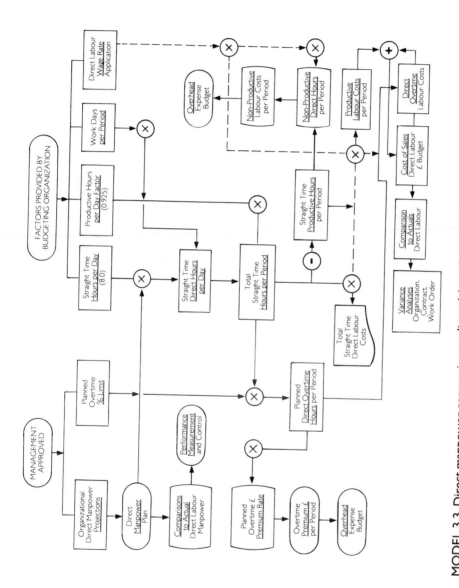

MODEL 3.3. Direct manpower conversion to direct labour hours and costs: a computerized planning process.

The productive hours per day factor is applied to the period's straight time hours. This yields the productive hours per period, which, when subtracted from straight time hours, results in non-productive hours per period.

The planned overtime percentage limit is applied to straight time hours by period to obtain the planned direct overtime hours by period.

Non-productive direct hours are multiplied by the appropriate wage rate(s) to obtain non-productive labour costs by period. These are reflected in the overhead expense budget.

The period productive hours are multiplied by the appropriate wage rate(s) to derive the productive labour costs by period, which are reflected in the cost of sales.

The overtime premium cost rate is applied to the planned direct overtime hours to obtain the overtime premium costs by period, which are reflected in the overhead expense budget.

The appropriate rate is applied to the planned overtime hours to obtain the direct straight time labour costs for reflection in the cost of sales. To obtain the total cost for overtime activities, combine the overtime premium costs with the overtime straight time labour costs.

Computerised reporting

- The actual headcount by organization is compared with the planned manning to provide the deviations by period for analysis, assessment of performance, and initiation of controls when feasible and appropriate.
- The actual direct labour hours and costs are compared to the planned projections to ascertain variances for corrective action. The labour hour and cost reporting can be by organization, contract, project, product, and/or work order.
- The developed overhead expense budget items (overtime premium costs and non-productive costs) are compared to actuals to determine variances.

Automated processing and reporting in the manpower system, as shown in Model 3.3, enables you to develop a direct manpower plan with the associated labour hours and costs. The data are segregated to achieve varied reporting objectives, particularly performance analysis, measurement, and control. Variance development and isolating problem situations highlight the system.

Reporting manpower actuals for assessment and planning

Model 3.4 displays a format for reporting manpower actuals. You can readily compare manpower projections, in terms of headcounts and ratios, to the actuals to ascertain variations and causes when significant.

Establishing ratios of indirect to direct manpower

Model 3.4 presents the actual direct factory and engineering manpower, although

MODEL 3.4. Reporting manpower actuals for assessment and planning

Direct manpower

Period	Factory	% of total direct	Engineering	% of total direct	Total direct
Jan.	14,410	64.6	7,902	35.4	22,312
Feb.	14,322	64.5	7,887	35.5	22,209
Mar.	14,712	64.5	7,959	35.5	22,671
Apr.	14,645	64.8	7,943	35.2	22,588
May	15,268	65.6	8,003	34.4	23,271
Jun.	15,274	65.7	7,987	34.3	23,261
Jul.	15,255	65.7	7,958	34.3	23,213
Aug.	15,190	65.5	7,997	34.5	23,187
Sep.	14,972	65.2	7,989	34.8	22,961
Oct.	14,789	65.1	7,916	34.9	22,705
Nov.	14,576	64.8	7,922	35.2	22,498
Dec.	14,482	64.7	7,910	35.3	22,392

Indirect manpower

Period	Factory	% factory direct	Engineering	% engineering direct	D&A selling	% total direct	Total indirect	Total headcount	% indirect to direct
Jan.	6218	43.2	992	12.6	3,387	15.2	10,597	32,909	47.5
Feb.	6211	43.4	978	12.4	3,384	15.2	10,573	32,782	47.6
Mar.	6287	42.7	988	12.4	3,398	15.0	10,673	33,344	47.1
Apr.	6278	42.9	981	12.4	3,392	15.0	10,651	33,239	47.2
May	6334	41.5	908	11.3	3,411	14.7	10,653	33,924	45.8
Jun.	6341	41.5	903	11.3	3,408	14.7	10,652	33,913	45.8
Jul.	6349	41.6	894	11.2	3,396	14.6	10,639	33,852	45.8
Aug.	6352	41.8	898	11.2	3,409	14.7	10,659	33,846	46.0
Sep.	6301	42.1	902	11.3	3,401	14.8	10,604	33,565	46.2
Oct.	6292	42.5	891	11.3	3,397	15.0	10,580	33,285	46.6
Nov.	6271	43.0	893	11.3	3,399	15.1	10,563	33,061	47.0
Dec.	6196	42.8	887	11.2	3,391	15.1	10,474	32,866	46.8

other direct functional classifications can be included for consideration in ratio analyses. The factory direct manpower approximates two-thirds of the total direct headcount. The ratio between periods for the factory direct ranged from a low of 64.5 per cent to a high of 65.7 per cent. The engineering percentages varied accordingly from a low of 34.3 per cent to 35.5 per cent.

The *factory indirect to direct ratio* varied among the reported periods from a low of 41.5 per cent (May and June) to a high of 43.4 per cent (February). The *engineering indirect to direct* period ratios ranged from 11.2 per cent to 12.6 per cent, with an average of approximately 11.6 per cent.

The *D&A and selling indirect to total direct* headcount averaged 15 per cent by period. Because the ratio is fairly consistent among periods, it provides a reasonable ratio for preliminary D&A and selling organization's headcount planning. The ratio may also be used as a validity check when the indirect manpower is developed by more detailed processes (such as unit organization and job classification).

Importance of indirect to direct headcount

The most important overall ratio statistic is the percentage of *total indirect to direct headcount* (provided by period at the extreme right of Model 3.4). Most organizations establish an indirect to direct ratio goal for the total organization, particularly if the operation is substantially orientated towards manufacturing and engineering. Generally, a low ratio is assumed to be a prime indicator of more productive and effective utilization of indirect personnel. Further, if indirect manpower is reasonably reduced and controlled, the effect on total overhead expenses and rate (relative to product cost and competitive sales price) can be signfiicant.

In Model 3.4 the lowest calculated ratio percentage of 45.8 per cent occurred in the May, June, and July periods, whereas the highest percentage of 47.6 per cent was in February. In comparing May's low percentage to February's ratio, note the following differences:

	Total direct manpower	Total indirect
May	23,231	10,653
February	22,209	10,573
Difference	1,062 ÷ 22,209 = +4.8%	80 ÷ 10,573 = +0.8%

The primary cause for the lower ratio in May is a combined effect of 1062 higher direct manpower base (or 4.8 per cent) and only 0.8 per cent increase in the indirect headcount. This is a desirable situation from the standpoint of cost control and manpower management, as long as the lower indirect support does not penalize the direct operational environment.

Final caution

Although ratios offer a succinct method for analysing operational results, you must use them with caution: they can misdirect your interpretation and use of them. Be sure to assess thoroughly the historical experience and trends to establish their validity. As a financial analyst, you must be aware of the underlying principles and circumstances that influence ratio fluctuations and, as a result, their approriate use.

4 How to monitor and control those elusive overhead costs

Chapter highlights

Monitoring, planning, and controlling overhead expenses can be particularly difficult. Yet they need not present a problem if you make use of the overhead expense ratios explained in this chapter.

As any ratios, these depend on an effective accumulation system for their accuracy. The chapter therefore begins by describing a computerized expense processing system. Also shown is how the overhead data flow interfaces with the balance sheet and cash flow. The models here illustrate factory overhead and D&A/selling expense comparisons, as well as the expense ratios for sound analysis and planning guidelines. Other models help you to assess advertising and sales promotion expenses, with special emphasis on their budgeting and effect on sales volume.

Overhead expenses are then correlated to direct labour costs. The focus is on period expense ratios to direct labour costs, expense category ratios to direct labour costs, and, finally, the correlation of indirect to direct labour costs.

Ultimately, you will see how to assess comparisons of factory overhead budgets and actual expenses, as well as how to use these analyses in budget planning.

Overhead expenses represent indirect services and support for operational activities. These expenses generally do not contribute directly – nor are they readily identified – to the manufacture of a product, performing direct services or to achieving direct project requirements. Instead, overhead expenses are accumulated in detailed accounts, budgeted, and reported by each organization. The expenses are then summarized into primary control accounts (as specified by the chart of accounts), such as manufacturing (factory), engineering, quality assurance, administrative, selling, research and development (if applicable), plus other categories depending on organizational requirements.

Certain expense ratios can help you to assess these indirect costs and control excessive expenditures. The key factors in monitoring these expenses are ongoing supervision, control measures, and performance measurement.

How to process overhead accumulation

Model 4.1 displays a basic mechanical system for processing overhead expense. In

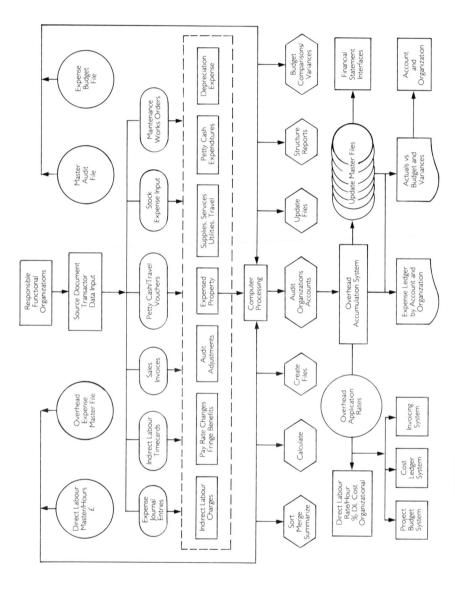

MODEL 4.1. How to process overhead expense accumulation by computer

many organizations, computerized expense processing is cost effective, providing a timely vehicle for expense accumulation, supervision and control. Periodic data are compared to the budget, significant variances are analysed to determine causes, and corrective action is taken. In developing the overhead budget plan, the possibility of invalid assumptions always exists, so the assumptions may have to be revised to reflect existing realities in overhead expense projections.

Utilizing input from the source documents

In an automated system, expense data from source documents is input by means of a station transactor device, as shown in Model 4.1. The basic documentation consists of indirect labour timecards, sales invoices, petty cash vouchers, travel expense reports, stock expense requisitions, repair and maintenance work orders, miscellaneous journals, and so on. The input information, including the date and the amount involved in the transaction, is identified and charged to a document number, a valid expense account, and an organizational number.

The various categories of the input expenses are then identified. The classifications of the model are only general examples; their type and detail may vary among organizations depending on their respective needs and control objectives.

Inputting additional information for processing

Information from the master files

In addition to the source data, the automated system needs other information before it can perform processing and meet its requirements. This information is fed into the computer from other master files (see Model 4.1).

The *actual direct labour master file* provides direct labour hours and cost data to develop an overhead rate per direct hour and/or overhead expense percentage of direct labour costs. This computation can be done for an individual organizational unit (cost centre, department, overhead centre) and for the overall organization. Rates can be developed by contract or by sales order – whichever the established needs are.

The *overhead expense file* provides prior period expense information, arranged by account and organization and summarized year to date. As new period actuals become available, the computer program adds the data to the file and summarizes them. The program can generate rates by direct labour hour and as a percentage of direct labour costs, which are compared with the overhead expense budget and variances calculated for reporting purposes.

The *expense budget file* contains the annual budget by period and by year to date totals for comparison with actuals and calculating variances.

How the computer processes the data

Before accepting data into the system, the computer program audits the input to verify the validity of expense and organizational identifier numbers. It rejects invalid information, which is returned to the input organization for corrective action and re-input.

Computer processing involves a number of routines that clerks would perform in a manual system. The program segregates account information by appropriate organization, merges it, and summarizes it in the overhead ledger. It also performs the required calculation, such as adding subaccounts to their control totals and organization levels.

It creates file records when necessary to accommodate new information and/or to make changes in existing file information.

It updates the appropriate master files and structures data into pre-established report formats.

Identifying the elements of system output

As displayed in Model 4.1, the results of the overhead expense accumulation are as follows:

An updated expense ledger by account and organization with appropriate subtotal and total summations.

Development of overhead application rates per direct hour or a percentage of direct labour costs, which can be used in the cost ledger system, project budget reporting, and the customer invoicing process.

Updating of master files as appropriate to feed other system requirements – general ledger and financial statement interfaces (profit statement, cash flow, and balance sheet).

Actuals versus budget comparison (period and year to date) with variances.

Although not shown in Model 4.1 but in subsequent displays, the percentage of each account to the total overhead (both actuals and budget) would be calculated, indicating the variance percentage increase or decrease among period increments and/or annual totals. This type of report provides a comprehensive review of changes that occurred. Various ratios are also developed from this system which will be described in this chapter.

Putting the automated system to work

The computerized overhead expense accumulation system provides you with a number of useful outputs:

- timely accumulating and processing of expense information with minimal manual effort;
- expense ledger by organization;
- overhead application rates for the cost ledger and invoicing systems;
- reporting of budget versus actuals;
- various ratios for performance evaluation and operational control and planning.

It is a cost-effective process.

Interfacing overhead expense data flow

Classifying the expenses

Model 4.2 displays the overhead data flow interfaces that occur after the expenses have been accumulated and processed. At the top of the chart are the major expense classifications. In the bottom part of each of these boxes is a listing of the more detailed account identifiers within the categories. Through journals, the expense accounts are set up as liabilities in the general ledger. The exceptions are prepaid expenses (current asset) and reserve for depreciation/amortization (reduction to property, plant, and equipment – a noncurrent asset).

Expenses are classified and segregated as either factory overhead (cost of sales item) or D&A and selling expenses (period costs and charges against gross profit). These items are reflected in the profit statement.

Analysing the balance sheet

The automated general ledger/balance sheet system provides the account balances for the balance sheet statement (that is accrued salaries and wages, creditors, and the like). When the liabilities become due for payment, they are paid and become reductions to the outstanding balances. As prepaid expenses are spread over time, they are reduced accordingly.

The depreciation reserve account reflects the period accumulation of depreciation expense, which represents a reduction to gross fixed asset costs. In some organizations, depreciation expense is reflected as a source of funds from operations. This expense is not reflected in the cash flow system as it is *not an actual cash receipt* or expenditure, but rather a contingency fund for fixed asset replacements.

Analysing cash flow

As direct cash payments are made, the amounts are classified as cash payments. The same is done to other liabilities as they are paid over a longer time span.

Model 4.2 shows how the overhead system interfaces with other segments of the overall financial reporting system. It provides an insight as to how the expense

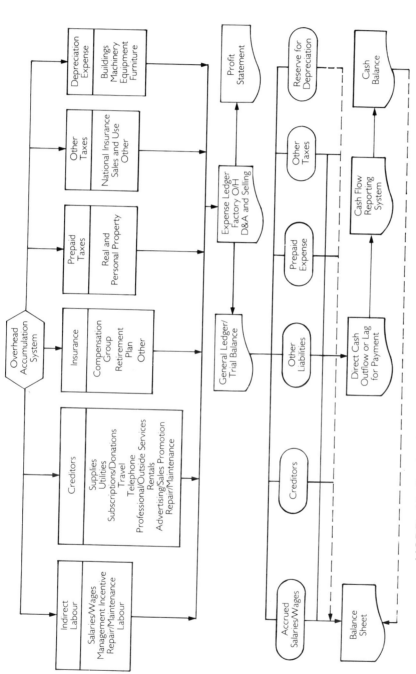

MODEL 4.2. Overhead expense data flow interfaces: a computerized approach

data are classified, collected, and reported from the overhead accumulation to the creation of liabilities and subsequently their payment. Some expenses are paid at the time of their occurrence and entered directly in the cash payments register.

Comparing individual expenses to total expense

The rates and ratios in Model 4.3 are the types used in analysing overhead expenses and in planning operational budgets, and its numerical data will augment our discussion. Comparisons and illustrations are provided for two annual time periods. Specifically, the model compares the *ratio relationships* among the individual expense accounts and the total for 19X4 and 19X3. Also presented are the variance amounts for the two years of actuals, along with the percentage change of increase or decrease among the accounts. The model's reporting format summarizes the pertinent factors involved in a thorough expense analysis of overhead expense performance. Highlights of the upper portion of the model are as follows:

Analysing individual expenses

- The total expense variance between the two years was £16 million, which represented a 6.3 per cent increase in 19X4 over 19X3. In cost terms, the largest variances occurred in indirect labour, pensions, and other labour benefits, which accounted for approximately 72 per cent of the total variance.
- In the other expense accounts, the relatively modest cost increases can be primarily attributed to a 5.6 per cent increase in direct labour hours and a 10.6 per cent greater sales activity, which indicates a higher production activity.
- The *ratios* of the individual expense accounts to their totals in both years were modestly consistent, indicating that the actual performance results were in accord with operational plan activity requirements.
- The comparative analysis data in Model 4.3, if reasonably consistent over time, provide a sound basis for developing an expense budget – or at least a preliminary assessment of budget data later to be developed by more detailed procedures. Budget to actuals comparisons can highlight significant variances for further analysis and possible corrective action.

These analyses, as well as monthly comparisons and timely performance assessments, can be readily accomplished using a computer.

How to use expense relationships

The expense relationships in the lower portion of Model 4.3 highlight the aggregate analysis of the actual overhead expenses:

MODEL 4.3. Factory overhead expense comparisons and ratio analyses

(in £000s)

Expense classification	19X4 actuals	% ratio to total expense	19X3 actuals	% ratio to total expense	19X4 Variances over (under)	19X4 % Variance over (under)
Indirect labour	125,000	46.3	120,000	47.3	5,000	4.2
Micellaneous labour benefits	50,000	18.5	45,000	17.7	5,000	11.1
Pensions	12,500	4.6	11,000	4.3	1,500	13.6
Management incentive	2,500	0.9	2,200	0.9	300	13.6
Supplies	18,500	6.9	18,000	7.1	500	2.8
Taxes and insurance	14,200	5.3	13,800	5.4	400	2.9
Repair and maintenance	12,500	4.6	11,800	4.7	700	5.9
Depreciation	13,200	4.9	12,500	4.9	700	5.6
Equipment rentals	2,400	0.9	1,900	0.7	500	26.3
Utilities	4,200	1.6	3,800	1.5	400	10.5
Telephone	4,000	1.5	3,900	1.5	100	2.6
Travel	3,800	1.4	3,700	1.5	100	2.7
Professional/outside services	4,700	1.8	4,200	1.7	500	11.9
Entertainment	900	0.3	800	0.3	100	12.5
Subscriptions and donations	800	0.3	700	0.3	100	14.3
Miscellaneous expenses	600	0.2	500	0.2	100	20.0
Totals	269,800	100.0	253,800	100.0	16,000	6.3

Overview of relationships

Values				
Direct labour (DL) hours	39,400	37,300	2,100	5.6
Direct labour (DL) cost	198,000	181,650	16,350	9.0
Sales volume	1,100,000	995,000	105,000	10.6
Cost of sales	945,000	865,000	80,000	9.2
Fringe benefits	65,000	58,200	6,800	11.7

Rates and ratios				
Expense rate/DL hour	6.85	6.80	0.05	0.7
Expense ratio to DL cost	136.2	139.7	(3.5)	(2.6)
Expense ratio to sales	24.5	25.5	(1.0)	(4.1)
Expense ratio to cost of sales	28.6	29.3	(0.7)	(2.4)
Indirect to DL cost ratio	63.1	66.1	(3.0)	(4.8)
DL cost to cost of sales	21.0	21.0	—	—
Fringe benefit rate/DL hour	1.65	1.59	0.06	3.6
Fringe benefit ratio to DL cost	20.1	19.3	0.8	4.0

- The *factory expense rate per direct hour* was £6.85 in 19X4 versus £6.80 in 19X3. This is a 0.74 per cent increase. Although there was an overall increase of 6.4 per cent in total overhead expenses, the effect of higher expenses was offset by the increased direct labour hour base of 5.6 per cent.

    The expense rate statistic can be useful when you are estimating product costs per direct labour hour. It may also serve as a planning guide for developing factory overhead budgets on an aggregate basis.

- The *expense ratio to direct labour costs* was calculated to be 136.2 per cent in 19X4 versus 139.7 per cent in 19X3, for a variance of 3.5 per cent or a 2.5 per cent decrease. The rate reduction is primarily attributed to a 9.0 per cent increase in direct labour costs versus an offsetting increase of only 6.3 per cent in total expenses.

    This ratio may be useful in bidding and estimating contract costs.

- Factory overhead is one of the direct cost elements in the product cost of sales composition, along with direct labour and material and other direct costs. In Model 4.3, the *overhead ratio to cost of sales* was 28.6 per cent and 29.3 per cent for 19X4 and 19X3, respectively. The small decrease was due to the higher cost of sales, which was only partially offset by a smaller increase in the factory overhead.

- The *overhead expense ratios to sales* for 19X4 and 19X3 were 24.5 per cent and 25.5 per cent, respectively. The decrease resulted from a 10.6 per cent increase in sales revenue versus a relatively smaller increase in overhead expenses. Look at the upper part of Model 4.3 to see which expense accounts declined as a ratio to total overhead.

- A frequently used control ratio assessment is the indirect to direct manpower and/or costs. In Model 4.3, the indirect to direct labour cost ratios were 63.1 per cent and 66.1 per cent for 19X4 and 19X3, respectively. The 3.0 per cent decrease in 19X4 represents a 4.8 per cent decline factor – a favourable trend in overhead expense control. As indirect labour generally represents the largest expenditure in overhead, reductions can become significant in both cost terms and in the overhead rate.

    The lower indirect ratio in 19X4 resulted from the relatively greater increase in the direct labour cost base of 9.0 per cent, as compared to the lower 4.2 per cent increase in indirect labour costs.

- The fringe benefit rates per direct labour hour for 19X4 and 19X3 were £1.65 and £1.59, respectively, with a difference of £0.06 per direct hour. The increase in 19X4 benefits (pensions, management incentive, and other labour benefits) were relatively higher than the increase in direct labour hours of 5.6 per cent, as shown in Model 4.3.

    These statistics are used to assess actual result performance and to plan overhead expense.

- The *ratios of fringe benefits to total labour costs* were 20.1 per cent and 19.3 per cent, respectively, for 19X4 and 19X3. The 19X4 ratio increased by 0.8 per cent, which resulted from a 9.0 per cent increase in direct labour costs. *Total labour costs* are used in the calculations because both direct and indirect personnel share in the retirement and other labour benefits (holidays, sick leave, insurance, and the like).

    This ratio highlights the proportion of fringe benefit expenditures in relation to total labour costs. These expenses are generally classified as non-controllable since the guidelines for expense allocation are governed by organizational policy and procedures. Results of union negotiations may also be a major consideration in organizations with strong union representation.

How to analyse D&A/selling expenses

D&A/selling and R&D expenses (if applicable) are generally accumulated and budgeted under their separate categories, particularly if they are of significant values. With this procedure, you can establish detailed controls and provide for detailed analyses.

- *D&A organizations* include general management, finance, and purchasing.
- *Selling organizations* include marketing and contract administration.

In Model 4.4, however, D&A and selling expenses are combined in the expense accumulation and reporting format. Like the factory overhead comparison in Model 4.3, the ratios in this model compare individual expenses to the total expenses, show over (under) variances for 19X4 and 19X3, and display the percentage of increase (decrease). This type of information provides a basis for detailed account analysis of the two time periods' results, and it may also be helpful in planning.

Let us look more closely at Model 4.4.

Analysing Model 4.4

- *Total D&A and selling expenses increased* by £3.65 million in 19X4 over 19X3, representing a modest increase in view of a 10.6 per cent growth in sales volume and a 5.6 per cent higher direct labour hour activity. The primary expense increases were in indirect labour, miscellaneous labour benefits, and the supplies account.

    The increase of £2 million in advertising and sales promotion expense was offset by a similar decrease in sales commissions. Since the exact details are unknown for the displayed data, the probability is that current customers increased their product purchase volumes.

- The *ratios of individual expenses to the total* in 19X4 and 19X3 are fairly consistent in the two time periods. The major exceptions were indirect labour and benefits, equipment rentals, and professional/outside services.

MODEL 4.4. D&A/selling expense comparisons and ratio analyses

(in £000s)

Expense classification	19X4 actuals	% ratio to total expense	19X3 actuals	% ratio to total expense	19X4 Variances over (under)	19X4 % Variance over (under)
Indirect labour	27,000	47.4	25,000	46.9	2,000	8.0
Micellaneous labour benefits	3,700	6.5	3,200	6.0	500	15.6
Pensions	1,300	2.3	1,200	2.3	100	8.3
Management incentive	700	1.2	600	1.1	100	16.7
Supplies	5,400	9.5	5,000	9.4	400	8.0
Taxes and insurance	2,700	4.7	2,400	4.5	300	12.5
Repair and maintenance	350	0.6	300	0.6	50	16.7
Depreciation	800	1.4	700	1.3	100	14.3
Equipment rentals	2,200	3.9	2,500	4.7	(300)	(12.0)
Utilities	800	1.4	700	1.3	100	14.3
Telephone	2,700	4.7	2,600	4.9	100	3.8
Travel	1,400	2.5	1,100	1.9	300	27.3
Professional/outside services	2,000	3.5	2,300	4.4	(300)	(13.0)
Entertainment	600	1.0	500	0.9	100	20.0
Subscriptions and donations	500	0.9	600	1.1	(100)	(16.7)
Miscellaneous	600	1.1	400	0.8	200	50.0
Advertising/promotion	3,000	5.3	2,800	5.3	200	7.1
Sales commissions	1,200	2.1	1,400	2.6	(200)	(14.3)
Total D&A and selling	56,950	100.0	53,300	100.0	3,650	6.8

Overview of relationships

Values				
Direct labour (DL) hours	39,400		37,300	2,100	5.6
Direct labour (DL) cost	198,000		181,650	16,350	9.0
Sales	1,100,000		995,000	105,000	10.6
Gross profit	155,000		130,000	25,000	19.2

Rates and ratios				
Expense rate/DL hour	1.45		1.43	0.02	1.4
Expense ratio to DL cost	28.8%		29.3%	(0.5%)	(1.7)
Expense ratio to sales	5.2%		5.4%	(0.2%)	(3.7)
Sales to expense ratio	19.3		18.7	0.6	3.2
Expense ratio to gross profit	36.7%		41.0%	(4.3%)	(10.5)

- The expense accounts increased or decreased considerably in 19X4 over 19X3, from a 50 per cent increase in miscellaneous expense to a 14.3 per cent decrease in sales commissions. Although most of the variances' sterling amounts appear to be significant for D&A and selling expenses, the 19X3 base figures were low compared to the factory overhead, as shown in Model 4.3.

Analysing expense relationships

In the lower portion of Model 4.4, pertinent rates and ratios are provided for the D&A and selling expense analysis. A few ratios are common to many organizations and others are rarely used, their usefulness depending on their applicability and the organization's practices.

Let us see how they are used:

- The *expense rate per direct hour* was calculated to be £1.45 for 19X4 as compared to £1.43 for 19X3. This trend appears to be consistent. The difference of £0.02 can be attributed to the relatively higher increase in expenses as compared to the direct labour hour base. As direct labour hour activity and sales volume increase, they affect D&A and selling expenses but not to the same degrees. The expense rate, if proven consistent, can be used as a control and planning factor.

- The *D&A and selling expense ratios* to direct labour costs were 28.8 per cent and 29.3 per cent, respectively, for 19X4 and 19X3.

    If you were to project direct labour costs and apply these ratios, you could derive approximate D&A and selling expense values for use as a check against their detailed expense development. Further, you could utilize the information for preliminary budget guidelines.

    The ratio for 19X4 of 28.8 per cent in Model 4.4 represents a 1.7 per cent decrease compared to 19X3. The cause for the decrease is a relatively greater increase in 19X4 direct labour costs (resulting from increased hours and higher labour rate) as compared to the expenses. Actually, the expense rate *per hour* is more commonly used as a factor because an increasing labour rate per hour does not distort the increased labour activity.

- For the sake of expediency in preliminary planning, you might sometimes project D&A and selling expense based on gross profit forecasts. In Model 4.4, the *expense ratios to gross profit* were 36.7 per cent and 41.0 per cent, respectively, for 19X4 and 19X3. If the expense ratio to gross profit is proven valid over time, you may apply it to the profit for preliminary values that can be used until other data become available. Periodic analyses will either verify this method's validity (and usefulness) or indicate inaccuracies.

    The 10.5 per cent decrease in the expense ratio for 19X4, as compared to 19X3, is attributed to the 19.2 per cent increase in gross profit in 19X4 with only a 6.8 per cent increase in expenses. The increase in the 19X4 gross profit is primarily due to the higher sales revenue with only a partial offset by the higher cost of sales.

● The *D&A and selling expense ratio to sales* was 5.2 per cent in 19X4 versus 5.4 per cent in 19X3. The expense variance difference in 19X4 was a negative (−0.2 per cent), which resulted from a higher sales volume.

    This ratio, if validated, can be very useful as a guideline in projecting D&A and selling expenses based on sales even before you develop the details by more conventional methods. If you determine that the expenses will approximate £0.052 on each pound of sales, then applying the factor to sales gives you the minimum amount of expenditures that will be incurred. Management controls must be exercised to reduce the expenses or constrain them within pre-established limits.

Analysing advertising and sales promotion expense

The cost for advertising and sales promotion can be significant, particularly if the organization's product is consumer-orientated. The public is deluged daily by advertisements about the merits of cars, pharmaceutical products, foodstuffs, tyres, and so on. Television, radio, newspapers, direct mail, and magazines all seek the consumer's attention.

Specifically and accurately measuring the sales growth and net revenue resulting from any sales campaign is often difficult. Unless the campaign is restricted to one type of advertising, the problem is to ascertain which of the media accounted for the sales gain and which contributed little to the effort. Even a detailed analysis of the varied advertising expenses may not reveal the answers to this question.

Budgeting for advertising and sales promotion

The budget represents an important tool in planning and controlling these expenses. Generally, organizations with substantial advertising budgets segregate and accumulate advertising expenses into detailed account classifications that can be compared to the budget plan on an analytical basis.

When establishing the budget, consider the organization's overall planning objectives relative to sales goals, marketing strategies, and projections. Historical experience codes may be developed in order that charges can be identified to specific product or product lines. Segregate major categories into expenditures for television, radio, newspapers, and so on as appropriate so that you can assess results.

Carefully consider the timing of the actual expenditures because of seasonal influences and also as a basis for projecting actual cash outflow.

In summary
Model 4.4 presents ways to analyse D&A and selling expenses, as well as to measure

performance and anticipate future results by means of applicable expense rates and ratios. The ratio of D&A and selling expenses to sales expresses the supervision and control measures that an organization exercises in relation to sales volume. These expenses have a major impact on gross profit. Changes in the ratio over time result from changes in business conditions and in the business environment, specifically changes the demand for a product and sales strategies.

If proven valid, the developed factors help you to establish expenditure controls. You can readily prepare the comparisons, rates, and ratios through rather simple mechanical routines. Exception reporting can highlight significant variances for corrective action and/or revised planning.

Assessing sales activity expenditures

As in other areas of analysis, you can develop factors, such as the ratio to sales and net profit, based on historical experience. These ratios then help you to limit and control advertising, promotion, and commission spending.

Assessing the data

In Model 4.5, note that the 19X4 advertising and sales promotion expenses increased 7.1 per cent versus a 10.6 per cent increase in sales. These expenses apparently have a decided influence on sales volume increases but not in the same proportions. (Such a conclusion has to be further supported by historical experience.) Generally, the effort and expense contributed to product/market exploitation results in higher sales volumes and increased profits.

MODEL 4.5. Illustrative approach in assessing and controlling sales activity expenditures

	(in £000s)			
Values	*19X4*	*19X3*	*Variance*	*% change*
Sales	1,100,000	995,000	105,000	+10.6
Net profit	49,025	38,350	10,675	+27.8
Advertising and promotion	3,000	2,800	200	+ 7.1
Commissions	1,200	1,400	(200)	−14.3
	Ratio to sales			
Advertising and promotion	0.27%	0.28%	−0.01%	− 3.5%
Commissions	0.11%	0.14%	−0.03%	−21.4%
	Ratio to net profit			
Advertising and promotion	6.1%	7.3%	−1.2%	−16.4%
Commissions	2.4%	3.7%	−1.3%	−35.1%

As shown in Model 4.5, the 19X4 profits increased by 27.8 per cent, but other factors may have also contributed to the increase, such as higher product prices, lower costs, more efficient operation, or improved cost control measures.

Why the 19X4 sales commission expenses declined by 14.3 per cent, however, is difficult to explain. The answer might have to do with reduced commissions on sales, direct customer purchases with no sales representative involvement, error in cost accumulation, or other circumstances.

Ratio to sales. The advertising and sales promotion ratio in 19X4 decreased by 3.6 per cent. This may be the result of a greater proportional increase in sales as compared to the expenses.

The 19X4 commission expense ratio declined by 21.4 per cent. Although the cost decrease was only £200,000, the greater 19X4 sales base volume undoubtedly accounted for the reduced ratio.

Ratio to net profit. Advertising and promotion decreased by 16.4 per cent in 19X4, primarily because of the 27.8 per cent increase in profit with only a 7.1 per cent increase in those expenses.

The cause for the 35.1 per cent decrease in the 19X4 sales commissions ratio is attributed to the 27.8 per cent increase in net profit versus a 14.3 per cent decline in commissions.

This type of analysis enables you to assess selling expenses in relation to the trends in sales volume and net profit. It might also help you to establish expense limits and controls. Further, the data provide guidelines based on historical experience for expense supervision and for planning a realistic selling expense budget. The proviso, of course, is that the ratio relationships prove to be valid over time.

How to correlate overhead expense to direct labour costs

Model 4.6 is a scattergraph correlation chart of overhead expenses related to direct labour costs using monthly data based on five-four-four week quarters. The values used in plotting the graph are provided with the chart. Note the following:

1. This is a common procedure used in establishing a correlation formula. The plotted points represent the *x* and *y* intersections of overhead at varying direct labour cost values as experienced in 19X4 (note the Model 4.3 totals).
2. The equations used to develop the formula are shown in Model 4.6. By substituting the cost values shown for *X*, *Y*, and *XY* into the equations, the *a* and *b* factors are calculated as illustrated.
3. The resultant formula is

$$Y \text{ (overhead)} = 2.683 \text{ (2.7 rounded)} + 1.2X \text{ (direct labour costs)}$$

EXAMPLE

Assuming projected labour costs of £17 million, what is the projected overhead?

$$Y = 2.683 + 1.2 \times 17.0$$
$$= 2.683 + 20.4$$
$$= £23.083 \text{ million}$$

Refer to the graph: The £17 million intersection on the regression line indicates an expense value of approximately 23 million.

4. The four plotted points at the extreme right of the chart indicate the five-week monthly periods, which reflect higher monthly values for direct labour and overhead. The four-week periods are represented by the plot points at the lower left in the graph.
5. If you draw the slope of the regression line, you can either make a visual inspection or use the formula at two labour base values. The labour values used are £15.5 million and £19.0 million. The calculation is illustrated in Model 4.6, with the results for points *A* and *B* £21.3 million and £25.5 million, respectively. A connecting line drawn between these two points represents the median among all of the plotted points.

Relating period expense ratios to direct labour costs

Model 4.7 is a graphic overview of total expense ratios to direct labour costs by period. By highlighting the changes in ratios, it pinpoints the deviations from the average, either for analysis and corrective action in the future or for establishing and revising planning criteria. In this chart, note that the largest *positive* deviation (0.07, in May) was due primarily to the increase in expenses for that period, but the direct labour costs remained relatively stable.

On the downside, the ratios for April and June are *negative* due to a high level of direct labour costs as compared to the expense values.

Commencing in April, every other month's ratio was either above or below the average for the year. This pattern follows the fluctuations in the direct labour costs base, while the period expense costs remained fairly constant. In a case like this, you might look for the causes of the changes in direct labour costs and of the constancy of expenses. The answers could form a basis for future planning.

Relating overhead expenses to direct labour hour activity

Model 4.8 displays the relationship between the weekly average of direct labour hours and overhead expenses by accounting period. The average rate per direct labour hour was £6.85, as shown in the data below the display. Note that for six months the expense rate was below the average and for six months it was above

MODEL 4.6. Correlating overhead expenses to direct labour costs

Least squares calculations*

	X(DL)	Y(OH)	XY	X^2	Y^2	Formula equations
J	18.6	25.7	478.0	346.0	660.5	$Y = Na + b\Sigma X$
F	15.6	21.6	337.0	243.4	466.6	$XY = a\Sigma X + b\Sigma X^2$
M	16.1	22.0	354.2	259.2	484.0	*Calculations*
A	19.8	25.9	512.8	392.0	670.8	$270.0 = 12a + 198.0b$
M	15.3	21.9	335.1	234.1	479.6	$4503.6 = 198.0a + 3307.8b$
J	15.9	20.9	332.3	252.8	436.8	$4455.0 = 198.0a + 3267.0b$
J	18.0	25.3	455.4	324.0	640.1	
A	15.5	20.5	317.8	240.3	420.3	$48.6 =$ $\qquad$ $40.8b$
S	14.5	20.1	291.5	210.3	404.0	$b = 1.2$
O	19.4	25.5	494.7	376.4	650.3	$270.0 = 12a + (198 \times 1.2)$ or 237.6
N	14.7	20.1	295.5	216.1	404.0	$12a = 32.4;\quad a = 2.7$
D	14.6	20.5	219.3	213.2	420.3	*Formula*
Totals	198.0	270.0	4503.6	3307.8	6137.3	$Y = 2.7 + 1.2X$
						Point A: $2.7 + 1.2(15.5)$ or $18.6; Y = 21.3 \leftarrow$
						Point B: $2.7 + 1.2(19.0)$ or $22.8; Y = 25.5 \leftarrow$

*Values based on five-four-four week quarters

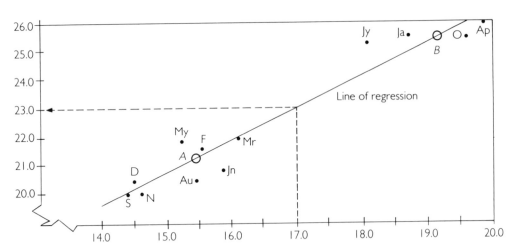

average. As a general observation, period expenses followed the increase and decrease in direct labour hours except in a couple of instances; this is considered to be a normal trend. As direct labour hour activity increases, the variable expenses tend to edge higher but not in the same relative proportion.

The objective of Model 4.8 is to show the relationship of expenses to the changes in the labour hour activity. This information provides a basis for measuring expense performance, initiating controls, and budgeting for future periods.

MODEL 4.7. Comparing total overhead expense to direct labour costs (by time periods)

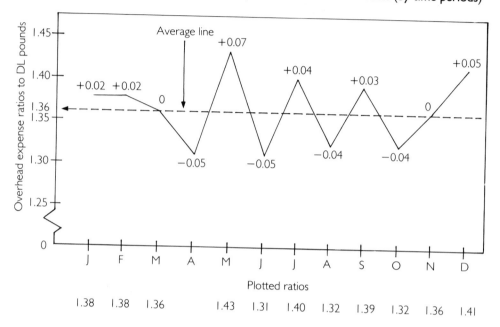

Plotted ratios											
1.38	1.38	1.36		1.43	1.31	1.40	1.32	1.39	1.32	1.36	1.41

MODEL 4.8. Correlating overhead expense to direct labour hour activity (year ended 19X4)

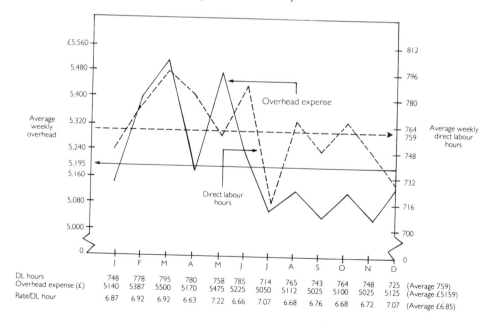

	J	F	M	A	M	J	J	A	S	O	N	D	
DL hours	748	778	795	780	758	785	714	765	743	764	748	725	(Average 759)
Overhead expense (£)	5140	5387	5500	5170	5475	5225	5050	5112	5025	5100	5025	5125	(Average £5159)
Rate/DL hour	6.87	6.92	6.92	6.63	7.22	6.66	7.07	6.68	6.76	6.68	6.72	7.07	(Average £6.85)

Comparing expense categories to direct labour costs

Model 4.9 displays in graphic form the ratios of individual expense categories to direct labour costs by time period. It shows the proportion and changes of the expense categories to the total overhead expense ratio per unit direct labour cost. The ratios were developed by dividing the period category expenses by direct labour cost.

Below the graph are the numerical data used in plotting. An analysis of the data leads to the following observations:

- *Indirect labour*: The highest ratios occurred in July, September, November, and December, as reflected by the upward thrust of the ratio line for those periods. The ratio differences are due principally to labour cost fluctuations.
- *Fringe benefits*: The highest ratio occurred in May, and the lowest ratios were experienced from August to November. The contributing causes for these changes were the fluctuations in fringe benefit expenses.
- *Supplies*: This expense ratio remained fairly constant by period, with the lowest ratio occurring in June.
- *Utilities, taxes, and insurance*: Approximately consistent for all periods, this expense ratio provides a reasonable factor for budgeting this category of expenses.
- *Repair and maintenance*: This ratio fluctuated between £0.06 and £0.07 per direct labour cost. These factors will be useful in assessing future performance and in projecting these expenses.
- *Depreciation*: The ratio factors were 6 per cent and 7 per cent of direct labour costs, with the exception of 8 per cent in December. The situation is primarily due to the below-average direct labour cost and above-average expense total.
- *Outside services, rentals, and miscellaneous*: These expenses remained relatively consistent throughout the periods. Modest fluctuations can be attributed primarily to the changes in the direct labour cost base.

Model 4.9 presents an overview of category expense ratios to direct labour costs with a proportionate analysis of period expense ratios. The display indicates how labour and expense changes affect the ratio from one period to another. If consistent and valid over subsequent time periods, the ratios enable you to monitor expenses and develop overhead budgets. They also aid in checking on planning data that is based on more detailed development procedures.

How to correlate indirect to direct labour costs

Model 4.10 was developed to demonstrate the correlation between indirect and direct labour costs. The data used for the calculations are shown below the plotted graph. The equations to derive the mathematical correlation formula, also shown in

MODEL 4.9. Comparing expense categories to direct labour costs

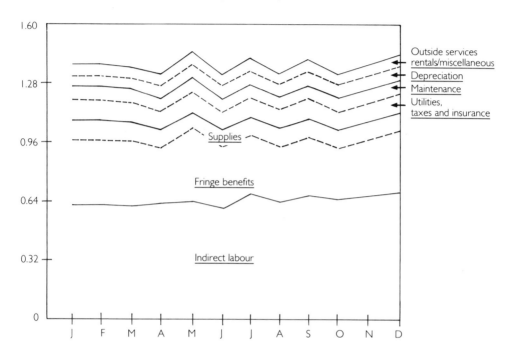

			Plotting data by period									
Ind. L.	0.62	0.62	0.61	0.61	0.63	0.60	0.67	0.62	0.66	0.64	0.65	0.67
Fringes	0.34	0.35	0.36	0.32	0.40	0.33	0.32	0.31	0.31	0.28	0.31	0.32
S/T	0.96	0.97	0.97	0.93	1.03	0.93	0.99	0.93	0.97	0.92	0.96	0.99
Supplies	0.11	0.11	0.10	0.09	0.09	0.08	0.09	0.09	0.09	0.09	0.09	0.09
S/T	1.07	1.08	1.07	1.02	1.12	1.01	1.08	1.02	1.06	1.01	1.05	1.08
Util./Txs.	0.12	0.11	0.11	0.11	0.11	0.11	0.12	0.11	0.12	0.11	0.12	0.12
S/T	1.19	1.19	1.18	1.13	1.23	1.12	1.20	1.13	1.18	1.12	1.17	1.20
R&M	0.06	0.07	0.07	0.06	0.07	0.06	0.06	0.06	0.07	0.06	0.06	0.07
S/T	1.25	1.26	1.25	1.19	1.30	1.18	1.26	1.19	1.25	1.18	1.23	1.27
Deprec.	0.06	0.06	0.06	0.06	0.06	0.06	0.07	0.07	0.07	0.07	0.07	0.08
S/T	1.31	1.32	1.31	1.25	1.36	1.24	1.33	1.26	1.32	1.25	1.30	1.35
O/S Svcs	0.07	0.06	0.05	0.06	0.07	0.07	0.07	0.06	0.07	0.07	0.06	0.06
Tot. Exp. ratios	1.38	1.38	1.36	1.31	1.43	1.31	1.40	1.32	1.39	1.32	1.36	1.41 (to £1 DL)

MODEL 4.10. Correlating indirect to direct labour costs

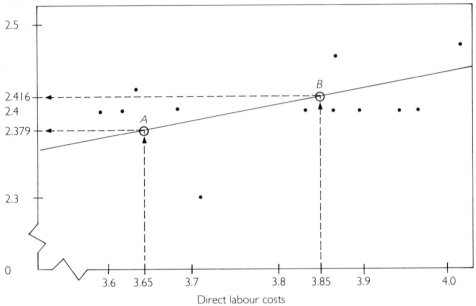

Indirect labour costs

Direct labour costs

Ratio % of indirect to direct labour costs

J	F	M	A	M	J	J	A	S	O	N	D	
62.2	61.5	62.5	60.0	63.2	60.0	66.7	61.5	66.7	64.1	61.5	66.7	(Average 63.2)

Weekly averages for computing correlation (Cost values rounded in £000,000s)

Periods	X	Y	XY	X²	Y²	Least squares equations
J	3.7	2.3	8.51	13.59	5.29	$Y = Na + b\Sigma X$
F	3.9	2.4	9.36	15.21	5.76	$XY = a\Sigma X + b\Sigma X^2$
M	4.0	2.5	10.00	16.00	6.25	
A	4.0	2.4	9.60	16.00	5.76	Calculations
M	3.8	2.4	9.12	14.44	5.76	$28.9 = 12a + 45.70b$
J	4.0	2.4	9.60	16.00	5.76	$110.10 = 45.7 + 174.30b$
J	3.6	2.4	8.64	12.96	5.76	$110.05 = 45.7 + 174.03b$
A	3.9	2.4	9.36	15.21	5.76	
S	3.6	2.4	8.64	12.96	5.76	$0.05 = 0.27b$
O	3.9	2.5	9.75	15.21	6.25	$b = 0.185$
N	3.7	2.4	8.88	13.69	5.76	$28.9 = 12a + 8.45$
D	3.6	2.4	8.64	12.96	5.76	$12a = 20.45$
						$a = 1.704$
Totals	45.7	28.9	110.10	174.33	69.63	

Locating points A and B for regression line

Point A: Y = 1.704 + 0.185 (3.650)
       Y = 1.704 + 0.675 = 2.379

Formula
Y = 1.704 + 0.185X
Point B: Y = 1.704 + 0.185 (3.85)
       Y = 1.704 + 0.712 = 2.416

the model, represent the commonly used process in the least squares method approach.

The calculations displayed solve for a, which was £1.704 million, and the variable b factor of 0.185. The resultant equation is expressed as follows:

$Y = 1.704 + 0.185X$

where

Y = indirect labour

X = direct labour costs

To locate the regression line, two labour values are used: point A, £3.650 and point B, £3.850 (both values in millions of pounds sterling). A line connecting these two points represents the regression or trend line.

Verifying the validity of the trend line

To validate the reasonableness of the trend line, select two or more labour values. Then, to determine the indirect labour value points on the regression line, use the following formula:

$Y = a + bX$

Direct labour values of £3.8 and 3.95 million are selected, and the results (£2.407 and £2.435 million of indirect labour) are located on the trend line. As an overview assessment, this indicates that the trend line is reasonably representative of the data correlation.

As a rapid means of estimating indirect labour costs based on direct labour, select any value for direct labour costs and draw a vertical line from the labour value to the trend line. At this intersection, draw a horizontal line to the left margin of the display. The result is the estimated indirect labour cost value.

Other methods used to test the validity of the correlation formula are to calculate the coefficient of correlation and the standard error of estimate.

Calculating the indirect to direct labour cost ratio

Model 4.11 presents another approach to the indirect to direct labour cost ratios, reflecting the time period deviations from the average. The display reveals that the ratios are below average in the first six months plus August and above average in the remaining periods. The primary cause for the below-average variances is the higher direct labour cost base combined with relatively consistent indirect labour cost values. The above-average ratios resulted from the below-average direct labour costs.

This type of presentation highlights at a glance the ratio fluctuations between periods. These fluctuations indicate problem areas requiring attention and control. Further, if the circumstances are valid, the factors may provide a basis for future planning.

MODEL 4.11. Indirect to direct labour cost ratios (weekly averages by periods)

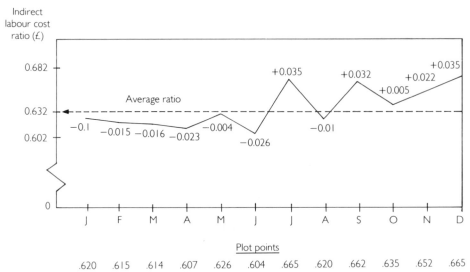

Indirect
labour cost
ratio (£)

Plot points

.620   .615   .614   .607   .626   .604   .665   .620   .662   .635   .652   .665

Analysing the supplies expense rate per direct labour hour

Model 4.12 displays the period supplies expense rate trend per direct labour hour. The high rate of £0.55 in February is attributed primarily to supply expenses being 20 per cent higher than the annual average and direct labour hours being only 2.5 per cent above average.

The lowest expense rate of £0.41 occurred in June. An analysis reveals that direct labour hours were 3.4 per cent above average, whereas supply expenses were 8.2 per cent *below* the annual average. The result of these two situations is the low rate per direct labour hour.

The next step in the analysis is to determine the cause for the high and low expenditure for supplies in the two periods. The question is: are the increase and decrease in the rate due to unusual circumstances or are they expected to prevail in the future? Since the supplies expense represents the third highest expense in the overhead total, you must give it appropriate attention to make sound budget projections.

Note that the first three months reflected a higher than average (£0.47/DLH) rate, whereas the succeeding months experienced a lower than average rate. The principal cause has to do with the expenses being below average in those periods.

Comparing factory overhead assessments

Model 4.13 reflects a type of analytical report used to assess and measure actual expense results against projected operational budget. This approach highlights the

MODEL 4.12. Supplies expense rate per direct labour hour (weekly averages by periods)

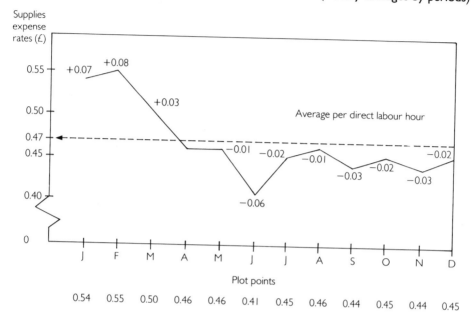

variances by expense account between the prior year's actuals and a proposed budget. The purpose is to determine the cause(s) for an 11.9 per cent increase (32.2 million ÷ £269.8 million) in the 19X4 budget over the 19X3 actuals.

As shown in the model, the two most significant value increases occurred in indirect labour (14.9 million) and in other labour benefits (£6.0 million), representing an 11.9 per cent and 12.0 per cent increase, respectively. There were higher percentage increases in some of the other expense accounts, but the relative comparable pound values were much smaller. The next step in the analysis is to determine why the 19X4 budget reflected the increases. There may be valid planning criteria for this situation, but you should conduct a detailed analysis to confirm the reasoning and budget decisions.

Generally, the budget increases can be explained at least partially by the anticipated increase in direct labour hours of 6.9 per cent. This increase, signifying greater operational activity, would influence a rise in indirect labour and other labour benefit expenses.

Calculating the overhead expense rate per direct labour hour

In total, the overhead expense rate per direct labour hour increased 4.7 per cent. The major increases occurred in indirect labour and in other labour benefits, followed by the supplies account. The rate factor provides preliminary and basic criteria for estimating and budgeting expenses predicated on past experience. In the budgeting

MODEL 4.13. Comparing factory overhead budgets: 19X4 operational budget versus 19X3 actuals

(in £000s)

Expense classifications	19X4 management budget	19X3 actuals	19X4 budget over (under)	% increase (decrease)	Rate per direct hour		Ratio % to DL costs	
					19X4 budget	19X3 actuals	19X4 budget	19X3 actuals
Indirect labour	139,900	125,000	14,900	11.9	3.32	3.17	64.68	63.13
Pensions	13,900	12,500	1,400	11.2	0.33	0.32	6.43	6.31
Management incentives	2,500	2,500	—	—	0.06	0.06	1.16	1.26
Other labour benefits	56,000	50,000	6,000	12.0	1.33	1.27	25.89	25.25
Supplies	21,150	18,500	2,650	14.3	0.50	0.47	9.78	9.34
Taxes and insurance	16,000	14,200	1,800	12.7	0.38	0.36	7.40	7.17
Repair and maintenance	14,300	12,500	1,800	14.4	0.34	0.32	6.61	6.31
Depreciation	14,700	13,200	1,500	11.4	0.35	0.34	6.80	6.67
Equipment rentals	2,550	2,400	150	6.3	0.06	0.06	1.18	1.21
Utilities	5,500	4,200	1,300	30.9	0.13	0.11	2.54	2.12
Telephone	4,200	4,000	200	5.0	0.10	0.10	1.94	2.02
Travel	4,200	3,800	400	10.5	0.10	0.10	1.94	1.92
Professional and outside services	5,050	4,700	350	7.4	0.12	0.12	2.33	2.37
Entertainment	800	900	(100)	(11.1)	0.02	0.02	0.37	0.46
Subscriptions and donations	800	800	—	—	0.02	0.02	0.37	0.40
Miscellaneous	450	600	(150)	(25.0)	0.01	0.01	0.21	0.30
Totals	302,000	269,800	32,200	11.9	7.17	6.85	139.63	139.24

Summary

Direct labour hours	42,100	39,400	2,700	6.9
Expense rate per direct hour	7.17	6.85	0.32	4.7
Direct labour cost	216,300	198,000	18,300	9.2
Overhead ratio to direct labour costs	139.6%	136.2%	3.4%	2.5

process, however, you must anticipate future expense and exercise good judgement when it comes to activity projections.

Analysing the expense ratio to direct labour costs

The ratio of expense to labour costs increased by 2.5% from 136.2 per cent to 139.6 per cent. The expense ratio factors, based on direct labour costs, can be and often are used in the budgeting process. Further, you can use the factors in preparing customer proposal estimates for product/contract pricing, particularly if experience has validated your budgeting in the past.

This type of comparative report provides a comprehensive review of expenses in detail not only for comparing the planned budget with the previous year's actuals, but also for measuring the actual data period by period. With this type of report, you can assess expense data and highlight major variances for further analysis and action.

In the model, note that the three most important ratios (because of the size of their costs) are indirect labour, other labour benefits, and supplies. They would be the major areas of concentration for control and planning. Shown at the bottom of Model 4.13 are the overall expense rates per direct hour and the overhead expense ratios to direct labour costs.

Comparing overhead to activity

Activity-based costing techniques (ABC) are being increasingly used for overhead control and product costing in both service organizations and high-overhead manufacturing concerns. As the name implies, the overheads are recovered on the basis of the activity as opposed to labour or machine hours. In some instances, however, it may be appropriate to use more than one basis for recovery. Overhead allocation bases such as labour and machine hours are regarded as volume related. For example, if you have a product that takes twice as long as another in the manufacturing process it picks up twice the overhead assuming overhead is recovered on the basis of £X per labour or machine hour. However, in many instances certain overheads are unrelated to volume, for example, setup times, drawing-office time, parts ordering, and so on, and therefore recovery of overhead on the basis of machine or labour hours leads to distortions.

The allocation systems used in ABC rely on identifying suitable *cost drivers*. Cost drivers are the activities that generate overhead cost. A typical cost driver might be machine setup times. The ratio of setup costs to setup hours would then produce an overhead recovery rate unrelated to volume and related instead to the actual set-up time incurred by that product or process. Drawing-office costs are also likely to vary disproportionately to volume. The work involved in producing drawings for one order may be the same regardless of the volumes of product run off from that order. The same applies to size. A double-decker bus is likely to consume more labour and machine hours than a single-decker bus, but the order-processing costs may be the same.

EXAMPLE

A company produces two products, A and B. Product A consumes 750 hours in manufacture, product B 250 hours. If overhead is charged out on the basis of £10 per labour hour, product A attracts a charge of £7500, product B £2500. However, part of the overhead, say £2000, may be machine setup costs, covering five setups. Assuming the setup times are constant we can calculate the cost per setup, in this case £400. If product A has three setups to product B's two then the overhead charge on an activity basis would be:

Product A $3 \times £400 = £1200$
Product B $2 \times £400 = £800$

On a labour hour basis the charge would have been:

Product A $£2000 \times \frac{3}{4} = £1500$
Product B $2000 \times \frac{1}{4} = £500$

Once the cost drivers have been identified and the ratio of expense to activity calculated, the result can be utilized for planning and control purposes. Industrial engineers may be able to identify ways of reducing setup times by redesigning the equipment involved. Measuring costs is an aid to controlling them.

5 How to assess and plan profit objectives by means of profitability ratio guidelines

Chapter highlights

Inasmuch as the aim of any business is to make a profit, profitability ratios are perhaps the most important in gauging a firm's success. How each element in a business's financial statements relates to the profitability of its activities is the key question. In this chapter, you will become acquainted with profitability ratios. You will learn how to calculate and interpret them in relation to the organization's overall financial position and operating progress.

First you look at the elements in the profit statement. Each item is analysed by means of a ratio, and the results are compared from one period to another. Where appropriate, possible explanations for variances are offered. You will familiarize yourself with the objectives and assessments of profitability ratios in terms of their composition and relationships to gross profit, profit from operations, and net profit – the 'bottom line', particularly in the context of business cycles.

Much the same is then done with the balance sheet. Each element is converted to a ratio, interpreted, and compared by periods. Explanations for variations are again offered when appropriate. You will be given some points to remember when analysing the turnover of capital employed.

You will then see how to calculate earnings per share and use this relationship in assessing financial data.

Finally, how do you evaluate the causes for profit variations? How do they relate to sales, production, expenses, or product mix? Which areas are involved in the variance? These questions are answered in the final section of the chapter.

Use of profitability ratios

Profitability ratios are generally the most useful to organizations directly involved in manufacturing and selling a product or in performing a service. For comparative purposes, the individual costs and profit ratios to sales are calculated by periods (monthly, quarterly, and so on). These comparisons provide insight into trends and further act as a tool for highlighting significant variances, which may be the occasion for investigation and possibly corrective action or changes in future planning. These ratios therefore enable you to gauge an organization's financial results and establish future objectives.

The use of profitability ratios for analysis and planning is primarily concerned with, but not necessarily limited to

- the rate of return from operations;
- gross margin;
- total assets;
- owners' equity;
- creditor contribution;
- price earnings;
- dividend yield.

The data used in developing the ratios are obtained primarily from both the profit statement and the balance sheet.

Analysing the profit statement

Model 5.1 displays a comparative profit statement analysis for the years 19X2–19X4. Each item in the statement is expressed in pounds sterling and as a percentage of net sales. For each data element, the percentage represents the element's relationship to the sales volume. Let us analyse each item on the left-hand side of the table:

- The *cost of sales* percentage decreased from 74.6 per cent in 19X2 to 73.6 per cent in 19X4, giving rise to a relative gross profit percentage increase from 25.4 per cent to 26.4 per cent. The improved profit could indicate increased manufacturing cost control, operating performance efficiencies, improved equipment output, or learning curve results.

- The *D&A and selling expense* percentage of sales declined between 19X2 and 19X4 in spite of increased sales volume. This is a favourable trend towards increased profitability.

- Although *interest charges* increased slightly, they are attributed to the additional financing requirements for sales growth. However, the overall impact on profits was partially offset by an increase in other *non-operating income*.

- The net result of these relevant factors is a 7.9 per cent net income to sales ratio in 19X4, as compared to the 7.05 per cent in 19X2. Although the percentage increase appears to be minor, the net profit amount was 1.07 times greater in 19X4 than 19X2. This situation resulted from the much larger sales volume and relatively lower manufacturing costs and D&A and selling expenses.

The percentage ratios help you to visualize changes from one period to another, investigate unusual circumstances, and possibly take managerial action. These ratios further focus on the need for management to adjust to varying operational changes, such as an increasing or declining sales volume and their associated cost trends.

MODEL 5.1. Comparative profit statement analysis

(in £000,000s)

| Description | 19X4 | | 19X3 | | 19X2 | | Determining changes for analysis | | | |
| | | | | | | | 19X4 versus 19X3 increase (decrease) | | 19X3 versus 19X2 increase (decrease) | |
	Amount	% sales	Amount	% sales	Amount	% sales	amount	%	amount	%
Net sales	240.00	100.0	190.00	100.0	130.00	100.0	50.00	26.3	60.00	46.2
Cost of sales	176.60	73.6	141.00	74.2	97.00	74.6	35.60	25.2	44.00	45.4
Gross profit	63.40	26.4	49.00	25.8	33.00	25.4	14.40	29.4	16.00	48.5
D&A expense	13.90	5.8	11.40	6.0	8.06	6.2	2.50	21.9	3.34	41.4
Selling expense	11.30	4.7	8.90	4.7	6.50	5.0	2.40	27.0	2.40	36.9
Subtotal	25.20	10.5	20.30	10.7	14.56	11.2	4.90	24.1	5.74	39.4
Profit from operations	38.20	15.9	28.70	15.1	18.44	14.2	9.50	33.1	10.26	55.6
Other income	0.48	0.2	0.19	0.1	0.13	0.1	0.29	152.6	0.06	46.2
Interest charges	0.72	0.3	0.38	0.2	0.26	0.2	0.34	89.5	0.12	46.2
Subtotal	(0.24)	(0.1)	(0.19)	(0.1)	(0.13)	(0.1)	(0.05)	(26.3)	(0.60)	(46.2)
Pretax profit	37.96	15.8	28.51	15.0	18.31	14.1	9.45	33.1	10.20	55.7
Provision for taxes (50%)	18.98	7.9	14.255	7.5	9.155	7.05	4.725	33.1	5.10	55.7
Net profit	18.98	7.9	14.255	7.5	9.155	7.05	4.725	33.1	5.10	55.7
Retained earnings (BB)	17.51	7.3	10.255	5.4	4.50	3.46	7.255	70.7	5.755	127.9
Cash dividends	(8.50)	(3.5)	(7.000)	(3.7)	(3.40)	(2.60)	1.500	21.4	3.600	105.9
Retained earnings (EB)	27.99	11.7	17.510	9.2	10.255	7.91	10.480	59.9	7.255	70.7

Note: BB = Beginning balance; EB = Ending balance

Retained earnings (EB) = Net income + Retained earnings (BB) − Cash dividends

Analysing comparative statement changes

Model 5.1 also reflects the extent of changes, in terms of percentages, in the various operating line items between 19X2 and 19X3, and between 19X3 and 19X4. This type of reporting forms a basis for horizontal analysis of the profit statement.

Note the following from Model 5.1:

- *Net sales* in 19X3 increased a significant 46.2 per cent over 19X2, compared with only a 26.3 per cent increase in 19X4 over 19X3.
- The *cost of sales percentages* were comparable to the increase in sales volume, and thus the differential effect on gross profit was nominal in both periods compared.
- *Profit from operations* showed a gain of 55.6 per cent in 19X3 over 19X2, while the gain in 19X4 over 19X3 was only 33.1 per cent. The increase is attributed primarily to the higher gross profit with a relatively minor offset in increased D&A and selling expenses.
- The 55.7 per cent increase in *net income* in 19X3 over 19X2 was due to the 7.5 per cent return on sales, compared to 7.05 per cent in 19X2.

Summary

The comparative profit statements are analysed by means of two complementary approaches:

1. *Vertical analysis* provides the *distribution of profit from sales* among the functions involved in producing it.
2. *Horizontal assessment* indicates the *rate or ratio of change* in the criteria affecting profit.

You should use both methods when analysing the profit statement since changes in the vertical assessment influence the horizontal evaluation.

How to interpret changes in net profit as percentages of sales

Model 5.2 presents another approach to analysing net profit changes between annual periods (19X3 and 19X4 in this instance) and ascertaining the net variation as a percentage of sales. In Model 5.1, the net profit as a percentage of sales is calculated to be 7.9 per cent in 19X4 versus 7.5 per cent for 19X3. The lower section of the model indicates that the 19X4 profit increased by £4.725 million, which is 33.1 per cent greater than in 19X3. Model 5.2, the alternative analysis, outlines the specific factors causing the increase or decrease between the two annual periods and their *resultant effect* as a percentage of sales.

Let us look at Model 5.2 item by item:

- The calculated differences between the 19X4 and 19X3 profit statement items represent increases or decreases to the profit variations.
- Initially, net profit increased because of a higher gross profit, the difference between a greater 19X4 sales volume of £50 million and a related cost of sales

MODEL 5.2. Changes in net profit as percentages of sales

(in £000,000s)

Description	19X4	19X3	Increase (decrease)	increase (decrease) % of sales
Net profit increases due to:				
Gross profit increases				
Sales increase	240.00	190.00	50.00	
Cost of sales increase	176.60	141.00	35.60	
Gross profit increase			14.40	0.06
Operating profit decreases				
D&A increase	13.90	11.40	(2.50)	
Selling expense inc.	11.30	8.90	(2.40)	
Operating profit decrease			(4.90)	(0.02)
Operating profit result			9.50	0.04
Pretax profit decreases				
Other income increase	0.48	0.19	0.29	
Interest expense increase	0.72	0.38	0.34	
Profit decrease			(0.05)	Negligible
Profit result			9.45	0.04
Net profit decrease				
Increase for taxes	18.98	14.255	(4.725)	(0.02)
Net profit increases			4.725	0.02

4.725 ÷ 240.0 sales = 2% (19X4 over 19X3)

of £35.6 million. The higher gross profit was £14.4 million or a *6 per cent ratio* to sales.

- Compared to gross profit, the *profit from operations* was reduced by increased D&A and selling expenses in the amount of £4.9 million or a *2 per cent ratio* to sales. To obtain the ratio of profit from operations to sales (4 per cent, as shown in Model 5.2), deduct the 2 per cent factor from the 6 per cent gross profit to sales increase.
- The *pretax profit ratio* to sales remained the same as profit from operations. Although miscellaneous other income increased by £290,000, it was more than offset by the increase in interest charges of £340,000. The resultant difference is negligible in terms of ratio to sales.
- As reflected in the model, the pretax profit increase of £9.45 million led to a tax increase of £4.725 million, which represented a *2 per cent decrease* in the sales ratio. By subtracting the 2 per cent tax increase allowance from the

pretax profit increase on sales, you get the 'bottom line' increase of 2 per cent in net profit as a ratio to sales.

The procedure used in Model 5.2 complements the one in Model 5.1. Non-technical in nature, it can be readily understood by the layman due to its narrative format, which highlights the causes for profit variation in comparative statement analyses. Further, it presents each of the actual variations between two periods in terms of a ratio to sales volume, a major criterion in profitability assessment.

How to assess profitability ratios

The profitablity ratio helps you to measure management's ability to manage and control costs. This ratio assesses whether there is a profitable return on sales activity and other resources invested in the business. The evaluation and planning of profitability involves many facets of the operational and financial results, which are categorically reported in both the profit statement and the balance sheet. Since the opinions of accounting professionals vary on this subject, we will take an integrated approach in discussing profitability ratios, their objectives, and their use.

Analysing gross profit to sales ratio. This basic ratio represents the percentage difference between net sales and the associated cost of sales. The cost of sales represents the direct costs associated with producing a product or for performing services: the labour activity, the material usage, and the associated indirect expense support, such as factory overhead (operating supplies, maintenance, repairs, utilities, and the like).

To succeed, business must achieve and maintain a profitable gross margin to sales ratio. Product demand and the competitive climate govern the magnitude of the gross margin. As competition increases, affecting the product/service demand, gross profit contracts and narrows. Conversely, as demand increases in proportion to supply, prices and profit margins tend to increase. This phenomenon is natural. The objective of every progressive organization is to sell its products/services at the highest prices consistent with volume and competitive offerings. Gross profits must not only support D&A/selling expenses and operational financing (interest expense) costs, but also yield an adequate net profit on sales and return on investment.

Weighing gross profit ratio considerations. As shown in Model 5.1, the gross profit to sales ratio is the difference between the sales percentage of 100 per cent and the cost of sales. In other words, when calculated as an individual item, it is simply the gross profit value divided by the net sales in pounds sterling. The gross profit ratio is governed by the variations in the cost of sales relationship to sales. In turn, each of these variables is affected by product demand and price. An assessment of the changes in *sales and cost of sales* includes the following considerations:

1. *Changes in sales values result from:*
   (a) The magnitude of product volume, assuming that there is *no change in selling price*. Thus, to obtain the resultant sales volume in pounds sterling, multiply the change in volume by the individual product selling price (or by the average product price if more than one product is involved).
   (b) If the variation in the sales volume is attributed to a *change in the selling price*, then multiply the product volume by the price differential to obtain the increase or decrease in the sales value.
   (c) If the variation in sales value *involves both volume and selling price*, then multiply the volume or quantity by the price differential to arrive at the change in sales value.
2. *To calculate changes in cost of sales*, follow the same steps.

Influencing factors on gross profit are as follows:

- Business conditions or the environment can change market conditions and influence product demand, thereby affecting gross profit.
- Material/supplies purchasing. Effective purchasing policies relative to quantity and price levels govern product cost and therefore affect the magnitude of the gross profit.
- Effectiveness of operational efficiencies and sales results. In terms of manpower utilization and quality/quantity output, operating efficiencies affect labour costs which, in turn, definitely influence product cost and gross profit. Strict supervision and control of operating expenses are mandatory for competitive product pricing which affects both product demand and gross profit results. (See Chapter 3 for direct product costs and associated ratios.)
- Need to create enough margin to cover high R&D costs.

Deriving the profit from operations ratio to sales

This ratio is of major significance in the assessment of the profit statement. To derive it, reduce gross profit by D&A/selling expenses, by R&D requirements, and by any other charge on gross profits. The ratio represents the return from operations prior to its adjustment for other income, interest and taxation.

Analysing D&A/selling expense ratio. This ratio to sales indicates the control and supervision exercised over these expenses relative to sales activities. Even in periods of financial difficulties, these expenses must be paid before fixed interest, principal, or dividends take their bite out of profits.

The ratio of each of these expenses to sales generally decreases with increased volume. Expenses that increase proportionately with sales generally indicate that management is not exercising proper attention and control, although extenuating circumstances could support increased expenditures.

Analysing the research and development (R&D) ratio. R&D costs, like D&A/selling expenses, are charges against gross profit before obtaining profit from operations. Investment in R&D, as a planned/controlled cost, can be increased or decreased depending on the nature of the 'need'. Many organizations divert funds and effort either to enhance their current product design or to develop new products for future exploitation. This investment can be substantial, particularly in the highly competitive automotive, aircraft, and defence industries. Although reduced expenditures can lead to improved short-term profits, they can adversely affect profitability in the long run, particularly if their competition's R&D activities are maintained at higher levels. External analysts need to pay particular attention to the R&D ratio in making comparisons between companies in the same industry. The accounting standard on R&D has been updated several times in an attempt to introduce some degree of uniformity as the 'capitalization' of certain costs frequently causes problems. In late 1991 the International Accounting Standards Committee issued an exposure draft on the subject (E37).

How to calculate the pretax profit ratio

To obtain the pretax profit value:

1. Add other miscellaneous income (exceptional items gains, gain on sale of fixed assets, interest income) to the operational income.
2. Then reduce this amount by other deductions, such as interest charges, loss on the sale of fixed assets and exceptional items losses.
3. Divide the result by net sales to obtain the pretax profit ratio.

Other income and deductions represent non-operating items in most organizations. The items of other income and deductions vary among organizations depending on their types of business and the accounting procedures.

Calculating the net income to sales ratio

Every business is managed and controlled to make profit, and its success is reflected in terms of its 'bottom line' – the net income after taxes in the profit statement. The ratio of *net profit to sales* measures the sales profitability. Although sales represent a dynamic force in the business enterprise cycle, profitability is a major criterion in assessing operational performance.

Variations in net profit. The variations over a period of years in the ratio of net profit to sales result from the same type of circumstances that affect the ratio of operating profits: the state of the business environment, competitive influences, management attention and controls, and the cost of borrowed capital. Relative to borrowing funds, a sound and profitable financial structure generally enables an organization to obtain adequate financing at favourable rates.

How business cycles affect net profit. To a degree, changes in the business cycle – periods of normality, of high earnings, and of depressed situations – affect every organization. In normal and high earning periods, management must therefore conserve its resources and maintain profitability so that it can cope financially with future adverse situations. To achieve its goals, management must be ever on the alert to take advantage of technological advances, investment opportunities, cost control, and maintain sound financing practices. It must continually assess competition to avoid an unfavourable operating/marketing position. Profitability, stability, survival, and progress all result from constructive financial policies with a continuing appraisal of their objectives and status.

Limitations of financial statements in ratio analysis

There are certain common limitations associated with the use of financial statement data for ratio analyses that should be recognized and understood in the assessment process and the acceptance of results from conclusive findings for decision making. The major limitations and problem areas are highlighted as follows.

- The contents of financial statements are predicated on *accounting policies* which have been developed and refined over a period of years by accounting professionals. The relevant exactness of the reported data is nearly impossible to achieve because the statements represent circumstances and conditions that cannot be precisely postulated. There exist differences of opinion in the accounting profession relative to the various complex aspects of accounting procedure. For example, *unrealized profits* should not be included in earnings but *accrued expenses* should be included in the liabilities. What one organization might classify as an exceptional item (a cost within normal business activities) another will classify as extraordinary (outside normal business activities, such as the costs involved in the closure of a subsidiary). Extraordinary items are shown in the balance sheet after profit on ordinary activities after taxation, that is, they go below the line used for the calculation of earnings per share. A UK exposure draft issued in 1991 is seeking to tighten up these definitions.

- Financial statements *use historical costs* and thus, in most instances, ignore the inflation factor. Inventories, for example, can be undervalued; therefore, by using the FIFO costing method, higher income would generally be experienced during periods of inflation.

- The net profit reported in the profit statement is *not absolute but rather relative* depending on the particular conventional procedures used by the organization in its accounting practices. Profit figures can be manipulated, either intentionally or unintentionally, by improper reflection of non-recurring gain on the sale of land or other resources, declining trends in repairs to existing fixed assets (a possible cost control objective), method of stock valuation in relation to cost of sales, use of diluted profit rates on contracts to provide for management contingency pools, use of estimated overhead rates that are not representative of actual expenses, and so on.)

- The statements reflect the *position of the financial accounting* for an organization but may not show the *true financial condition* of the operational results since there are many factors that are not a part of the financial data reporting. *Informative footnotes* could provide clues to existing or anticipated financial adjustments.

- There are *inherent estimations* in the accounting measurement process such as the life of the individual fixed assets and associated depreciation values, which affect operating expense and profit, warranty provisions, estimated corporation tax provisions, projected disallowances (particularly on government contracts), and write-offs of expected project failures.

The statement limitations pose a problem in reliably analysing an organization's financial position, developing meaningful ratios, and comparing operational results with other organizations even in a similar type of industry.

Analysing the comparative balance sheet

Model 5.3 will help us see how some common practices are employed in analysing the increases and decreases among assets, liabilities, and equity. It also highlights information that is pertinent to other aspects of profitability and that can be used in conjunction with the profit and loss account.

Examining the balance sheet

The balance sheet in Model 5.3 reports data for the years ending 19X3 and 19X4. The recommended format has been changed to match assets with liabilities. The item classifications may also vary somewhat among organizations depending on their types of operations and specific reporting requirements. The single balance sheet emphasizes an organization's *financial position*, whereas comparative reporting concentrates on the *changes* between two or more time periods and financial *trends*.

The changes in the balance sheet items are the effects of the period's operational activities, and they reflect the interactions among assets, liabilities, and capital accounts. Most significantly, the comparisons provide an opportunity to analyse and evaluate the trends in financial position of an organization in terms of the specifics reported.

Analysing comparative statements

In the vertical approach to balance sheet analysis, *each of the total asset items is*

MODEL 5.3. Comparative balance sheet analysis

(in £000,000s)

	19X4 £	19X4 %	19X3 £	19X3 %	19X4 increase (decrease) £	19X4 increase (decrease) %
Fixed assets						
Tangible assets						
Land and buildings	22.3	19.1	22.0	18.8	0.3	1.5
Plant and machinery	31.4	26.7	29.4	25.0	2.0	6.8
Less depreciation	(17.9)	(15.3)	(16.8)	(14.3)	(1.1)	(6.5)
Net fixed assets	35.8	30.5	34.6	29.5	1.2	3.5
Current assets						
Stocks						
Raw materials	26.8	22.9	19.2	16.4	7.6	39.6
Work in progress	10.7	9.1	19.7	16.8	(9.0)	(45.7)
Finished goods	7.3	6.2	5.6	4.8	1.7	30.4
Subtotal	44.8	38.2	44.5	38.0	0.3	0.7
Debtors	28.7	24.5	32.7	27.9	(4.0)	(12.2)
Prepayments	0.25	0.2	0.3	0.2	(0.05)	(16.7)
Deferred charges	0.90	0.8	1.7	1.4	(0.80)	(47.1)
Cash in hand and at bank	3.5	3.0	2.5	2.1	1.0	40.0
Investments	3.3	2.8	1.0	0.9	2.3	230.0
Total current assets	81.45	69.5	82.7	70.5	(1.25)	(1.5)
Total assets	117.25	100.0	117.3	100.0	0.05	
Creditors due within one year						
Trade creditors	20.85	17.8	16.5	13.9	4.35	26.4
Bank loans and overdrafts	2.50	2.1	2.3	2.0	0.20	8.7
Bills of exchange	1.40	1.2	6.0	5.1	(4.6)	(76.6)
Accruals	3.60	3.1	2.9	2.5	0.7	24.1
Taxation	2.60	2.2	2.4	2.0	0.2	8.3
Total current liabilities	30.95	26.4	30.1	25.5	0.85	2.8
Creditors due after one year						
Debenture loans	26.7	22.8	28.8	24.6	(2.10)	(7.3)
Provisions for liabilities and charges						
Deferred taxation	1.9	1.6	2.2	1.9	(0.30)	(13.6)
Total liabilities	59.55	50.8	61.10	52.0	(1.55)	(2.5)
Capital and reserves						
Called up share capital	29.71	25.3	38.69	33.1	(8.98)	(23.21)
Profit and loss account	27.99	23.9	17.51	14.9	10.48	59.9
Total liabilities/capital	117.25	100.0	117.3	100.0	0.05	
Working capital	50.5	—	52.6	—	(2.1)	(4.0)
Current ratio	2.6	—	2.7	—	(0.1)	
Ratio to sales	—	20.7	—	26.8	—	(6.1)

divided by the total asset value. This computation provides the quantitative positional relationships among the reported items at a particular point in time. *Each liability and equity item* is divided by the *aggregate total* which equals the total asset value.

Let us take a look at the comparative values and their percentages:

- Debtors and stocks represented the major elements in the current assets. Although the debtors decreased £4.0 million or 12.2 per cent in 19X4 over 19X3, the decrease was offset primarily by a £3.3 million increase in cash and securities. Relative to stocks, raw materials and finished goods increased by £9.3 million; the increase, however, was mostly offset by a £9.0 million decrease in work in progress.

- The total overall current assets for the two reporting periods remained in a static position with only a 1.5 per cent decrease in 19X4 versus 19X3.

- Net fixed assets increased by £1.2 million or 3.5 per cent in 19X4 over 19X3.

- Creditors represented the largest current *liability*, indicating that there was £4.4 million or a 26.4 per cent increase in 19X4 as compared to 19X3. This situation is generally considered to be unfavourable unless production/sales requirements increased accordingly (which they did, as shown in Model 5.1). Further, the increase was more than offset by the £4.6 million decrease in bills of exchange payable – a favourable trend in liability reduction.

- In the aggregate, total current liabilities increased by £0.85 million or 2.8 per cent in 19X4 versus 19X3. Such an increase, in relative terms, is not significant when production costs increased by 25.2 per cent, as shown in Model 5.1.

- As a result of decreased current assets of £450,000 and increased current liabilities of £0.85 million, the net effect on working capital in 19X4 was a decrease of £2.1 million or 4.0 per cent. The *current ratio* (current assets ÷ current liabilities) was 2.6 in 19X4 versus 2.7 in 19X3. These ratios are considered favourable, particularly in manufacturing operations.

- The decrease in *total liabilities* of £1.55 million or 2.5 per cent is primarily attributed to the reduction in long-term debt of £2.1 million or 7.3 per cent. This is a favourable trend in light of the £50,000 increase in total assets and a £1.5 million increase in shareholders' equity, as displayed in Model 5.3.

Summary
Using both the vertical and horizontal approaches to financial statement analysis, you can thoroughly assess operating results. Either type of analysis contributes uniquely to data assessment. Use the calculated percentages as result indicators, which may require additional interpretation and further use in analysis and planning. You must determine whether the various proportions and changes are favourable or unfavourable to the organization's objectives.

Making comparative assessments of external organizations

You can use the same process to compare the financial positions of two or more *external* organizations in related industries at a point in time. Comparisons expressed in pounds sterling may be misleading due to the relative sizes of the organizations. Converting to percentages clarifies the relative proportions of the financial elements.

Caution

Be careful. The balance sheet data must be compatible and comparable in terms of basic accounting procedures. Follow the guidelines set forth by the ASB (Accounting Standards Board) as common standards.

Applications

Comparative balance sheet analysis provides informative insight into the overall financial position/percentage changes (increases or decreases) between periods. It also reflects the interactions among assets, liabilities, and capital, as well as the respective trends of each.

How to analyse changes in shareholders' equity

The changes in shareholders' equity schedule highlight and summarize financial variations and report their effect on the capital position.

Model 5.4 displays an assessment of capital changes. *Increases in assets* and *decreases in liability accounts* represent the factors causing an *increase in capital*. Conversely, *decreases in assets* and *increases in liabilities* result in *capital reductions*. As shown in Model 5.4, the change in the 19X4 capital position is the difference between the increases and decreases resulting in the extra amount of £1.5 million or 2.7 per cent over 19X3. In other words, the factors that increase capital represent the source for the increases (cash, investments, and so on), whereas the reductions to the capital account are considered to be capital applications (increased creditors and decreased debtors, as examples).

If you require more detail on fixed assets and accumulated depreciation than is given in the model, you would show the individually categorized *gross asset increases* as *increases in assets* and the increases in classified depreciation groupings as *increases* under major item 2 – 'Factors decreasing capital'.

How to use shareholders' equity ratios. In Model 5.4 are examples of equity ratios that can be used in assessing the capital position and changes. In some organizations, these ratios may be relevant and useful, but in others they may be considered inconsequential. By evaluating your own organizations, you can determine which ratios are significant in assessing the capital position.

With respect to the ratios in Model 5.4, note the following:

MODEL 5.4. Assessing changes to shareholders' equity*

31 December 19X3–19X4 (in £000,000s)

Summary of shareholders' equity		19X4	19X3
Called up share capital		29.71	38.69
Profit and loss account		27.99	17.51
Subtotal		57.70	56.20
Increase in capital		—	1.50
Totals		57.70	57.70

1. *Factors increasing capital*				
Increases in assets				
Cash	1.00			
Investments	2.30			
Net stocks	0.50			
Net fixed assets	1.20	5.00		
Decreases in liabilities				
Bills of exchange payable	4.60			
Deferred taxes	0.30			
Debentures	2.10	7.00	12.00	
2. *Factors decreasing capital*				
Decreases in assets				
Debtors	4.00			
Prepayments	0.05			
Deferred charges	0.80	4.85		
Increases in liabilities				
Borrowings	0.20			
Accruals	0.70			
Creditors	4.55			
Taxation	0.20	5.65	10.50	
Increase in capital			1.50	

Capital ratios	%	%
Capital to sales	24.0	29.6
Net profit to capital	32.9	25.4
Retained earnings to capital	48.5	31.2
Capital to total assets	49.2	48.0
Capital to total liabilities	96.9	92.3

*Refer to Models 5.1 and 5.3 for operating and balance sheet detail.

The formula

$$\text{Investors' capital to sales ratio} = \frac{\text{Shareholders' equity}}{\text{Sales}}$$

As shown in Model 5.4, the equity capital relationships to sales for 19X4 and 19X3 were 24.0 per cent and 29.6 per cent, respectively. The decrease in the 19X4 ratio is primarily attributed to a 26.3 per cent increase in 19X4 sales over 19X3 with only a 2.7 per cent increase in capital.

Applications

Although not commonly used, this ratio may have useful application in certain organizations to indicate the proportion of sales financed by shareholders' equity. A further 25 per cent of sales is financed by creditor liabilities, and the operational activity is supported by the cash flow from operations. Let us analyse this relationship from another perspective: The ratio of sales to capital in 19X4 is 4.16 to 1.00 (£240 million sales ÷ capital equity of £57.7 million). The comparison indicates that the sales volume exceeds the stockholders' equity by four times the investment.

The formula

$$\text{Net profit to capital ratio} = \frac{\text{Net profit}}{\text{Capital}}$$

The net profit to capital ratio was 32.9 per cent and 25.4 per cent for 19X4 and 19X3, respectively. These ratios indicate the *returns* on stock equity achieved in 19X4 and 19X3. The increase in 19X4 is primarily attributed to a 33.1 per cent increase in net profit (Model 5.1) with a relatively modest increase (2.7 per cent) in equity.

Special note

When developing ratios involving balance sheet items (assets, liabilities, equity) versus operational data (sales, net profit, and the like), you generally obtain more reliable results by using *averaged balance sheet data* and *annualized operational data*.

Application

This analysis represents the capital or equity *profitability* for the periods ending 19X4 and 19X3. The 19X4 ratio indicates a favourable trend of capital investment return.

The formula

$$\text{Retained earnings ratio to capital} = \frac{\text{Retained earnings}}{\text{Capital}}$$

The retained earnings ratio in Model 5.4 was 48.5 per cent in 19X4 and 31.2 per cent in 19X3. The large increase in 19X4 resulted from a 59.9 per cent increase in net profit, which was only partially offset by a small increase in capital.

Application

This ratio indicates a favourable situation: The major contributing factor to capital financing is being achieved from operational results and thus reducing the pressure on outside investor contributions and dividend payments.

The formula

$$\text{Capital ratio to total liabilities} = \frac{\text{Capital}}{\text{Total liabilities}}$$

This ratio reports the amount of the total liabilities, creditors due within one year and over one year supported by outstanding capital, both the investors' and retained earnings.

As displayed in Model 5.4, the ratio factor was 96.9 per cent and 92.3 per cent, respectively, for 19X4 and 19X3. The higher ratio in 19X4 is primarily attributed to decreased total liabilities and a modest increase of £1.5 million in capital.

Application

This ratio presents to creditors an organization's financial stability in terms of contracting and meeting its debt obligations. For example, an analytical assessment of the ratio in the model indicates that every pound of the total liabilities is supported by £0.97 and £0.92 in capital for 19X4 and 19X3.

Comparing equity capital to non-current assets

To obtain this ratio, divide the capital value by the non-current assets.

EXAMPLE

The following factors are derived from data in Model 5.3:

	(£000,000s)			
	19X4	*19X3*		
Net fixed assets*	35.8	34.6	19X4	57.7 ÷ 35.8 = 161%
			19X3	56.2 ÷ 34.6 = 162%

*Some organizations may use gross fixed costs depending on their situations. The calculated ratios are 157 per cent and 155 per cent, respectively, for 19X4 and 19X3.

Application

The significance of this ratio is that the shareholders' equity supports the non-current assets and that the surplus is available for current asset operating requirements. Generally, the greater the ratio is over 100 per cent, the more favourable is the

organization's financial position from the standpoint of meeting creditor commitments and debts.

How to gauge turnover of total capital employed

The ratio of sales to average total assets represents the turnover of the total capital
employed in operations. The turnover formula is as follows:

The formula

$$\text{Total assets employed ratio} = \frac{\text{Net sales}}{\text{Average total assets (fixed and current)}}$$

Included in the total assets are the typical balance sheet items as shown in Model 5.3,
such as cash, debtors, stocks, net fixed assets, and so on. Investments are excluded
because they do not contribute directly to operational requirements and are separate
producers of non-operating income. Note that the asset distribution represents all of
the sources of capital both borrowed (short- and long-term), as well as the
shareholders' capital plus profit and loss account.

EXAMPLE
The following calculations are made from Model 5.3 data:

(in £000,000s)

	19X4	19X3		Asset turnover	
Total capital	117.25	117.10	19X4	240.00*	= 2.11
Less: investments	3.30	1.00		113.95	
Adjusted capital	113.95	116.10	19X3	190.00*	= 1.64
				116.00	

*Net sales data from Model 5.1.

The annual sales and year-end asset figures are used instead of the average in
order to compare the two years. If only 19X4 sales were compared with the two years'
asset average, the resultant ratio would be 2.08. If monthly or quarterly comparative
data were used, you would use annualized sales and average assets.

The increase in the capital employed turnover rate in 19X4 over 19X3 indicates
that assets are being utilized more effectively in 19X4 (2.11 versus 1.64). In other
words, the assets supported more sales per pound in 19X4 compared to 19X3.

Calculating the rate of return on total capital employed. In addition to analysing the
asset turnover status, you have to determine and evaluate asset profitability. To
make this assessment, combine the asset turnover with the profit rate on sales.

Depending on organizational practices and requirements, you can calculate two rates of return for analysing operational results: (1) profit from operations and (2) net profit. The calculating formulae are as follows:

1. *Approach A:*

$$\text{Rate of return on total assets} = \frac{\text{Rate on profit from operations or net profit}}{} \times \text{Asset turnover}$$

a. Profit from operations
   $\dfrac{38.2}{240.0} = 15.9\%$ return on operating profit
   19X4 sales

   Asset turnover $2.11 \times 15.9\% = 33.5\%$ Operating return on adjusted total assets

b. Net profit
   $\dfrac{18.98}{240.0} = 7.9\%$ return on net profit
   19X4 sales

   Asset turnover $2.11 \times 7.9\% = 16.7\%$ Net profit return on adjusted total assets

2. *Approach B:*

$$\frac{\text{Operating profit}}{\text{Total assets}} = \frac{\text{Profit}}{\text{Sales}} \times \frac{\text{Sales}}{\text{Total assets}}$$

a. Profit from operations
   $\dfrac{38.20}{113.95} = \dfrac{38.2}{240.0} \times \dfrac{240.00}{113.95}$
   19X4 total assets
   $33.5\% = 15.9\% \times 2.11$
   33.5% Operating return on total assets

b. Net profit
   $\dfrac{18.98}{113.95} = \dfrac{18.98}{240.0} \times \dfrac{240.00}{113.95}$
   19X4 total assets
   $16.7\% = 7.9\% \times 2.11$
   16.7% Net profit return on total assets

Points to remember about return on total capital employed. Here are some things to remember about this relationship:

- An improved asset turnover generally means an increase in the rate of return on total assets employed.

EXAMPLE
Using the 19X4 and 19X3 results already developed, the following comparison is made:

	19X4	19X3	
Adjusted capital employed	113.95	116.00	
Net sales	240.00	190.00	
Turnover ratio	2.11	1.64	
Operating profit	15.9%	15.1%	
Return on capital employed	33.5%	24.8%	(8.7% increase in 19X4)
	(2.11 × 15.9%)		(1.64 × 15.1%)

- The *increased sales* in 19X4 of 26.3 per cent over 19X3 and a decrease of 1.9 per cent in total capital employed resulted in an 8.7 per cent increase in the asset return.
- Generally, an organization selling higher-priced items (motor vehicles or machinery, for example) has a *lower turnover rate* than one selling lower-priced units. The *lower-priced units have a higher-profit margin* in order to achieve a favourable return on the capital assets employed.
- A *high rate of turnover* in capital employed usually indicates efficiency in the utilization of capital.
- *Use of average total assets and appropriate annualized sales* provides a realistic assessment of profit return on total capital employed despite unusual fluctuations among time periods.
- As a measure of return on total capital employed this ratio has advantages over those that relate operating profit to total assets minus current liabilities. This is because the inclusion of bank overdrafts in current liabilities can lead to distortions. For example if profits are falling but net operating assets are falling more, due to increasing overdraft, then the company's profitability measured by that ratio may appear to be increasing. Distortions due to changes in the current ratio are avoided by using total assets. Furthermore, where the interest charge is a significant amount in relation to profits before interest it may be sensible to deduct it from operating profit in order to see the amount of profit that is really available for equity providers.

A word of caution
The above ratio is satisfactory in asssessing the same company over several years. However, when compared to industry averages the investment base needs to be considered. The following example will make the position clear.

EXAMPLE
Company A has a profit (after depreciation) of £500,000.
It has invested in new plant costing say £5 million less depreciation to date of £1 million. Current assets stand at £2 million.

Company B has a profit (after depreciation) of £500,000.
Its older plant is in the books at £2 million less depreciation of £1 million. Current assets stand at £2 million.

The return on capital employed (ROCE) is as follows:

Company A $= \dfrac{500,000}{5m - 1m + 2m} = \dfrac{500,000}{6,000,000}$

Company B $= \dfrac{500,000}{3,000,000}$

B may be twice as profitable as A until it has to replace its plant.

Calculating earnings per ordinary share

Investors in ordinary shares are generally more interested in and concerned with the earnings per share (influencing factor on market price) of their shares than with the dividend return. (The exceptions might be shareholders who depend on their dividends for their livelihoods.) The shareholders assume the ultimate risk in the business enterprise if it should fail since all creditor claims must be satisfied before any investment reimbursement is made to the owners. The investors' share ownership represents tangible evidence of their claim against the net assets of the organization.

To derive earnings per share, divide the net profit by the number of ordinary shares outstanding in the possession of the shareholders.

EXAMPLE

Assume that the main and only concern is ordinary shares since no preference or other equivalent type stock is involved in this situation:

Earnings per share (in £000,000s)

	19X4	19X3
Net profit	18.98	14.255
Average shares outstanding	$\dfrac{}{3.43} = 5.53^*$	$\dfrac{}{3.43} = 4.16^*$

*Earnings per share

Rate of return on shareholders' equity (in £000,000s)

	19X4	19X3
Net profit	18.98	14.255
Shareholders' equity	$\dfrac{}{57.70} = 32.9\%$	$\dfrac{}{56.20} = 24.4\%$

The increase in earnings per share in 19X4 is attributed to a 33.1 per cent higher income.

The ordinary shareholders' equity is generally the total shareholders' equity less the par value of the preference shares. So, if there were dividend requirements for *preference shares*, deduct the amount from the net profit before calculating the earnings per share on ordinary shares. The net profit is currently taken after tax and preference dividend but before extraordinary items. Where new shares are issued during the year or where a company has securities in issue which may rank for future dividends then the earnings per share (eps) is adjusted in accordance with Standard Statement of Accounting Practice number 3, which is intended to apply to the accounts of listed companies. A further complication may arise on the calculation of eps when a company pays a dividend. United Kingdom dividend payments incur a payment of advance corporation tax (ACT) – relievable (within rules) against the mainstream tax liability. However, some companies may have difficulty in fully relieving ACT and finish up with a higher tax charge.

Three alternative methods of computing eps have therefore arisen. The 'nil basis' assumes no ordinary dividends are distributed. The 'net basis' assumes that all the elements of the taxation charge are taken into account. The 'maximum' method is based on the post-tax profit plus the maximum amount of ACT that could be offset against corporation tax in the event of a notional total distribution of profit by way of dividends. At present this amounts to twenty-five thirty-fourths, the current basic income tax rate over the current corporation tax rate. For most companies both the nil and net calculations will produce the same result and they are required to report on the 'net basis'. Companies which have income taxed overseas are likely to produce different figures and are required to show both calculations. Where a company at the balance sheet date has contracted to issue further shares after the end of the period, or where it has already issued shares which will rank for dividend later, the effect may be to dilute future earnings per share. The fully diluted eps is therefore calculated.

If new equity shares have been issued during the year either for cash at full market price or as consideration for the acquisition of an asset the earnings should be apportioned over the average number of shares ranking for dividend during the period weighted on a time basis. Where new equity shares have been issued by way of capitalization during the period, the earnings should be apportioned over the number of shares ranking for dividend after the capitalization.

Calculating the price–earnings ratio per share

This ratio represents the relationship between earnings per share and the market price. To obtain it, divide the market price per share by the comparable earnings per share.

EXAMPLE
The market prices per ordinary share are £16 and £14, respectively, for 19X4 and 19X3.

	19X4		19X3	
Market price per share	£16	= 2.89	£14	= 3.37
Earnings per share*	£5.53		£4.16	

*Calculated in previous example.

The price–earnings ratio is calculated to be 2.9 and 3.4 times earnings, respectively.

EXAMPLE
The London Stock Exchange requires the 'net' distribution method to be used for calculating price–earnings ratio. The market price is divided by the net earnings per share.

Calculating the dividend cover
The 'maximum' distribution method gives the most suitable indication of a company's dividend-paying ability. Dividend cover is obtained by dividing the maximum earnings per share by the gross dividend per share.

$$\text{Ratio } \frac{\text{eps}}{\text{dps}}$$

If company A has dividend cover of 1 and company B cover of 4 what can we deduce? The implication for company A is that if a downturn in earnings occurs A might be forced to cut its future dividend. For B there appears to be more cover to maintain the present level of dividend payments in the future. However, dividend cover may give a misleading indication of ability to pay dividends. Dividends are paid in cash so it is important additionally to examine ratios concerned with liquidity.

Assessing the causes of profit variation

By using cost variation analyses, you not only determine the reasons for the variance in planned profit goals, but also ascertain whether some type of corrective action is required or whether profit forecasts were too optimistic. Essentially, you try to answer such questions as these: Can the cost assessment provide the necessary insight as to where and how cost deviations occurred? Can the deviations be reduced and profits increased?

Most progressive and successful organizations plan their profit objectives in advance rather than accept whatever results materialize at the end of a reporting period. With a 'planning' philosophy, you must initiate cost control standards for cost of sales and D&A/selling expenses. You must also carefully plan and then assess anticipated sales volumes and product profit margins.

The basic causes of variations

At the end of the reporting period, compare the planned profits to the actuals and then calculate the difference in terms of increases or decreases. Next, determine the cause or causes. Some of the common reasons for profit variations are changes in

- sales volume;
- sales mix of products;
- sales prices of products;
- direct production costs;
- distribution and administration costs.

Look at each of these causes more closely:

Sales volume. The planned sales objective may be either not achieved or exceeded, with generally a resultant increase or decrease in profits. An analysis would help you to pinpoint the problem: an 'unaccepted' product line, an accelerated or delayed production schedule, a 'blown' contract or sales order, a 'tough' sales territory, and so on.

Direct production costs (cost of sales). Variations in these costs can be attributed to a number of factors, such as machine downtime, poor learning curve results, wage increases, fluctuations in the price of raw materials and operating costs, excessive rework, production schedule delays, and so on. The detailed work order and cost sheets can generally provide the reasons for these variations.

D&A. These expenses may have exceeded estimates due to increased advertising, acceleration and expansion of sales activity, higher than anticipated administrative costs, increased head office expense allocations, and so on.

Sales prices of products. Product prices can be lower than expected due to many factors, such as price concessions to favoured customers because of competitive pressures, large-quantity sales at discount prices, poor estimates of product cost and gross margin markup, exploitation of new market outlets, and so on. The marketing organization is undoubtedly aware of the details.

Sales mix of products. In an organization with varying product lines and different gross margins, the estimated sales for the individual product lines may or may not materialize. In other words, low-priced items, with their low profit margins, may have represented most of the projected sales. A detailed analysis of the sales by product line would reveal 'what happened' to dilute profit.

Analysing gross profit variance

Model 5.5 displays the formulae used to derive the gross profit variances and to determine their specific causes. As shown in the model, the overall gross profit variance is the difference between the actual and standard gross profits. To ascertain the causes for the difference, use the following formulae:

Cost of sales	= Standard cost of sales − Actual cost of sales
Sales price list at discount	= Actual net sales − Price list sales at standard discount
Standard gross profit variation by product line	= Standard gross profit on cost of sales − Standard gross profit on actual price list sales by product line
Standard gross profit variation on sales volume	= Standard gross profit on actual price list sales by product line − Standard gross profit

MODEL 5.5. Analysing gross profit (GP) variance

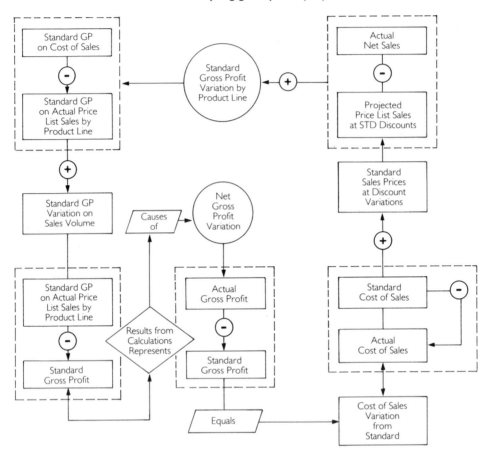

The sum of the increases and decreases derived from these calculations represents the causes of the net profit variation, as shown in Model 5.5. Note that the D&A/ selling expenses are not displayed since they do not generally influence gross profit; they are rather subsequent deductions to derive profit from operations.

Segregating gross profit variations by causes

Model 5.6 demonstrates the calculations for product lines A and B and their totals. Segregation of the variance analyses is by *cause*. The sum total of the gross profit variations resulted in a decrease of £670,000 for product line A and an increase of £1.34 million for product line B, with a net total increase of £670,000 for the combined product lines.

The bottom of the model displays a summary of the gross profit variations by causes for each product line. This type of analysis and reporting provides

MODEL 5.6. Calculating gross profit variations by causes

(in £000,000s)

	Product line A	Product line B	Combined total
Gross profit (GP) variation			
Actual	2.23	9.04	11.27
Standard or estimated	2.90	7.70	10.60
Increase (decrease)	(0.67)	1.34	0.67
Analysis of GP increases (decreases)			
Cost of sales			
Standard	3.20	12.40	15.60
Actual	3.32	11.96	15.28
Increase (decrease)	(0.12)	0.44	0.32
Sales at price list or discounted			
Actual net sales	5.55	21.00	26.55
Price list sales at discount	5.80	20.70	26.50
Increase (decrease)	(0.25	0.30	0.05
Standard GP variation by product line			
Cost of sales	2.60	8.30	10.90
Actual price list sales discounted	2.50	6.70	9.20
Increase (decrease)	0.10	1.60	1.70
Standard GP variation on sales volume			
Actual price list sales discounted	2.50	6.70	9.20
Standard gross profit	2.90	7.70	10.60
Increase (decrease)	(0.40)	(1.00)	(1.40)
Summary of variation analysis			
Actual gross profit	13.85	48.40	62.25
Standard gross profit	14.52	47.06	61.58
Increase (decrease)	(0.67)	1.34	0.67

Variation analysis by causes

	Product line A	Product line B	Combined total	Percentage increase (decrease)
Cost of sales	(0.12)	0.44	0.32	0.478
Sales price or discounted	(0.25)	0.30	0.05	0.075
Standard GP variation by product line	0.10	1.60	1.70	2.537
Standard GP variation on sales volume	(0.40)	(1.00)	(1.40)	(2.090)
Net increase (decrease)	(0.67)	1.34	0.67	1.000

management with a rapid overview of the causes of gross profit variations and permits positive action, if required, to correct unfavourable situations.

The variations indicate that product line B had favourable variations in gross profit with the exception of sales volume results, which indicate that actual discounted prices were £1.0 million less than the projected standard.

6 How to use ratio analysis for industry comparisons

Chapter highlights

Financial analysts, as well as managers, may utilize comparison ratios to assess and interpret data for planning and controlling operations. Industry comparisons can be extremely helpful, but their use has its pitfalls. As an analyst, you must be familiar with the role of ratio guidelines in making comparisons, as well as with the possible deficiencies in data reliability.

Some ratios are used to uncover problems relative to debtors, stock, profit, sales, financing, and fixed assets.

Other ratios examine the company's solvency relative to fixed assets to net worth, woking capital to sales, and stock to working capital.

These ratios also play an important role in trend analysis. The procedure for their use is explained, as is the significance of similar industry comparisons.

Coping with the dilemma in the initial use of ratio analysis

Ratio analysis was initially used to assess an organization's financial position and performance in the early 1900s by financial and banking institutions. The purpose was to determine an organization's financial stability, particularly its ability to meet debt obligations on schedule. This assessment provided a basis for an organization's decision to extend credit to a borrower. Originally, the lender's concern was with the organization's *current ratio* – the relationship of current assets to current liabilities. The borrower's ratio was analysed individually and with respect to the related industry.

Subsequently, both investors and financial analysts realized that their prevailing ratio approach was, by itself, not an adequate assessment of an organization's financial stability, progress, and performance. They then scrutinized other ratios for their usefulness in data analysis to supplement and validate the financial status indicated by the current ratio.

A series of applicable ratios was developed. Although many users were captivated by the newly found possibilities of these ratios, analysts were unfamiliar with their significance and limitations. As a result, these ratios were often misapplied

Table of industry average ratios

Average industry ratios for the year ended 31 March 1991 – quoted companies

SIC code	17	427	321	371
Industry	Water production	Beer/ malting	Tractors/ agricultural m/c	Measuring instruments
Description of ratio				
1. Current ratio	1.45	1.20	1.71	1.18
2. Liquidity ratio	1.31	0.68	1.01	0.85
3. Solvency ratio (%)	71.86	50.23	40.13	38.56
(equity to total capital employed)				
4. Gearing (%)	20.19	61.97	73.60	83.94
5. Interest cover	11.17	4.43	8.18	7.76
6. Profit margin (%)	28.24	11.93	6.37	11.82
7. Return on shareholders' funds	13.69	18.85	19.08	34.62
8. Return on total assets	9.83	9.47	7.65	13.35
9. Stock turnover	15.74	6.51	4.54	7.73
10. Debtors turnover	5.26	7.15	4.24	4.32
11. Turnover per employee (£)	76,505	64,284	50,805	68,652
12. Total assets turnover	0.34	0.79	1.2	1.12
13. Fixed assets turnover	0.45	1.10	3.45	2.39
14. Collection period (days)	69.00	51.00	86.00	84.00
15. Credit period	93.00	54.00	27.00	71.00

Source: The FAME database, Jordan & Sons Limited

and misinterpreted. Users found that the application and use of the broad ratio approach to evaluate an organization's performance and financial progress were not the panacea originally envisaged. Care and judgement had to be exercised in using and interpreting ratios.

Recognizing the inherent weaknesses in ratio analysis

A number of factors can influence the reliability and validity of ratio performance indicators, thus placing limits on their unqualified utilization for management's financial and operating decisions. Here are some of the major limitations and possible drawbacks. If you are to use ratio analysis on a firm basis and accept the results with confidence and finality, you should bear the following in mind:

- In business problem solving and planning, quantitative data analyses are not the sole criterion. Management's judgement and its operating effectiveness play vital roles in decision making and assessing performance results.

- To interpret the implications of changes in ratios reliably, you must analyse the variations in the two or more variables representing the relationship. For example, given unusual fluctuations in the current ratio, you must investigate the individual current assets and liabilities to determine whether the trend of change is temporary or permanent.

- Inherent exceptions can be involved in any ratio interpretation since the standard of content and calculation is not absolute. If data compatibility is not assured, comparisons with industry averages may be misleading and invalid.

- Persons involved in the reporting and analysis processes may overlook or 'gloss over' significant information. Consequently, ratios do not necessarily provide a *thorough and accurate overview* of the financial statement content, relationships, and results.

- Profit is a key area of analysis. Yet the ratio assessment of profit return on equity and total assets can be distorted. The reported profit figures might include profits before or after deducting depreciation and interest expenses, or corporation taxes might not have been given consideration. For a generally sound criterion in judging the profit generated, you might use pretax profit from operations.

- Ratios are sometimes accepted as the 'final say' in result analysis. However, do not overlook other relevant and influencing criteria, such as (1) the effects of inflation, (2) changes in product mix and its effect on the operating/sales environment, (3) debtor/stock turnover factor, (4) adverse cash flow, (5) changes in credit policy, (6) prevailing sales/orders outstanding position and trends, and (7) excessive investment in capital facilities.

- Although you may use ratios for planning, do not ignore the fact that they represent historical experience and past relationship. Although past performance is and should be of considerable interest, the emphasis is on correcting deficiencies and improving future results. The prevailing ratios aid in reconciling and developing projections for the future. Nevertheless, the key requirements for success and profit are judgemental decisions, marketing intelligence, anticipated operating environment, planned goals, and effective management control.

- Ratios of similar types of organizations can be so misleading that they hamper a realistic comparative analysis of data results and meaning. You should consider (1) the relative sizes of the organizations, (2) their uniformity in accounting procedures, (3) lengths of accounting periods being reported, and (4) type of customers. Each of these factors can influence the inter-industry comparison of performance results by means of ratios.

How to use periodic trends to measure performance

By using ratio analyses as representatives of past experience, you can effectively plan financial objectives and gauge future operating environments. In so doing, your concern must be directed towards the underlying direction and intensity of changes in operating results. The situation may be static and quiescent, requiring only minor changes in future operating decisions. Major trend changes would call for a thorough review of the operating plan and perhaps significant changes to meet new challenges.

Types of measurement
The common measurements in financial data analysis fall into two primary groups:

1. The first type of assessment is concerned with the *item element relationships* in current performance reporting.
2. The second is directed toward the *item changes* in a series of time-reported statements.

Current or single report analysis measures results only at a point in time. Assessing a series of time reports is a dynamic approach in performance evaluation because you can determine patterns of progess and trends for establishing future planning goals. Further, you can redirect operational trends that are inconsistent with management's prerogatives and objectives.

The use of trend measurement, in conjunction with ratio comparisons and data evaluation, provides a supplemental and logical basis for sound planning. Trend measurement and projections are affected by estimates or approximations and their computation. The latter method involves the principles of semi- or moving averages and the least squares procedure.

The progressive organization depends on successful operating performance results, their appropriate assessment and interpretation, sound financial planning, and adequate controls. When an organization lacks financial success or fails, it generally has not paid enough attention to data result analyses, and possibly the financial accountants and analysts who prepare the reports for management review might have erred. Sound, factual, and relevant communication between management and staff is often they key to successful operational activities.

Understanding the role of ratio guidelines

Presenting your analysis to management
As the financial analyst, your assessment of operating results may indicate that debtor and/or stock balances are too high, that fixed assets are excessive when compared to sales and net worth, that bank loans are disproportionate to asset requirements, and so on. Although your presentation may be perfectly valid, your viewpoint could be overruled by management. However, if you point to prevailing situations and results in other similar organizations, you make your point more convincingly. At least, you obtain supportive interest and attention from management, who might further explore and analyse the causes for the data results and differences. To show management, therefore, that certain components of the financial structure are out of balance or represent problem areas, compare the organization's data with those of similar organizations and/or similar industry averages.

Yet data comparisons even among similar industry organizations can be difficult to support due to the following important factors:

- uniformity of accounting systems, procedures, and time periods;
- dissimilarity in size and organizational structures;
- different types of customers with their particular effects on credit terms and extension and debt collections;
- age, cost, composition, and utilization of fixed assets;
- capitalization requirements and availability;
- leased versus purchased assets;
- somewhat different products which affect various elements in the financial structure;
- different sub-contracting policy;
- failure of past results to indicate the future and its trends;
- management effectiveness;
- varying external standards and goals among organizations, rendering comparisons invalid and incompatible in assessing internal results and planning future objectives.

Comparing the pound value results among organizations is very often unsatisfactory and meaningless. Generally, more effective and reliable comparisons can be effected through the *use of ratios*. Ratios may not be the panacea, but they serve a useful purpose. The major drawback occurs when an individual organization's ratios are compared with averages.

A *ratio* is a computation that expresses the relationship of two or more sets of data in terms of a *percentage* or a *multiple*, as in the case of the common *current ratio*. Ratios are usually classified as

- *static* – balance sheet items, point in time;
- *operating* – costs versus sales;
- *velocity* – relationship of certain income and expense items to balance sheet items.

Where to obtain comparative ratios

List of sources
The major sources of ratio information are as follows:

- Dun & Bradstreet Ltd
- Extel Financial Ltd
- ICC Information Group Ltd

On line databases
- Datastream International Ltd
- FAME.

In addition, organizations whose shares are listed on the stock exchanges file annual reports at Companies Registration Office, containing more information than non-listed companies are obliged to produce.

Prime ratios published

- current ratio (current assets to current liabilities);
- net profit return on tangible net sales;
- net profit as a percentage of net working capital;
- net profit as a percentage of tangible net worth;
- net sales as a percentage of net working capital;
- debtor collection period (length of);
- net sales to stock;
- fixed assets to tangible net worth;
- current debt to tangible net worth;
- total debt to tangible net worth (equity ratio);
- stock to net working capital;
- current liabilities to stock;
- funded debt to net working capital.

These ratios are published for retail, wholesale, and manufacturing companies in Dun & Bradstreet publications.

Reporting requirements for the Stock Exchange

All organizations who have securities listed with the Stock Exchange are required to file an annual report and accounts within six months of their year end unless they have significant overseas interests in which case they can apply for an extention.

The report and accounts are prepared in accordance with the Companies Act 1985 formats supplemented by additional information required by the Stock Exchange. Model 6.1 shows the two most common profit and loss formats and alternative balance sheets. Certain of the additional information is extremely useful in industry comparisons.

1. If there are any significant departures from standard accounting practices the directors have to provide reasons.
2. A geographical turnover analysis and contribution to trading results of operations outside the UK and Ireland.
3. Details of bank loans, overdrafts and other borrowings.
4. The amount of interest capitalized by the company (or group) during the year.

Use of the additional information and the information contained in the standard formats has to be treated with care. If unusual gains and losses are included in

MODEL 6.1. The Companies Act 1985: standard formats

Profit and loss account formats

SCH. 4
PART I

Format 1

1. Turnover
2. Cost of sales (*14*)
3. Gross profit or loss
4. Distribution costs (*14*)
5. Administrative expenses (*14*)
6. Other operating income
7. Income from shares in group companies
8. Income from shares in related companies
9. Income from other fixed asset investments (*15*)
10. Other interest receivable and similar income (*15*)
11. Amounts written off investments
12. Interest payable and similar charges (*16*)
13. Tax on profit or loss on ordinary activities
14. Profit or loss on ordinary activities after taxation
15. Extraordinary income
16. Extraordinary charges
17. Extraordinary profit or loss
18. Tax on extraordinary profit or loss
19. Other taxes not shown under the above items
20. Profit or loss for the financial year

MODEL 6.1. The Companies Act 1985: standard formats *Contd*

Profit and loss account formats

SCH. 4

PART I

Format 2

1. Turnover
2. Change in stocks of finished goods and in work in progress
3. Own work capitalized
4. Other operating income
5. (*a*) Raw materials and consumables
   (*b*) Other external charges
6. Staff costs:
   (*a*) wages and salaries
   (*b*) social security costs
   (*c*) other pension costs
7. (*a*) Depreciation and other amounts written off tangible and intangible fixed assets
   (*b*) Exceptional amounts written off current assets
8. Other operating charges
9. Income from shares in group companies
10. Income from shares in related companies
11. Income from other fixed asset investments (*15*)
12. Other interest receivable and similar income (*15*)
13. Amounts written off investments
14. Interest payable and similar charges (*16*)
15. Tax on profit or loss on ordinary activities
16. Profit or loss on ordinary activities after taxation
17. Extraordinary income
18. Extraordinary charges
19. Extraordinary profit or loss
20. Tax on extraordinary profit or loss
21. Other taxes not shown under the above items
22. Profit or loss for the financial year

MODEL 6.1. The Companies Act 1985: standard formats *Contd*

Balance sheet formats

Format 1

A. Called up share capital not paid (*1*)

B. Fixed assets
  I 1. Development costs
     2. Concessions, patents, licences, trade marks and similar rights and assets (*2*)
     3. Goodwill (*3*)
     4. Payments on account

  II Tangible assets
     1. Land and buildings
     2. Plant and machinery
     3. Fixtures, fittings, tools and equipment
     4. Payments on account and assets in course of construction

  III Investments
     1. Shares in group companies
     2. Loans to group companies
     3. Shares in related companies
     4. Loans to related companies
     5. Other investments other than loans
     6. Other loans
     7. Own shares (*4*)

C. Current assets
  I Stocks
     1. Raw materials and consumables
     2. Work in progress
     3. Finished goods and goods for resale
     4. Payments on account

  II Debtors (*5*)
     1. Trade debtors
     2. Amounts owed by group companies
     3. Amounts owed by related companies
     4. Other debtors
     5. Called up share capital not paid (*1*)
     6. Prepayments and accrued income (*6*)

  III Investments
     1. Shares in group companies
     2. Own shares (*4*)
     3. Other investments

  IV Cash at bank and in hand

D. Prepayments and accrued income (*6*)

MODEL 6.1. The Companies Act 1985: standard formats *Contd*

E. Creditors: amounts falling due within one year
    1. Debenture loans (7)
    2. Bank loans and overdrafts
    3. Payments received on account (8)
    4. Trade creditors
    5. Bills of exchange payable
    6. Amounts owed to group companies
    7. Amounts owed to related companies
    8. Other creditors including taxation and social security (9)
    9. Accruals and deferred income (10)

F. Net current assets (liabilities) (11)

G. Total assets less current liabilities

H. Creditors: amounts falling due after more than one year
    1. Debenture loans (7)
    2. Bank loans and overdrafts
    3. Payments received on account (8)
    4. Trade creditors
    5. Bills of exchange payable
    6. Amounts owed to group companies
    7. Amounts owed to related companies
    8. Other creditors including taxation and social security (9)
    9. Accruals and deferred income (10)

I   Provisions for liabilities and charges
    1. Pensions and similar obligations
    2. Taxation, including deferred taxation
    3. Other provisions

J. Accruals and deferred income (10)

K. Capital and reserves
    I   Called up share capital (12)
    II   Share premium account
    III Revaluation reserve
    IV   Other reserves
         1. Capital redemption reserve
         2. Reserve for own shares
         3. Reserves provided for by the articles of association
         4. Other reserves
    V   Profit and loss account

MODEL 6.1. The Companies Act 1985: standard formats *Contd*

Balance sheet formats   SCH. 4
Format 2   PART I

ASSETS

A.   Called up share capital not paid *(1)*

B.   Fixed assets
  I   Intangible assets
        1. Development costs
        2. Concessions, patents, licences, trade marks and similar rights and
            assets *(2)*
        3. Goodwill *(3)*
        4. Payments on account
  II   Tangible assets
        1. Land and buildings
        2. Plant and machinery
        3. Fixtures, fittings, tools and equipment
        4. Payments on account and assets in course of construction
  III   Investments
        1. Shares in group companies
        2. Loans to group companies
        3. Shares in related companies
        4. Loans to related companies
        5. Other investments other than loans
        6. Other loans
        7. Own shares *(4)*

C.   Current assets
  I   Stocks
        1. Raw materials and consumables
        2. Work in progress
        3. Finished goods and goods for resale
        4. Payments on account
  II   Debtors *(5)*
        1. Trade debtors
        2. Amounts owed by group companies
        3. Amounts owed by related companies
        4. Other debtors
        5. Called up share capital not paid *(1)*
        6. Prepayments and accrued income *(6)*
  III   Investments
        1. Shares in group companies
        2. Own shares *(4)*
        3. Other investments
  IV   Cash at bank and in hand

D.   Prepayments and accrued income *(6)*

MODEL 6.1. The Companies Act 1985: standard formats *Contd*

LIABILITIES

A.   Capital and reserves
   I   Called up share capital (*12*)
   II   Share premium account
   III Revaluation reserve
   IV   Other reserves
       1. Capital redemption reserve
       2. Reserve for own shares
       3. Reserves provided for by the articles of association
       4. Other reserves
   V   Profit and loss account

B.   Provisions for liabilities and charges
       1. Pensions and similar obligations
       2. Taxation including deferred taxation
       3. Other provisions

C.   Creditors (*13*)
       1. Debenture loans (*7*)
       2. Bank loans and overdrafts
       3. Payments received on account (*8*)
       4. Trade creditors
       5. Bills of exchange payable
       6. Amounts owed to group companies
       7. Amounts owed to related companies
       8. Other creditors including taxation and social security (*9*)
       9. Accruals and deferred income (*10*)

D.   Accruals and deferred income (*10*)

---

the financial statements, comparisons with other organizations are destroyed. The problem with using financial statements data is that the information is limited to what is recorded in the books of account. Other reported data supplement the information contained in the traditional financial statements.

How to use ratio analysis to ascertain possible problem areas

Uncovering problems
You can use various ratios to assess and highlight current and potential operational problem areas. To gauge the significance of a ratio, you must test the it to determine its applicability, relevance, and use in the organization's operations.

Some areas that require constant supervision and have a decided influence on financial stability are:

- debtors;
- stock;
- net profit;
- sales activity;
- financing;
- fixed assets.

Applications

Debtors ratio. This aspect of an organization's operations is important because funds are rendered unavailable until collected. The ratio that reveals the most about the status and acceptability of the debtors position is the *average collection period*, an informative guide in comparing an organization's collections with the industry as a whole. This average is used in evaluating the effectiveness of its credit and collection functions. If there is a collection problem, review the credit policies and/or take corrective actions to accelerate customer payments.

Stock ratios. One of the prime causes of business failures and involuntary liquidations is either excessive or unbalanced stock. Only with constant and aggressive monitoring can you avoid this type of situation. Except for possible speculation, management would seldom intentionally plan to build an excessive stock. Ratios do not reveal an unbalanced stock. They can, however, be used as a guide in determining if the stock totals are in line with those of other organizations in the industry or with goals set by management in projecting financial requirements.

The most recognized and used ratios in stock assessment and control include the following:

- *Cost of sales to stock*, which indicates stock turnover.
- *Sales to stock*, which is a prime indicator of too much or insufficient stock to meet the sales volume demands and objectives.
- *Days of sales in stock*, which reveals stock turnover and is also an indicator of too much or too little stock.
- *Stock to working capital*, which shows how the least liquid portion of current assets compares to the total position.

The *disadvantages of excessive stock* are:

1. To much *working capital* is being utilized. As a result, the organization may not be able to meet current obligations, which are primarily supported by the cash and debtors.
2. *Obsolescence* may be a problem. When the stock does not turn over within a reasonable time, it can deteriorate or a new product may require a different type of stock.

3. The *price* of raw materials may decline. In this case, the stock has to be written down to reflect the true value. This situation may cause larger losses than if the stock were at a nominal level.
4. Excessive stock creates *additional costs*, such as interest on investment, storage, insurance, and taxes. Further, excessive stock may necessitate plant expansion. These factors lead to increased costs without adding value to the product.

The *problems with insufficient stocks* are:

1. When a company finds itself *continually out of stock*, small purchase orders have to be placed, thus increasing paper work and handling costs. Eventually, these conditions lead to higher production costs, resulting from additional setups, short runs, and the like.
2. *Delays in customer deliveries* and possibly cancellation of orders may result.
3. Work activity and machine usage may *slow down or even stop* since there is inadequate stock to be processed in the manufacturing environment.

Net profit ratios. These ratios, used to assess profitability, are under constant supervision by most organizations. Net profits represents the bottom line of operational achievement. Useful ratios for comparing the profitability of an organization with others in the industry include net profit to sales, to net worth or equity, and to total assets.

● The *net profit to sales ratio* is used to answer two questions: (1) Are the profit margins compatible with those of other comparable organizations? (2) Do they meet organizational goals? If the information is available, a more detailed and realistic comparison is *gross profit to sales*.

● The *net profit to net worth (equity)* ratio indicates whether management has the ability to earn a reasonable return on the owners' investment. As an assessment guideline, compare the profit return achieved to the prevailing interest rates on accepted *secure investments*, such as government bonds, money market certificates, bond savings, and the like. The earnings on those investment instruments should be considered as the break-even point of acceptability. You should have profit above this figure to attract investor capital since investment in any organization poses a greater risk than that of the so-called 'safe and secure' investments.

● The *net profit to total assets* ratio tests whether management can achieve a favourable rate of return on all assets employed in the business enterprise.

Here are some considerations in profit ratio comparisons and analyses:

1. Know whether the profit figures are before or after taxation. The comparative results make quite a difference in profit assessment.
2. Another problem in making profit comparisons relates to the owner-manager salaries in closely held companies. Owners may be drawing more

or less than the prevailing salaries for comparable managers. The owner should determine what he or she would pay a professional manager to perform the job. This figure is then substituted for the actual owner's salary and reflected in the pretax and after-tax income figures for making comparisons. A true salary figure must be reflected in the data used for comparisons.

Applications

Sales activity ratios. These ratios are used to determine whether an organization is over- or undertrading (selling). The primary ratios used are:

- The *sales to working capital* ratio is used to indicate the amount of working capital required to support varying sales volumes.
- The *sales to equity ratio* is used to determine if the owners are investing too much or too little for the sales volume involved. Further, it is a valid check on whether the owner's equity is being employed effectively.

The *sales to total assets* ratio actually supplements the sales to equity ratio. It is an indicator of whether the organization is using an excessive amount of creditor capital.

Major financial ratios. Financing for an organization is divided into two major categories:

- *Acquisition of funds* from owners/investors, long-term financing, and short-term creditor sources.
- *Appropriate allocation and proper balance* of available funds among cash, debtors, stock, and fixed assets.

Certain ratios are used in evaluating the relative balance in the *source of funds*, as follows:

- Current ratio.
- Current debt to owners' equity, which indicates whether the suppliers may be providing too much capital.
- Total debt to owners' equity, which supplements the current debt to equity ratio and highlights whether an organization is undercapitalized.
- Funded debt to working capital, which is a reasonable test to determine if an organization could liquidate its long-term debt from the prevailing working capital. A ratio that exceeds 100 per cent is a criterion that an organization may have invested too much in fixed assets.

Fixed asset ratios. As a generally recognized management principle, only a certain amount of equity should be invested in fixed assets. Two common and basic ratio guidelines are used to highlight the soundness of an organization's financial structure and investment policy relative to fixed assets.

- The *fixed asset to capital equity* ratio indicates the proportion of total equity that is invested in property, plant, and equipment. Comparison to other organizations in a similar industry can provide a basic guideline as to whether an organization is over invested or 'in-line' with average practices.

- The *sales to fixed asset ratio* may disclose that an organization has too large or too small a facility for the prevailing or anticipated sales volume. In making comparisons of sales to fixed assets, give consideration to another possible problem. Normally, fixed assets are carried at the original value less depreciation. If the assets were purchased in years when the value of the pound was higher and thereafter was heavily depreciated, this would result in a very high ratio.

    Conversely, a low ratio reflects an excessive valuation of fixed assets. So if an organization's ratios are out of line with the industry ratios, you must apply considerable judgement before drawing specific conclusions or initiating actions based on the comparisons.

Using ratios for assessing solvency

Generally, these ratios are considered to be the tests for and the *keys* to solvency. With them, you can ascertain the ability of an organization to withstand such adverse situations as a recession, strikes, declining sales demand, and/or other major setbacks. The pertinent ratios are:

- fixed assets to net worth or equity;
- working capital to sales;
- stocks to working capital.

Net fixed assets to net worth

Net fixed assets include the book value of land, building, machinery, and furniture/fixtures less the accumulated depreciation (not on land). *Net worth* is the invested owners' equity and excludes all intangibles such as patents, trade marks, and goodwill. An organization's investment should be in proper relationship to the owners' equity.

What is the 'right' relationship? There is no specific guideline. It generally depends on the type of operational requirements and/or industry. A major consideration, however, is that a buildup in fixed assets results in higher costs such as taxes, insurance, maintenance, depreciation, and storage. Further, increased costs raise the *break-even point* which, in turn, may create profit problems for the organization if sales decrease substantially.

Some organizations may reason that they are successful if they maintain an expanded facility and the most advanced equipment. The general assumption is that, if demand increases for their product(s), they can readily capitalize on this demand and increase profits. What may be overlooked in this thinking is that, when a great proportion of equity is invested in fixed assets, then less funds are available for working capital requirements such as debtors, stock, and cash. On the optimistic side, the organization may be in a position to meet increased product demands, but may not have sufficient working capital to support the greater sales volume. Naturally, the adverse situation is a higher break-even point and possibly the need for *reducing sales volume* due to insufficient capital to support debtor and stock requirements.

Net working capital to sales

The ratio of working capital to sales should be in proper proportion. Yet there is no specific guideline as to the 'proper' proportion. The relative size of an organization and its operational requirements generally govern the magnitude of the working capital needs. To determine relative averages and to guard against 'overtrading', you can compare similar types of organizations in the same industry. The assumption is that, the more an organization sells, the more profits it reaps. In some cases this may be true, but additional sales may tie up more capital in debtors and stock.

If the organization does not provide the additional capital, it must then borrow the capital fund requirements either by making short-term borrowings or by delaying creditor payments. Borrowing can create serious problems for the organization, particularly if the sales volume declines significantly and the organization cannot meet its outstanding obligations. An accepted adage is that business failures can occur just as quickly by *selling too much* as by *selling too little*.

Stocks to working capital

The stock investment should be compatible within the structure of the organization's net working capital. When stocks exceed net working capital, the current liabilities may exceed cash, marketable securities, and debtors. Under these circumstances, the organization is forced to liquidate some of its stock to meet its current obligations, particularly if the organization is faced with operating losses.

The importance of ratios in trend analyses

Generally, comparing a single ratio for an organization against published information may not reveal a significant trend. Because preparing, compiling, and publishing industry financial statements takes considerable time, the data may be unavailable for months. Usually, industry averages do not vary substantially from year to year unless general economic conditions change considerably as a result of recession, inflation, relevant government regulations, and so on. To assess trends, therefore, plot ratios for a number of years on graph paper. Enter each ratio on an individual sheet of graph paper, on which comparable industry ratios are also plotted. You can then make a realistic comparison with other organizations in a similar industry based on years of experience. Model 6.2 shows the Dun & Bradstreet ratio figures plotted for the upper, median, and lower quartiles. This type of visual comparison provides an immediate view of an organization's ratio and trends relative to similar industry results as a whole.

Advantages of plotting
Plotting these ratios enables you to highlight the trend so that management can review and assess it. Whereas a one-year comparison with industry averages might indicate a healthy situation, the trend may actually be in the wrong direction. Plotting presents an immediate overview of the situation and the annual trend direction.

Inevitably, the question is: How do you know if the ratio is out of line? For the answer, you have to determine the specific reasons for deviations when the organization's ratio is outside the upper to lower quartile range. Generally, the organization's ratios are assumed to be in line with the average results when they are

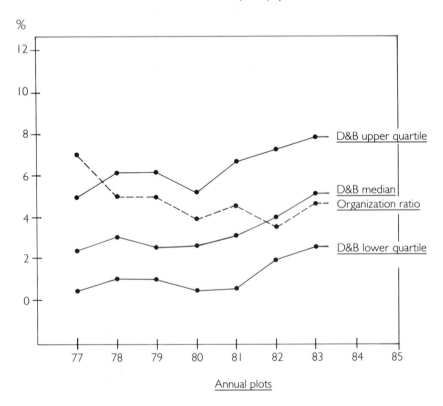

MODEL 6.2. Net profit to net sales ratio: organization versus
Dun & Bradstreet (D&B) quartiles

between the upper and lower quartiles. In Model 6.2, the organization's ratio trend begins above the median, dips in 19X2, but continues to climb in 19X3. Why did the trend decline in the annual periods shown? Only a detailed assessment will reveal the cause of the variations.

The significance of similar industry comparisons

Ratio comparisons with organizations in the same industry may be valid, but you must exercise analytical assessment before accepting this assumption completely. Some of the ratio figures may be approximately the same in many manufacturing lines, but peculiar industry characteristics can invalidate a comparison with a composite of all industry. Since some ratios can have wide variations based on the nature of the industry, make your comparisons within the industry rather than with any composite overall average.

A well-balanced financial structure is a *must* for the successful operation of any organization. Rarely is capital unlimited, so the available funds must be allocated judiciously. Naturally, when too much is invested in one segment of the business, then another function/operation is neglected. Inefficient use of capital can result from too much *overall investment* in the enterprise. Relatively few formulae indicate the optimum use of capital.

Yet valuable guidance can be obtained by comparing organization ratios with industry and determining the causes for unusual variances. An excellent presentation tool for highlighting varied and unusual situations to management is a display graph of pertinent organization and industry ratios, which emphasizes both trends and variances.

Using comparative ratios

Ratios represent only guidelines in assessing financial data and in operational planning. There may be valid reasons for an organization's ratios to vary significantly from those in a similar industry. Most important, be aware that differences do exist and that you must determine the reasons for them.

Ratios should not be used as absolutes. For example, it may be totally justifiable to build up stock if a material shortage is threatened. Even if the fixed asset to equity ratio varies from industry averages, *plant expansion* may still be logical and desirable, and the investment may be based on the anticipated growth in sales volume. If properly interpreted and used, ratios can serve as revealing and valuable guides for analysing financial results, planning operations, and making management decisions.

Ultimately, the usefulness of ratios depends on a thorough understanding of ratio logic, data compatibility, operational objectives, and analytical investigation regarding their appropriateness.

Summary of limitations involving ratio analysis

- A ratio is only as reliable as the quality of its component makeup. The question arises as to the validity of the data being used. For example, a high current ratio may be reflecting poor-quality debtors, stocks, and securities. There could be intentional delays in stock replenishment, which could affect creditors and funding.

- *Varying accounting procedures* among external industry organizations can complicate and distort valid industry comparisons. Treatment and use of various period-end adjustments would invalidate reliable comparisons. For example, balance sheets may be untypical of normal average levels. If a firework manufacturer chooses 30 November as the accounting year end then stocks may be at their lowest levels. There is always the problem of *categorizing similar industries* due to differences in diversified products, objectives, and procedures. Through historical experience and monitoring over a period of time, selective organizations may be identified that have compatible accounting and reporting similarities that make them acceptable for valid comparisons.

- *Ratios involve quantitative data* which are not always indicative. They should not necessarily be used as sole criteria in assessing performance results or providing planning factors. Management expertise, judgement, and experience are the basic fundamentals in evaluating performance results and decision making.

- In making organization comparisons, it is very important that the analyst should know what the *ratio composition* is. In using net profit figures, for example, it must be ascertained whether the profit is before or after charging interest expense and depreciation.

- It is advisable to use a number of *different ratios* in making comparisons in order to gain a more realistic insight or perspective on actual performance analysis and results. The size of the organization may be relevant. Small high-tech businesses may have knowhow which can command high profit margins – particularly if they have found a niche in the market-place.

- *Caution and judgement* must be exercised in using ratios for *projecting* an organization's financial position and trends. Ratio development is predicated on historical performance and, as such, may not be a valid indicator of the future. A thorough ongoing review of past results based on prevailing operational circumstances plus future operating budgets must be considered in establishing financial goals and performance objectives. Under reliable circumstances, *ratios may provide valuable guidelines* in future planning.

● *Inflation influences* (*changes in purchasing power of the pound*) have a decided effect on ratio analysis. This factor is difficult to incorporate in the ratio assessment of performance results. A possible approach in overcoming this problem is to include price level adjustments as supplementary information to the ratio analysis. The inflation impact can distort performance trends and relevant individual ratios. Similar problems arise when there are significant changes in sales revenues – either in growth or a declining trend.

7 Evaluating an organization's financial position

Chapter highlights

What are the objectives of financial position reporting? How do both internal and external users employ such reports? This chapter deals with these questions. It offers an insight into the key ratios used in evaluating an organization's financial position. Model 7.1, an overview of one organization's financial status, provides the illustrative data for developing and analysing relevant ratios. This chapter discusses:

- the usefulness and importance of structural ratios;
- ratios relative to an organization's liquidity, such as current ratio, acid test, cash, and cash turnover;
- the relationships of working capital to current assets, sales, current liabilities, and stock balances;
- common fixed asset ratios, which are calculated relative to total assets, turnover, owners' equity, loan capital, and sales;
- various debt ratios, such as owners' equity to total liabilities, aspects of the capital structure, equity to total capital employed, loan capital, and so on.

Not all the ratios described are relevant to all organizations. Historical experience can suggest which ratios are relevant and helpful to an organization's performance assessment and operational planning.

The financial status of an organization at a particular point in time consists of the assets owned by an organization and the claims against the assets in the form of liabilities and the owners' or shareholders' equity. Specifically, the data are reported and identified in a balance sheet (or statement of financial position). Explanatory notes to this statement augment the monetary values in the formal report.

Users of financial position reporting

At any time, a number of concerned parties have an active interest in the financial position of an organization. Internally, various *management levels* use the information to review and evaluate the organization's current position and progress, to initiate corrective action as required, and to determine the course of their future planning. *Owners and investors* analyse the financial position data to determine the solvency of the operations, as well as the degree of risk in making or continuing an investment. *Creditors* (such as vendors or banks) and credit agencies have a marked interest in ascertaining an organization's debt-paying capability and its financial outlook. *Stockbrokers* may use the information to advise and influence the investments of their clients. Certain *government agencies* may take an interest in the reported information for regulatory enforcement, awarding contracts based on adequate financing for contract performance, and possible taxation aspects. *Similar industry organizations* use the information to compare results, thereby assessing their performance and progress relative to their competitors. These are the major users of financial position reports outside the organization.

Within an organization, and in addition to management, many other parties use and analyse balance sheet data: management accountants, financial planners, and certain operational personnel concerned with stock control and fixed asset acquisition and control. Executive operational management has a particular interest in the financial progress of an organization that results from operational activities.

Setting objectives for the balance sheet

Balance sheet reporting serves the following basic objectives:

1. The *identification* of the various types of *financial resources* (cash, debtors, stocks) that are available within an organization to meet operational goals.
2. The *means* (sources) by which the resources were obtained (investment by owners, borrowings, creditors, and so on).
3. *Valuation* of specific types of resources, such as
   - debtors less the reserve for doubtful accounts
   - gross fixed assets reduced by the reserve for depreciation/amortization
   - marketable securities at cost or current market value
   - stocks at lower of cost or net realizable value.
4. *Supplemental information* that is not reflected in the formal statement, such as contingencies and explanatory data, and that may be important to the report users in assessing the financial position for decision-making.

The balance sheet – the statement of financial position – reflects a static situation. It presents the data at a point in time, and will change immediately after the reporting date since new transactions are constantly occurring (cash receipts and payments, purchases, sales, and the like). The balance sheet reflects the results of all the activities, actions, and decisions since the organization's inception. As a record of the results from past performances, it can serve as an index to future events. Other reports, such as a profit and loss statement and cash flow statement, are required to provide the answers to 'how' the organization arrived at its current financial position.

MODEL 7.1. Structure of the statement of financial position

(in £000,000s)

Assets:	19X3 December	% of total assets	19X4 March	June	September	December	% of total assets
Fixed assets, gross	128.8	26.08	133.5	138.1	142.1	146.6	30.18
Accumulated depreciation	(65.4)	(13.24)	(68.6)	(71.8)	(75.1)	(78.4)	(16.14)
Net fixed assets (tangible)	63.4	12.84	64.9	66.3	67.0	68.2	14.04
Investment in subsidiaries	5.5	1.11	5.5	5.5	5.5	5.5	1.13
Deferred charges	5.3	1.07	6.2	6.0	6.9	7.0	1.44
Current assets							
Stocks	247.8	50.18	260.0	268.5	256.9	243.4	50.10
Debtors	125.0	25.31	110.4	111.5	102.3	105.1	21.63
Cash	22.9	4.64	38.0	32.9	36.6	35.5	7.31
Investments	8.0	1.62	7.5	8.5	8.0	6.0	1.24
Advances to subcontractors	5.9	1.20	5.1	4.2	3.0	3.4	0.70
Prepayments	10.0	2.03	9.5	8.6	15.7	11.7	2.41
Total current assets	419.6	84.98	430.5	434.2	423.2	405.1	83.39
Total assets	493.8	100.00	507.1	512.0	502.6	485.8	100.00

MODEL 7.1. Structure of the statement of financial position (*Contd*)

Liabilities	l/eq.	% of total l/eq.	l/eq.	l/eq.	l/eq.	l/eq.	% of total l/eq.
Creditors: amounts falling due within one year							
Bills of exchange	70.0	14.18	95.0	100.0	95.0	85.0	17.50
Trade creditors	91.5	18.53	84.4	83.1	76.9	76.7	15.79
Accrued salaries and wages	18.6	3.77	21.4	21.8	19.0	19.3	3.97
Estimated corporation taxes	15.8	3.20	12.8	10.7	10.8	9.3	1.92
Customer advances	75.0	15.19	66.8	68.8	65.0	64.0	13.17
Miscellaneous liabilities	29.3	5.93	30.4	28.8	34.9	29.5	6.07
Total current liabilities	300.2	60.80	310.8	313.2	301.6	283.8	58.42
Creditors: amounts falling due after more than one year							
Loans/debentures	42.6	8.62	42.6	42.6	42.6	42.6	8.77
Total liabilities	342.8	69.42	353.4	355.8	344.2	326.4	67.19
Shareholders' equity:							
Ordinary shares	50.5	10.23	50.5	50.5	50.5	50.5	10.39
Retained earnings	100.5	20.35	103.2	105.7	107.9	108.9	22.42
Total equity	151.0	30.58	153.7	156.2	158.4	159.4	32.81
Total liabilities/equity	493.8	100.00	507.1	512.0	502.6	485.8	100.00
Other relevant data:							
Working capital	119.4	—	119.7	120.0	121.6	121.3	—
Sales volume	—	—	252.8	274.9	276.2	273.1	—
Net income	—	—	4.9	5.7	4.7	3.0	—
Annualized sales	—	—	1011.0	1100.0	1105.0	1092.0	—

Viewing the balance sheet as an overview of financial status

Model 7.1 presents an overview format of an organization's financial position by quarterly periods. As reflected in the model, the financial structure of a business enterprise involves three primary elements: assets, liabilities, and owners' equity (share capital and retained earnings). The relationship of the three elements is represented by the equation:

$$\text{Assets} = \text{Liabilities} + \text{Owners' equity}$$

This equation can also be represented as follows:

Liabilities   = Total assets – Total equity capital
Equity capital = Total assets – Total liabilities
Total assets   = Total equities (owners' and creditors')

Understanding structural ratios

Reasonable relationships generally exist among the various items in the financial structure. In Model 7.1, ratios are developed among the reported items at year-end for 19X3 and 19X4. On the asset side, each individual asset is divided by the total asset value. Also, each liability and owners' equity is divided by the total liabilities and equity. This type of analysis provides not only a structural relationship among the various items for the two year-end periods being reported but also the *trend* between the time periods.

An illustration
A review of the data indicates that the current assets as a percentage of total assets decreased from 84.98 per cent in December 19X3 to 83.39 per cent in 19X4. The principal cause is the 19X4 increase in cash, which was more than offset by the decrease in debtors. Total assets decreased by 1.6 per cent in December 19X4 as compared to 19X3, due to a 3.5 per cent decrease in current assets (£419.6 to £405.1 million). Although fixed assets increased by 13.8 per cent in 19X4, much of the increase was diluted by a 20 per cent increase in accumulated depreciation.

As shown in the model, current liabilities decreased by 5.5 per cent in 19X4 as compared to 19X3 (£300.2 to £283.8 million). This situation is attributed to decreases in creditors, taxes, and customer advances, which were partially offset by an increase in bills payable. The long-term debt remained a relatively stable percentage, but the resulting net overall debt was a 4.8 per cent decrease in the 19X4 total liabilities.

Total equity increased by 5.6 per cent in December 19X4 over 19X3, which was attributed to an 8.4 per cent increase in retained earnings, while the original share capital remained consistent at £50.5 million. The overall liabilities and equity total (as in the case of total assets) was 1.6 per cent lower in 19X4 for reasons already discussed. Working capital increased by 1.6 per cent (£119.4 million to £121.3 million), indicating a favourable trend.

Applications

Structural and trend *ratios* can be very useful in assessing the basic characteristics of capital structure relationships, particularly if calculated by monthly and quarterly periods. Further, the trend indicators provide a basis for planning, at least on a preliminary basis. By analysing the developed ratio data, you can determine unusual highlights and deviations, which can lead to management actions and decisions.

Balance sheet limitations in ratio analysis

In assessing balance sheet reported data and calculating ratios, consideration should be given to the following information limitations that would be reflected in that type of reporting. The effect of the limitations could jeopardize the reliability of ratio development and utilization.

- The balance sheet may not reflect the *true market value of the assets*. Stocks may not be truly presented at the net realizable value or cost, whichever is lower (data value conservatism). Debtors may not be adjusted for doubtful accounts. Short-term investments may be over- or undervalued. Direct material costs may be over- or understated depending on the method of valuation.

- It is common management procedure to review the various items of the balance sheet at the period-end and *take appropriate steps* to enhance the organization's financial position and achievement (window-dressing) in the opinion of current shareholders, potential investors, credit agencies, and funding institutions. An important approach is to reduce or eliminate outstanding debt obligations. Therefore, in calculating debt and equity ratios, a weighted-average debt value would be used rather than a year-end balance. This action would generally reflect a more positive debt position. Further, year-end comparisons to other organizations could be distorted and misleading.

    A device used to create a high current ratio would be to delay the replenishment of stocks in the period preceding the closing of the books.

- *Liabilities could be undervalued* due to a pending or anticipated lawsuit for which information would not be reflected on the face of the balance sheet. Debt ratios would be distorted and comparative data with other organizations would be misleading and inappropriate for an adequate operational assessment.

- Certain *assets could be overvalued*; particularly in the case of obsolete stock or stock which has deteriorated. Changes in product mix may have resulted in certain material being surplus due to changed product requirements. Material prices may have declined substantially whereas the stock value is being carried on the books at the original higher prices. This situation would distort such relevant ratios as: current, stock to working capital, turnover, and average age. The reliability of industry stock comparisons would undoubtedly be questionable.

- Another limitation of balance sheet reports could involve the existence of *undervalued assets*, for example marketable securities may be reported at cost value when market prices are higher. This situation would affect both the current and acid test ratios. Net working capital would be understated. Other ratios such as current and total assets to sales and equity would be affected.

- *Ratios are static* and do not necessarily reflect future conditions and expectations. Careful evaluation of past experience, anticipated future events (from market intelligence and trends, management objectives, identification of potential problem areas) and judgement must prevail in their usefulness in the planning process.

If a financial analyst were aware of specific under- or overvaluations he would comment accordingly. This would alert management as to the true significance and inherent limitations that were being reported. In making industrial comparisons between organizations, manipulation of internal data is unlikely to be revealed in their financial statements. Due allowance has to be made, therefore, for the inconsistencies existing between companies.

How to use the liquidity ratios

The *liquidity* of a business organization is its potential to meet current debt obligations. A reasonably sound liquidity position permits an organization to obtain financial resources to take advantage of investment opportunities and adequately respond to operational emergencies.

The degree of liquidity is generally linked to the size of the working capital position at a given point in time. The *ratio* of current assets to current liabilities – rather than the monetary difference between them – is the measure of liquidity. (The difference between current assets and current liabilities represents the *net working capital*, whereas the single identification of current assets indicates the *aggregate working capital*.) Working capital represents the portion of current assets that is not supplied by current creditors. If no funded debt exists, then the working capital is the owners' equity in the current assets, as differentiated from the owners' equity in the fixed assets.

Using the current (working capital) ratio

The calculation

$$\text{Current ratio} = \frac{\text{Current assets}}{\text{Current liabilities}}$$

This traditional ratio is commonly used in the business environment as a guideline to the financial margin of safety or solvency. It indicates the *number of times* current assets will pay off the current liabilities. Historically a two-to-one ratio has been considered the ideal minimum. Yet there may be exceptions. Some organizations with a 'two-to-one' ratio may have more varied and difficult problems than those with a lower ratio.

EXAMPLE

From the information provided in Model 7.1 the following *current ratios* are developed:

19X3		19X4		
December	*March*	*June*	*September*	*December*
1.40:1	1.39:1	1.39:1	1.40:1	1.43:1

This indicates a fairly consistent pattern for the periods reported. Any unusual deviations among periods are cause enough to investigate the differences to determine whether a trend (up or down) will prevail in the future or will result from unusual circumstances. The 1.43 factor in December 19X4 represents a favourable trend in liquidity.

Using the acid test ratio

This ratio determines an organization's *immediate* capability to pay its current obligations. Quick assets generally include cash, marketable securities, and debtors. Stocks are excluded because they must first be sold and customer invoices collected before they become assets capable of being used to pay current debts. The equation for calculating the acid test ratio is as follows:

The calculation

$$\text{Acid test radio} = \frac{\text{Cash} + \text{Marketable securities} + \text{Debtors}}{\text{Current liabilities}}$$

EXAMPLE

From the information provided in Model 7.1, the following acid test ratios are derived:

19X3		19X4		
December	*March*	*June*	*September*	*December*
0.519 (155.9 ÷ 300.2)	0.502	0.488	0.487	0.517

The size of the ratio (approximately 50 per cent of current liabilities) highlights the fact that the stock values represent the major current asset item. Conversely, the current liabilities could be excessively high in comparison to the quick assets.

The low ratio of 48.7 per cent in September resulted from a relatively low quick asset period value of £146.9 million, compared to prior periods, which was not offset by a low current liabilities amount. The higher ratio in December 19X3 is attributed to the greater quick asset value versus the lower current liabilities. The same comment applies to the December 19X4 period.

You must exercise caution in the use and interpretation of the acid test ratio. Although the ratio implies that only three current assets will be available to pay current liabilities, such may not always be the case. Some of the stock may very well be converted into cash before all of the current obligations mature for creditor payment. Further, bills of exchange and creditor payments could be deferred to coincide with the quick asset position. Payment of miscellaneous and other liabilities may be delayed with possibly no major consequences. The material purchase schedule may be extended. So before making any decisions based on the application of the acid test ratio, be sure you have thoroughly assessed its applicability to your organization.

Using cash ratios

The calculation
Some organizations may use another liquidity test ratio. In this instance, the formula is as follows:

$$\text{Cash ratio} = \frac{\text{Cash} + \text{Marketable securities}}{\text{Current liabilities}}$$

EXAMPLE
Using the data in Model 7.1, the following ratio data are prepared by quarterly periods:

19X3			19X4	
December	March	June	September	December
10.3% (30.9 million ÷ 300.2)	14.6%	13.2%	14.8%	14.6%

These cash ratios indicate that, using this method (which is far more conservative than the acid test ratio), there is enough liquidity in the cash and marketable securities to pay only 10.3 per cent to 14.8 per cent of the current obligations. In some cash-sales-orientated organizations that maintain minimum debtors, the usefulness of this ratio is justified. Yet its universal acceptance as a criterion for assessing an organization's position to meet current debts on schedule is doubtful.

Making use of the cash turnover ratio

With this ratio, you can analyse and assess the effectiveness of an organization's use of its cash position. The equation is as follows:

$$\text{Cash turnover} = \frac{\text{Sales volume}}{\text{Cash balance}}$$

EXAMPLE

Using the 19X4 *quarterly* data in Model 7.1, the following ratios are obtained for comparative purposes. (The more precise method is to use annualized sales.)

		19X4	
March 6.65:1 (252.8 million ÷ 38.0)	*June* 8.36:1	*September* 7.55:1	*December* 7.69:1

The highest ratio, in June 19X4, is attributed to a below-average quarterly cash position versus a high sales volume of £276.2 million. The low turnover rate in March 19X4 resulted from a low sales volume of £252.8 million, whereas the quarterly cash position was above average.

The increase in the turnover rate in December 19X4 over March indicates an increased effectiveness in the use of cash in supporting the sales volume. The turnover rate is useful in determining preliminary cash balance forecasts based on sales projections. In March, for example, the £252.8 million sales, divided by the 6.65 factor, results in a £38 million cash balance.

The annual cash turnover ratio is calculated to be approximately 30:1. This value is obtained by dividing the annual sales of £1077 million by an average cash balance of £35.75 million.

Employing the total asset turnover ratio

This ratio assesses how effectively an organization is utilizing its total assets. It gauges management's efficiency in controlling the use of assets based on sales volume activity. The equation is as follows:

$$\text{Asset turnover} = \frac{\text{Sales (usually annualized)}}{\text{Average total assets}}$$

EXAMPLE

For purposes of illustration, the quarterly balances for total assets are the averages for the period. The following quarterly ratios are developed from the basic data in Model 7.1.

		19X4	
March 49.9% (252.8 million ÷ 507.1)	*June* 53.7%	*September* 55.0%	*December* 56.2%

These ratios indicate that the asset turnover is improving – 56.2 per cent in December versus 49.9 per cent in March. The high ratio in December is attributed to declining total assets, whereas sales volume remained relatively constant. The decrease in total assets resulted primarily from lower stocks.

average turnover for the year is 2.15, a rate derived by dividing the annual £1077 million by the annual average assets of £501.8 million. The annual ratio more indicative and informative of the actual total asset turnover position because the annual sales volume was used versus the annual average assets. Note that if the four quarterly ratios are totalled (214.8 per cent – note the figure of 2.15 above) and divided by four, the average quarterly ratio is 53.7 per cent.

Using the total asset relationship to sales

With this ratio, you can determine the total asset requirements based on sales volume. This approach is the inverse of that of the asset turnover ratio. To obtain this ratio, simply divide total assets by sales volume.

EXAMPLE
The following quarterly ratios were developed from data in Model 7.1:

	19X4		
March	June	September	December
2.01:1 (507.1 million ÷ 252.8)	1.86:1	1.82:1	1.78:1

Given an annual quarterly average of total assets of £501.8 million and total annual sales of £1077 million, the ratio is 2.15:1. Totalling the ratios (7.47) and dividing this value by four results in a ratio of 1.87:1. The difference is due to the use of the annual average of total assets versus total sales volume, as opposed to quarterly period calculations.

The low average ratio of 1.78:1 in December indicates a favourable trend in that reduced assets are used in supporting the sales volume.

As a preliminary planning guide (if historically consistent and adjusted for trends) the estimated asset requirements based on sales would be projected by multiplying sales volume by the ratio factor; for example, as shown above £252.8 million sales times 2.01 would approximate total assets to £508.1 million.

Making use of working capital relationships

Influences on working capital
The working capital ratio, one of the most widely used in business, reveals the proportion of capital provided by the enterprise and the contribution made by creditors, hence its importance to creditors and short-term funding institutions. The working capital position is affected by a number of operating/financial factors, such as the turnover velocity of debtors and stock, the size of the credit obtained from suppliers, and the amount of capital provided by the investment owners.

Debtors and stock turnover is of prime importance in the adequacy of the working capital position. Debtors turnover is affected by business conditions in general, by credit terms, and by the organization's collection policy, control, and enforcement. Stock turnover is primarily influenced by product price, by the extent of stock obsolescence, by production demands, and by the size of the stock in relation to sales. To achieve a desirable turnover ratio management must keep a constant watch on the organization's debtor/stock position.

Comparing working capital to current assets

To derive this relationship, divide average working capital by average current assets.

EXAMPLE
The following quarterly ratios are calculated using data in Model 7.1.

19X3	*19X4*			
December	*March*	*June*	*September*	*December*
28.5% (119.4 million ÷ 419.6)	27.8%	27.6%	28.7%	29.9%

    These ratios indicate that working capital represented an annual average in 19X4 of 28.5 per cent (annual average working capital divided by annual average current assets) of the current assets. The high ratio of 29.9 per cent in December 19X4 is primarily due to the relatively lower current asset value of £405.1 million, whereas the working capital remained fairly constant when compared to prior period results.

This type of ratio, if proven historically to be reasonable and valid, can be used to assess current versus past performance in terms of the working capital/current asset relationship. Further, you can use it as a planning guide to future projections in the development of the annual operating plan. In other words, having projected current assets, you apply the average working capital position. By subtracting this value from planned current assets, you obtain the projected current liability values.

Using the current assets to working capital ratio

The ratio of the current assets to working capital is simply the inverse of working capital to total current assets. To obtain this ratio, divide average current assets by the average working capital.

EXAMPLE
The following results are obtained using data in Model 7.1.

19X3	*19X4*			
December	*March*	*June*	*September*	*December*
3.51:1 (419.6 million ÷ 119.4)	3.60:1	3.62:1	3.48:1	3.34:1

    The decreased ratio in December 19X4 resulted from a relatively low current asset value in comparison to the rather consistent working capital position of prior periods. The principal contributing factor is the reduction in stocks (a high of £268.4 million in June 19X4 to £243.4 million in December).

On the current liability status, there was a favourable decrease in the December 19X4 bills payable when compared to the quarterly periods in 19X4. Creditors was reduced to £76.7 million in December 19X4 as compared to the high of £91.5 million in December 19X3.

Applications

These ratios can be used in planning and/or in assessing data projections developed by more detailed conventional methods. Here is a method for forecasting current liabilities. If working capital values were initially projected (although this is generally not the planning sequence), you can estimate current assets by multiplying the working capital value by one of the preceding ratios to obtain the expected current asset values. Then subtract the projected working capital from the developed current asset values to obtain the projected current liabilities.

Comparing working capital to current liabilities

In analysing the current position of a business enterprise, you must determine the adequacy of working capital. One such approach is to determine the ratio of working capital to current liabilities. This relationship enables you to compare the resources supplied by the current creditors versus the proportion provided by the owners, long-term creditors, or both. You should interpret this ratio in the context of the turnover rate of current assets versus that of current liabilities.

As a general rule, a rapid turnover of current assets with a slower turnover of current liabilities requires a lower working capital ratio. The opposite is true with a rapid turnover of current liabilities and a slow turnover of current assets; you need a higher working capital ratio.

To determine the ratio between working capital and current liabilities, divide average working capital by average current liabilities.

EXAMPLE

The following ratios are calculated using data in Model 7.1.

19X3		19X4		
December	March	June	September	December
39.8% (119.4 million ÷ 300.2)	38.5%	38.3%	40.3%	42.7%

The high ratio in December 19X4 is attributed to a relatively low current liability position compared to prior periods, whereas the working capital remained at one level.

Another approach is to determine the inverse relationship of *current liabilities to working capital*. To calculate this ratio, divide the average current liabilities by average working capital.

EXAMPLE

The developed relationships are as follows:

	19X3			19X4	
	December	*March*	*June*	*September*	*December*
	2.51:1 (300.2 million ÷ 119.4)	2.60:1	2.61:1	2.48:1	2.34:1

These ratios indicate that the current liabilities are at an average of 2.51 times the working capital. Note that the current asset ratio to working capital averaged about 3.5 times working capital – a more favourable relationship than if the current liabilities ratio were higher.

Application

This type of ratio can be used to assess financial performance and to evaluate the validity or reasonableness of data developed by more detailed methods.

Comparing stock to working capital

This ratio is an indicator of the stock position at a point in time. It reflects the portion of working capital invested in stocks. In other words, it shows how the least liquid part of current assets relates to its total. Stocks that are greater than net working capital signify that current liabilities exceed the liquid current assets represented by cash, marketable securities, and debtors. In this type of situation, the organization might have to consider decreasing, at least in relative proportion, a part of its stock.

From another viewpoint, this relationship represents the ratio of the stock to the owners' equity in the current assets, providing there are no fixed liabilities to consider. Establishing a universal standard ratio is difficult because it depends on the type of business and its requirements, asset turnover, and the sales demands. Further, this ratio is an indirect statistical situation, compared to the acid test which is both understandable and direct in concept and use.

To develop this ratio, divide average stock by average working capital.

EXAMPLE

The following ratios are developed using the data in Model 7.1:

	19X3			19X4	
	December	*March*	*June*	*September*	*December*
	2.08:1 (247.8 million ÷ 119.4)	2.17:1	2.24:1	2.11:1	2.01:1

The average is 2.12:1, with the highest ratio of 2.24 occurring in June 19X4. The principal reason is the increased June stock in comparison to the other quarterly periods, while the working capital position remained relatively constant.

Application

As always, exercise evaluation and judgement in using this ratio for any practical benefit. It may be suitable in some organizations as a preliminary planning factor and/or as a means of comparing performance results among periods. While the ratio represents a possible analytical guideline, segregating working capital into its individual component parts is difficult, if not unrealistic.

Relating sales to working capital

The sales volume of an organization bears a definite relationship to the amount of its working capital in support of sales. Generally, a substantial sales volume requires large working capital. With increased sales volumes, debtors, and cash, the organization has to invest more in maintaining adequate stocks. The increases in current assets, however, are somewhat offset by increased current liabilities, such as purchase requirements (material and supplies). This results in greater creditor balances, as well as higher accrued salaries, due to increased labour activity and possibly short-term loans to support the higher volume. The owners' investment would also have to be greater to finance increased sales activity.

Establishing a standard for sales/working capital relationship in industries as a whole is difficult due to various influencing factors, such as the prevailing velocity of current assets and current liabilities among organizations. These and other factors must be given due consideration before you can establish ratio validity and accept it as a reasonable criterion for data assessment and planning.

To determine the relevance and usefulness of this ratio to an organization's performance assessment and planning, you should explore two versions of the relationship. The equations used in calculating the ratios are as follows:

$$\text{Working capital to sales} = \frac{\text{Average working capital}}{\text{Sales (usually annualized)}}$$

$$\text{Working capital turnover} = \frac{\text{Sales (usually annualized)}}{\text{Average working capital}}$$

Working capital to sales. Using this ratio, you can estimate working capital needs based on sales volume (sales multiplied by the ratio factor). The usefulness of this ratio is contingent on its being proven consistent and valid by experience.

EXAMPLE

The quarterly working capital ratio to sales is calculated using data in Model 7.1:

		19X4	
March	*June*	*September*	*December*
47.3% (119.7 million ÷ 252.8)	43.7%	44.0%	44.4%

The high ratio of 47.3 per cent in March 19X4 is attributed to the lower sales volume of £252.8 million as compared to the other periods. At the same time, the working capital position remained relatively constant with the other periods.

Working capital turnover. This version measures the number of times working capital is employed or turned over during a given period. The use of working capital becomes more efficient as the turnover rate increases. A low ratio generally signifies poor performance in the use of working capital, whereas a high ratio usually indicates efficient capital employment.

EXAMPLE
Model 7.1 provides the quarterly data for calculating the working capital turnover rates, as follows:

		19X3		
March		*June*	*September*	*December*
2.11:1 (252.8 million ÷ 119.7)		2.29:1	2.27:1	2.25:1

If the *period sales are annualized*, the capital turnover ratios are calculated as follows (they also represent four times the quarterly ratios):

		19X4		
March		*June*	*September*	*December*
Annualized sales	1011.2 million	1099.6	1104.8	1092.4
Ratios	8.44:1	9.16:1	9.08:1	9.00:1

The low ratio in March 19X4 is attributed to a lower sales base in comparison to the subsequent periods, while the working capital remained practically constant.

This ratio may be useful in some organizations, if verified to be relatively consistent, in determining or planning approximate working capital requirements based on sales volume. To use it in this way, divide the quarterly annualized sales by the appropriate ratio factor. The use of sales and working capital trend ratios over an extended period may be the most effective means of establishing or verifying their relevance.

How to analyse fixed asset relationships

Net fixed assets to total asset ratio

This ratio enables you to determine the relationship of net fixed assets to total assets based on past experience. To calculate the ratio, divide average net fixed assets by average total assets.

EXAMPLE
The following quarterly ratios are calculated using data in Model 7.1:

19X3		*19X4*		
December	*March*	*June*	*September*	*December*
12.8% (63.4 million ÷ 493.8)	12.8%	12.9%	13.3%	14.0%

The increasing trend in the ratio is due to increased investment in fixed assets, while total asset value was declining, particularly in the September and December 19X4 quarterly periods (partially offset by increasing depreciation reserve). The main cause for the decrease in total assets is a low current asset position. The significance of this situation is that fixed assets represent a greater share of the total assets and that the current working assets, which directly support operational activity, are declining. This can be an unfavourable trend unless additional fixed assets are required for expansion, more efficient or new equipment, or the modernization of existing facilities.

Applications

You may use these ratios in a couple of ways: (1) as guidelines in estimating expenditure on fixed assets based on projected total assets, (2) as a tool for measuring fixed asset growth or decline in relation to fluctuations in the total asset position.

Computing the fixed asset turnover

The objective of this ratio is to annalyse the use of fixed assets based on sales volume activity. It generally indicates how effectively an organization is employing its fixed asset investment in relation to sales volume and objectives. The equation is as follows:

$$\text{Fixed asset turnover} = \frac{\text{Sales (usually annualized)}}{\text{Average net fixed assets}}$$

EXAMPLE
The following quarterly turnover ratios are developed based on the data in Model 7.1:

	19X4		
March	*June*	*September*	*December*
3.90:1 (252.8 million ÷ 64.9)	4.15:1	4.12:1	4.00:1

The high turnover ratio of 4.15 in June is attributed to increased sales (£274.9 million) versus a minor increase in fixed assets to £66.3 million. The decrease in the turnover ratio in December resulted from a decrease in quarterly sales with an increase in net fixed assets. The increase and decrease amounts are conservative but sufficient to reduce the turnover ratio.

This type of ratio may be somewhat misleading if used for comparison with other organizations in the same industry, particularly if an organization, for example, leases buildings rather than owning them. The effect is a more favourable ratio. In another instance, the gross fixed assets might greatly depreciate over a period of time (such as in long-established organizations), and thus the net fixed asset values are lower with a resultant higher turnover rate. The opposite is true – the net value (allowing for depreciation) is larger – with a heavy investment in new facilities.

Applications

You must exercise judgement when using this ratio. These ratios may be used to assess performance among periods, as long as they prove to be consistent and realistic. The ratios may not only indicate valid trends, but they may also act as planning guidelines in projecting the need for fixed asset acquisitions. They can reveal too much capacity – or too small a plant with insufficient machinery and equipment to support a given sales volume.

Calculating the net fixed assets to owners' equity

With this ratio, you can analyse and assess the proportion of an organization's fixed assets financed from the owners' equity capital. Large fixed asset investments result in greater fixed costs (depreciation, maintenance, and the like), with its predictably increased break-even point. If the sames volume is reduced substantially, other related problems, such as the attendant effect on profits, may result.

Generally, as the proportion of fixed asset investment increases from owners' equity, less funds are available for working capital requirements, such as debtors, stock, and cash. Although the investing organizations enhance their capacity to meet increased product demand, they may not have sufficient working capital to support the larger sales volume. Thus, an organization may actually have to decrease its sales volume due to a lack of funds to support its operations. Too much investment in a business, if not properly justified, usually indicates an inefficient use of capital.

To calculate this relationship, divide average net fixed assets by average tangible owners' equity.

EXAMPLE
The following ratios are developed using data in Model 7.1:

19X3		19X4			
December	*March*	*June*	*September*	*December*
42.0% (63.4 million ÷ 151.0)	42.2%	42.4%	42.3%	42.8%

These ratios indicate a consistent trend in net fixed asset investment. Fixed assets increased from £63.4 million in December 19X3 to £68.2 million in December 19X4. The owners' equity increased from £151.0 million in 19X3 to £159.4 million in December 19X4.

Verifying the ratio

To evaluate the reasonableness of the fixed asset investment ratio, compare it to those of other organizations of comparable size in the same line of business. Management must exercise judgement, however, in such comparisons. There may be extenuating circumstances accounting for major differences, such as current large investments in plant modernization or unusual expansion expenditure to meet projected new product demands. Excessive fixed asset investments can lead to insufficient working capital adequately to meet operational needs, the accumulation of expensive long-term indebtedness, and possibly financial instability. The prime value of fixed assets to a business depends on their earning power.

Ratio of net fixed assets to loan capital/debentures

This comparison is a reasonable indicator, to a lending organization, of the integrity of its investment. To determine this ratio, divide the average net fixed assets by the average loans.

EXAMPLE
The following quarterly ratios are calculated using data in Model 7.1:

	19X3		19X4		
	December	*March*	*June*	*September*	*December*
	1.49:1 (63.4 million ÷ 42.6)	1.52:1	1.56:1	1.57:1	1.60:1

For every £1.00 of loans, there is £1.60 (December 19X4) net book value of property, plant, and equipment. The upward trend in the ratio is attributed to an increase in fixed asset acquisitions, whereas the loans remained constant.

To determine the reliability and usefulness of this relationship, make comparative analyses and management judgements relative to other organizations in the same industry.

Relating sales to net fixed assets

Use this ratio to measure the size of the fixed asset investment relative to the sales volume activity. This ratio may give you an insight as to whether an organization has too much capacity and associated machinery/equipment or too small a plant for a given sales volume. In making this comparison with other organizations in the same industry, give consideration to the age of the assets, price levels when they were purchased, and the depreciation policies with their effect on fixed asset valuation. If the assets were acquired in years when the value of the pound was high and thereafter heavily depreciated, the result is a higher ratio. This situation is due to the lower net fixed asset value. Conversely, a low ratio indicates an excessive valuation of the fixed assets without a comparable increase in sales. If the organization's ratios are out of line with the industry as a whole, then you must make a judgement on the differences and causes before drawing specific conclusions.

Fixed assets in themselves do not produce sales, but generally without them only limited sales can be made in a manufacturing organization. Sales result from many factors, such as product demand, favourable markets, effectiveness and efficiency of sales promotion, and so on. To calculate this ratio, divide annualized sales by the average net fixed assets.

EXAMPLE

The following quarterly ratios are developed using data in Model 7.1:

		19X4	
March	*June*	*September*	*December*
3.90:1 (252.8 million ÷ 64.9)	4.15:1	4.12:1	4.00:1

The low ratio of 3.90 in March is attributed to the relatively low sales volume, whereas net fixed assets had a conservative increase over December 19X3. The high ratio of 4.15 in June resulted from an 8.7 per cent increase in sales over March, but the fixed assets were only 2.2 per cent greater.

These ratios indicate that the sales volume is approximately four times as great as the net fixed asset position. In other words, fixed assets averaged 25 per cent of sales value.

Depending on whether they prove valid, these ratios can be used in assessing period performance, in planning asset requirements, and in making comparisons with other organizations in the same industry.

How to evaluate key debt ratios

Assessing risk

When a business is financed by creditors, a considerable degree of risk is involved. For example, if there is a significant decrease in sales activity or in debtor turnover, the business may be unable to meet its obligations. Substantial interest on loans (borrowed capital) may even exceed earnings, giving rise to losses.

The high overall industry debt in 1991 is attributed to excessive borrowing during the 1980s, low stock market prices, and high inflation rates. Many organizations assumed that they could repay borrowed capital with cheaper pounds if inflation continued at double-digit rates. The reasonableness of many an organization's debt capacity was underestimated. As a result, a number of organizations had to seek to restructure their debts, seek relief from creditors in the form of extending debt payment schedules, and further negotiate with creditors for reduced interest rates. In the early 1990s, bankruptcies were at their highest levels since the 1930s. Major firms encountering financial problems included Coloroll, Polly Peck, Brent Walker, and Maxwell Communications.

Relating owners' equity to total liabilities

This ratio relates the amount of investment resources provided by the owners to that provided by creditors. Creditors are investors in an organization because, in essence, money is borrowed and/or other debts incurred in order to achieve a higher rate of return from operational activities.

To calculate this ratiof divide the average owners' equity by average total liabilities.

EXAMPLE

The following quarterly ratios are developed using data in Model 7.1:

19X3			19X4	
December	*March*	*June*	*September*	*December*
44.0% (151 million ÷ 342.8)	43.5%	43.9%	46.0%	48.8%

The owners' investment equity is 48.8 per cent in December 19X4. The primary cause for the favourable trend is decreasing liabilities with an increasing owners' equity (greater retained earnings). The increased owners' equity, in comparison to the creditors', is one indicator of a stronger financial position trend.

Computing the capital structure ratio

This ratio indicates the proportion of long-term debt to the owners' equity plus long-term debt. To calculate this ratio, use the following equation:

$$\text{Capital structure ratio} = \frac{\text{Average long-term debt}}{\text{Owners' equity} + \text{Long-term debt}}$$

EXAMPLE

Using data in Model 7.1, the following quarterly ratios resulted:

19X3			19X4	
December	*March*	*June*	*September*	*December*
8.6% (42.6 million ÷ 493.8)	8.4%	8.3%	8.5%	8.8%

The variations in the ratios are due to the fluctuations in the total liabilities plus owners' equity.

Relating owners' equity to total capital employed

This ratio indicates the relative proportions of invested and borrowed capital to the total capital employed in the business enterprise. *Owners' equity* includes the owners' investment (primarily share capital) plus retained earnings. *Borrowed capital* includes both current liabilities and long-term debt commitments (debentures, for example).

Application

This ratio acts as a guideline in evaluating the adequacy of invested capital and the security of borrowed capital. Generally, the greater the proportion of owners' equity that an organization possesses in terms of resources, the more assurance the creditor has that debt obligations will be met. An accepted baseline is that invested capital should exceed borrowed capital, but this criterion may not be valid in some organizations depending on their type of operations. Borrowed capital in excess of invested capital indicates that there is a sharing of proprietary risk with the creditor and that the security of debt repayments may result in financial jeopardy.

To calculate this ratio, divide the average owners' equity by the average total capital employed.

EXAMPLE

The following quarterly ratios are developed using data in Model 7.1:

19X3			*19X4*	
December	*March*	*June*	*September*	*December*
30.6% (151 million ÷ 493.8)	30.3%	30.5%	31.5%	32.8%

The ratio of owners' equity to total capital employed over a period of time usually reflects an organization's financial policy and objectives – and gives an insight into management's fiscal responsibility. Operating with excess creditor investment, however, may be fully justified and acceptable under certain circumstances.

Relating working capital to loan capital

Use this ratio to evaluate and determine if an organization could liquidate its long-term debt obligations from working capital. Although an organization may have a more than adequate earnings' position, it still may not have maintained enough liquid capital to meet long-term debt obligations. To calculate this ratio, divide the average working capital by average funded debt.

EXAMPLE

The following quarterly ratios are calculated using data in Model 7.1:

19X3			*19X4*	
December	*March*	*June*	*September*	*December*
2.80:1 (119.4 million ÷ 42.6)	2.81:1	2.82:1	2.85:1	2.85:1

The ratio of 280 per cent for December 19X3 indicates there is £2.80 of working capital for each £1.00 of funded debt. The ratio increased to 285 per cent in September and December of 19X4, which is more conservatively favourable to meet debt obligations.

Analysing loan/debenture disposition

Here is another approach to working capital versus loan evaluation.

EXAMPLE

The data are extracted from Model 7.1:

	December 19X4		
	£m		*£m*
Current assets	405.1	Current liabilities	283.8
Non-current assets	80.7	Loans	42.6
		Capital	159.4
Totals	485.8		485.8

Current assets of £405.1 million, less current liabilities of £283.8 million, provides a working capital of £121.3 million. Since the loans are £42.6 million, the total amount of the loans is represented by current assets – £121.3 million versus £42.6 million. None of the long-term debt has to be supported by the non-current assets. This financial position is favourable both for the organization concerned and for its long-term creditors because of the degree of liquidity.

Relating current debt to owners' equity

Use this ratio to determine whether the short-term creditors are providing too much in capital resources to support the operational environment relative to material, supplies, and services. To calculate this ratio, divide the average current liabilities by the owners' equity.

EXAMPLE

The following quarterly ratios are calculated using data in Model 7.1:

19X3	*19X4*			
December	*March*	*June*	*September*	*December*
1.99:1 (300.2 million ÷ 151.0)	2.02:1	2.01:1	1.90:1	1.78:1

The 19X3 ratio signifies that suppliers were providing £1.99 (December) of credit support for each £1.00 of owners' equity. A more favourable trend was experienced in December 19X4, which resulted from decreasing current liabilities as compared to an increasing owners' equity (higher retained earnings).

Determining a reasonable ratio is difficult because it depends on several factors, such as the velocity of debtor and stock turnovers, characteristics of the operational environment, working capital position, and the comparative ratio averages being experienced by other organizations in a similar industry. Continual periodic analyses and historical experience may help you to make a judgemental decision on acceptable ratio guidelines.

Comparing total debt to total assets

With this ratio, you can evaluate an organization's debt position in relation to its total asset position, both current and non-current. It is one indicator of how much debt an organization can incur and still cope without financial difficulty. To develop this ratio, divide the average total debt by average total assets.

EXAMPLE
The following quarterly ratios are calculated using data in Model 7.1:

19X3		*19X4*		
December	*March*	*June*	*September*	*December*
69.4% (342.8 million ÷ 493.8)	69.7%	69.5%	68.5%	67.2%

These ratios indicate that total liabilities represented 67.2–69.7 per cent of the total assets. In other words, approximately 70 per cent of the total assets are being financed by external suppliers and non-trade creditors.

On the surface, this situation implies possible difficulties in meeting scheduled debt obligations, but this may not be the case in reality. Current assets may turn over quickly, thereby permitting timely debt payments. Certain current liabilities, such as trade creditors, may extend the payment period. Long-term debts can be restructured for delayed payments. Increased earnings may be anticipated based on improved business outlook, and so on. As discussed in an earlier example, the organization's working capital was considered to be adequate based on industry-wide comparisons. Current assets were in a 1.4:1 ratio to current liabilities (common to this industry).

Calculating the total debt to owners' equity ratio

This ratio is another approach in evaluating whether an organization has enough capital to support its operations and debts. The merits of this measurement, however, can be misleading. To calculate this ratio, divide the average total debt by average owners' equity.

EXAMPLE
The following quarterly ratios are derived from data provided in Model 7.1:

19X3		*19X4*		
December	*March*	*June*	*September*	*December*
2.27:1 (342.8 million ÷ 151)	2.30:1	2.28:1	2.17:1	2.05:1

The developed ratio for December 19X4 indicates that the total debt is twice (2.05) the amount of the owners' equity. The trend is downward, as current liabilities decrease and owners' equity increases. In view of the reasonably strong position, financial difficulties are unanticipated. Current assets are adequate to support the total debt, with undercapitalization of minor importance in this particular organization.

Pros and cons of debt ratios and financing

Trading on equity – or on what is known as 'gearing' in some organizations – refers to the use of borrowed capital to achieve a higher rate of return on the owners' equity than could otherwise be accomplished without the use of the creditors' capital. For example, if funds can be borrowed at a rate that is lower than can be earned with the capital, then borrowing is considered to be both practical and profitable. Conversely, if the organization's earning power is lower than the interest cost on the borrowed capital, then the owners will earn less than if part of the capital had not been borrowed.

Trading on equity involves the risk of some losses, but it can also be rewarding. This ratio represents the relationship between the amount of borrowed capital and the owners' equity. Creditors' capital must be repaid, and so must interest expense, whether earned or not. When liquidation is a possibility, creditors have first claims against the assets over those of the owners. Thus the inappropriate use of creditors' capital presents risks both to the creditors and to the owners. The point is that operating capital is affected by the maturity dates of the creditors' capital.

The prime objective of debt ratios is to focus management's attention on potential problems associated with the use, size, and repayment of creditors' capital. You must also give consideration, however, to other influencing ratios, such as earnings, cash flow, working capital, capital structure, and so on. This is the only way to review properly financial objectives and operational planning in terms of creditors' impact on an organization's financial stability.

8 Understanding data relationships for effective cash flow planning

Chapter highlights

Cash flow might be described as the blood flow of an organization. Cash flow can be reduced, when required, or increased. The opening section of the chapter explains how you can do either.

You are then acquainted with a computerized cash collections and ratio analysis process, including cost-incurred contracts, sales deliveries, and progress payments. The development of progress payments, to provide available funding and improved cash flow, are very important in connection with fixed price contracts, particularly government contracts.

The step-by-step outline of an automated cash flow and reporting process is presented, although the procedures may vary somewhat among organizations.

Using an illustrative model, you will familiarize yourself with a numerical cash schedule, with ratios among the cash receipts, payments, and balances. By means of the two other models, you will come to understand the relationships among sales, receipts, and debtors. A similar approach is used for creditor costs, payments, and creditor balances. Finally, accrued salaries/wages and creditor costs, payments, and balances are outlined and highlighted.

The cash flow statement and its associated data reveal the in- and outflow of cash, its availability, the need to borrow funds to support operational activities, and problem areas.

Cash flows into the organization as the result of product sales and/or performance of services. Typical input for cash flow systems arises from such systems and processes as sales deliveries, debtors, and progress or partial payments. Receipts are also provided by customer advances, borrowings, and issuance of share capital.

Cash flows out of the organization in the form of major cash payments for salaries/ wages, creditors, capital asset expenditures, interest expenses, taxes, loan repayments, dividends, and so on.

The amount of cash available at any point in time can be calculated. First obtain the prior period's cash balance from the cash book. Combine that total with the current period's receipts. From this total, deduct the cash disbursements. The result is an ending cash balance for the period.

The next question is whether cash is indeed available, or if borrowing is in order. To answer this question compare the cash balance to the organization's pre-established cash requirements.

Understanding the dynamics of cash flow

In recent years, many organizations, both large and small, have experienced inadequate cash flow, with its characteristic problems – one of which is their inability to meet their debt obligations. A few notable examples of the early 1990s are Polly Peck, Brent Walker, and the Maxwell group. Many others are forced into liquidation. These problems can be attributed to overextension of credit, selling to poor credit risks, delays in collecting debtors, large interest commitments on borrowings, overexpansion, acquisitions, economic reversals, cut-throat competition, and possible reductions in sales volume.

This chapter is concerned with the various aspects and details of invoicing, collections, and cash positions. The ratios and other guidelines in the following sections can aid your organization in achieving and maintaining financial stability, as well as in cash planning.

How to reduce cash outflow

If you determine that a cash shortage is imminent, then, outside of borrowing, certain actions are feasible. One you should consider is *reducing cash outflow* (at least temporarily). Cash outflow can be reduced as follows:

Steps for reduction

Defer, where possible, the payment of specific creditor commitments to a later period through negotiations with suppliers.

Delay normal creditor payments to the last possible date or as long as you can without jeopardizing purchase discounts.

Restructure long-term debts to delay scheduled due date payments.

Reschedule capital expenditure projects until funds become available. (In some instances, this is not feasible because of immediate operating needs.)

Postpone dividend payouts if cash flow becomes an acute problem.

Try to negotiate with suppliers to establish payment dates during peak receipt periods.

How to increase cash receipts

Certain situations lend themselves to *increasing cash flow*:

Steps for increasing

1. Emphasize the collection of debtors, particularly if they are past the due dates. A more stringent credit policy may be necessary.

2. Initiate prompt customer invoicing, such as invoicing the customer on the same working day that product delivery has been made or service performed.
3. Make a concerted effort to reduce debtor and stock balances to conservative levels. This may mean a change in the customer credit policy and a delay in making major purchases.
4. Provide payment incentive discounts to selected customers.
5. Reduce advances to subcontractors and subsidiaries.
6. Dispose of surplus assets and consider sale/leaseback of assets.

Implications of cash flow from operations

Cash flow from operations represents *cash receipts from sales* (product/services) less the costs and expenses associated with producing a product or performing services. This would include supervisory, administrative/selling expenses. The financial reporting information provided would include a profit and loss account, balance sheet and undoubtedly changes in financial position in terms of a cash flow statement. The objective in this process is to determine the net increase or decrease in working capital resulting from sales revenues versus expenses.

The general procedure followed in the calculations is to adjust net working capital to reflect the changes that occurred in the current asset and liability accounts as a result of operational sales revenues. In essence, increases in current liabilities are combined with asset decreases and from this resultant value is deducted the combination of liability decreases and asset increases.

A simplified illustration of this procedure is noted as follows:

Pound sterling values in millions			
Net working capital from operations		*Cash flow from operations*	
Net profit	10.0	Increase in debtors	5.0
Depreciation/amortization	1.5	Decrease in stocks	(3.0)
Other (deferred debts)	0.1	Decrease in prepaid expense	(0.5)
		Increase in creditors	2.5
		Increase in accrued expenses	1.0
Net working capital	11.6	Net total	5.0

The £11.6 million less £5.0 million equals £6.6 million net cash flow from operations. It should be noted that the cash balance (to meet operational requirements) and fixed asset accounts (replacement/expansion) are generally also affected by fluctuations in sales revenues but these items are not usually reflected in the accepted format of changes in financial position.

It is pointed out that interest and fixed charge ratios should not only be based on profit but also the cash from operations as illustrated above since favourable cash flow is what pays the expenses. Financial position ratios and cash flow planning are further discussed in Chapters 7 and 8, respectively. Future cash flows are the determinate factor in assessing an organization's projected capability in meeting its debt obligations.

Charting the computerized cash collection process

Model 8.1 shows how customer invoices and collections can be processed. The system includes:

1. cost-plus contract collections;
2. sales deliveries;
3. progress or partial payments.

Cost-plus contract invoices

Costs plus a fixed fee are rare nowadays but assume invoices are settled after 15 days. Costs invoiced in one period may fall into the following period for collection. To derive the total contract invoice collections for the current period, combine the *prior period's* lagged amount balance with the *current period's* collectable amount. The lagged amount, based on historical experience, may vary from one organization to another.

Delivery invoices/collections

First negotiate a payment factor with the customer. Then apply the factor to the sales invoices. The result represents the *current period's payment* value. Deduct that amount from the sales invoices to derive the net outstanding amount. To this value, apply the collection lag percentage to obtain the amount to be lagged to the subsequent period.

To derive the value that is *collectable* in the current period, subtract the developed lagged value from the invoices amount. This amount is combined with the prior period's lagged invoices to obtain the current period's *total sales collections*. Note that the value lagged into a subsequent period represents *debtors* in the balance sheet.

Progress payments

As shown in Model 8.1, the collection lag percentage is applied to the progress payment invoice to obtain the value of the progress payment to be lagged to the next period for collection. Deduct the lagged amount from the invoice to obtain the current period's cash receipts.

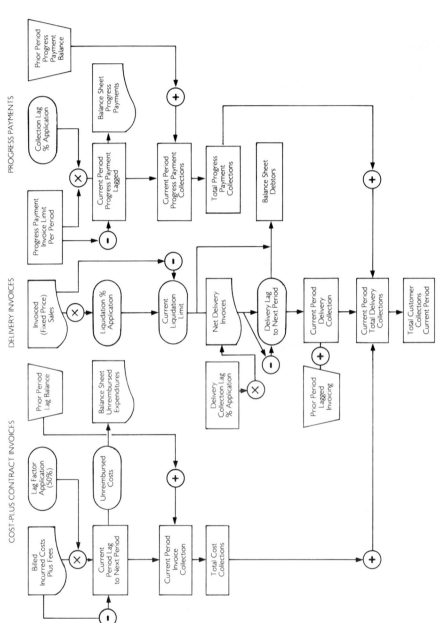

MODEL 8.1. Computerized invoicing and collection process

Combine the prior period's progress payment balance with the current period's collectable amount to obtain the total progress payment collections in the current period.

Total customer collections

To derive the total customer collections (bottom centre in Model 8.1), add cost-plus contract collections to the sales delivery and progress payment collections. The *lagged values* represent a current asset in the balance sheet.

Collection steps

Basically, the process involves four steps:

1. Determine the amount of the invoice that, based on experience, will remain unpaid until the following period.
2. Subtract the lagged amounts from the current period's invoices to derive the sum to be collected in the current period.
3. Combine the prior period's lagged amounts with the current period to obtain the current period collections in the invoice categories, displayed in Model 8.1.
4. Combine the three categories of collections to arrive at the total anticipated cash receipts in the current period.

Using ratios in connection with automated invoicing/collections

Model 8.2 reflects the information in the flow chart (Model 8.1). It provides examples for the three types of invoices: cost-plus, deliveries, and progress payments. The values may be used for the development of ratios, which in turn serve as a basis for comparative analyses in subsequent periods. The proviso, as always, is that the ratios must prove to be *consistent and valid* over a period of time under similar operational circumstances.

Calculating ratios to cost-plus invoices

As illustrated in Model 8.2, the process is simple. As costs are incurred and invoiced, you apply a collection lag percentage (or substitite a pound value). The lagged amount – £50,000 or 50 per cent of costs in this example – falls into the following collection period. The lagged portion represents *outstanding amounts due*.

An illustration

Deduct the lagged amount from the incurred costs (£100,000) to determine the amount to be collected in the current period (£50,000). To this value add the prior period's lagged amount (£45,000) to obtain the total collections for the period (£95,000).

MODEL 8.2. Ratio aspects of the invoicing/collection process

Cost plus contracts: assumptions (in £000s)		*Ratio development*	*%*	*£*
Total costs incurred	100.0	Current collections to costs	50.0	(50 ÷ 100)
		Prior invoices to total costs recovered	47.4	(45 ÷ 95)
Invoice collection lag	50.0	Prior lagged invoices to costs	45.0	(45 ÷ 100)
Prior lagged invoices	45.0	Current and prior invoices to costs	95.0	(95 ÷ 100)
Total costs recovered	95.0	Outstanding amounts to costs	50.0	(50 ÷ 100)

Delivery invoices: assumptions (in £000s)				
Invoiced sales	60.0	Payment limit to sales	60.0	(36 ÷ 60)
Payment limit	36.0	Current payment lag to sales	40.0	(24 ÷ 60)
		Delivery collection lag/payment limit	25.0	(9 ÷ 36)
Current payment lag	24.0	Delivery collections to sales	45.0	(27 ÷ 60)
Delivery collection lag	9.0	Prior invoices to total collections	30.8	(12 ÷ 39)
Current delivery collections	27.0	Current collections to total	69.2	(27 ÷ 39)
Prior invoices	12.0			
Total delivery collections	39.0			

Progress payment (PP) invoices: assumptions (in £000s)				
PP invoice limit	40.0	Collection lag to invoicing limit	50.0	(20 ÷ 40)
		Prior invoicing to total collections	47.4	(18 ÷ 38)
Current collection lag	20.0	Current collections to total	52.6	(20 ÷ 38)
Prior invoicing lag	18.0	Total collections to invoicing limit	95.0	(38 ÷ 40)
Total PP collections	38.0			

Customer collection summary (in £000s)

	Current period	*%*	*Prior invoices*	*%*	*Total collections*	*%*
Incurred costs	50.0	51.6	45.0	60.0	95.0	55.2
Invoiced deliveries	27.0	27.8	12.0	16.0	39.0	22.7
Progress payments	20.0	20.6	18.0	24.0	38.0	22.1
Totals	97.0	100.0	75.0	100.0	172.0	100.0

The following ratios can be developed for analysis and planning:

- The relationship of *current period collection to incurred costs* is 50 per cent (a 15-day lag in collection, generally based on historical experience and/or customer negotiations). The calculation process is illustrated in Model 8.2.
- The *prior period invoices to total collections* is calculated to be 47.4 per cent, which indicates a consistent pattern in the collection process based on the data provided.

- *Lagged prior period invoices to current period cost ratio* is determined to be 45 per cent. This ratio may not be valid or significant. Only experience can gauge or verify its usefulness.

- Total *current and prior invoices to current costs*, represented by a 95 per cent factor in the model, may provide a valid statistic for future planning and/or assessing the realities of collection and trends.

- *Current outstanding amounts ratio to incurred costs* is a reciprocal of current period collections to cost. This ratio, if proven valid over several periods, may be useful if projecting outstanding balances for a forecasted balance sheet, either in total or by specific contracts.

Computing ratios to delivery invoices

Model 8.2 displays the basic assumptions used in developing the total delivery collections and associated ratios.

To obtain the *current payment value* (£36,000), apply the payment application percentage (payment limit) to the invoiced sales. Subtract this value from the invoiced sales to derive the balance of the uncollectable (£24,000), which represents a debtor for the next period.

An illustration

The current payment limit of £36,000 represents net invoices due for payment in current month. Apply a collection lag of 25 per cent to the invoiced (£36,000) to obtain the uncollectable delivery portion of £9,000. The limit of £36,000, less the £9,000, represents the *amount to be collected this period*.

Combine the *prior period's lagged balance* of £12,000 with the current period's to obtain the *total delivery collections*.

The pertinent ratios are as follows:

- The *payment limit to invoiced sales* is 60 per cent (£36,000 ÷ £60,000). The payment limit percentage establishes the amount that can be collected or received in the current period. The limit is based on past experience and/or customer negotiations. This ratio can be used as a planning factor in establishing payment limits based on projected invoiced sales.
- The *current payment lag value to sales* is calculated to be 40 per cent, which is the complement of the 60 per cent payment limit noted above. (You can use either factor application to obtain the other.)
- The *delivery collection lag to the payment limit* is calculated to be 25 per cent, as shown in the model. The pound lag value may be a direct input, and it represents a debtor in the following period.
- The *current delivery collections to sales* is 45 per cent. This ratio may be useful in projecting current delivery collections based on forecast invoice sales activity.

- The *prior period invoices relationship to total sales* is calculated to be 30.8 per cent. The complementary percentage represents the current period collections (69.2 per cent). Either factor may be useful in planning current collections and prior period invoices based on anticipated total collections.

Calculating ratios for progress payments

An illustration

Model 8.2 displays the pound value assumptions used in developing the total progress payment collections and related ratios. The progress payment *invoicing limit* is developed as illustrated in Model 8.2. Or you can apply an applicable percentage to the cumulative *progress payment potential* to derive a period invoicing limit. To obtain the value of the *deferred* progress payments to be lagged into the following period, apply a *collection lag percentage* to the invoicing limit. The value of £20,000 (based on a 50 per cent collection lag) is deducted from the period progress payment limit of £40,000 to obtain the progress payments to be collected in the current period. Then combine these with the prior period's lagged amount of £18,000 to derive the total payments of £38,000 for the period.

Useful ratios can be developed from these data:

- The *current collection lag relative to an invoicing limit ratio* is calculated to be 50 per cent, as shown in Model 8.2. The ratio can vary among contracts depending on the terms of negotiation. This is a useful planning factor in projecting the current period's progress payment collections based on the invoicing limit.
- As shown in the model, the *prior period's invoicing to total collections* is calculated to be 47.4 per cent. The ratio of the current period's collections to the total collections is 52.6 per cent, which is the complement of the prior period's lagged collections. *Either factor* can be used in planning the anticipated component values of the total collections in a given period, provided they have been proven to be valid over a period of time.
- Comparing the *total collections to the invoicing limit* results in a 95 per cent ratio. Use this ratio in planning with caution due to possible changes in the operational environment and in the arrangements negotiated with customers.

Summarizing customer collection

The customer collection summary at the bottom of the model is based on the data detailed in the upper part. This summary indicates the relative proportions of incurred costs, deliveries, and progress payments as they apply to collections for the current and previous periods. The summary's objective is to determine the primary source of collections, which in this case were incurred costs with an overall 55.2 per cent. Current period invoices accounted for 56.4 per cent (£97,000 ÷ £172,000) of the total collections.

You can apply these factors, given similar operating circumstance, to total projected collections to obtain, at least preliminarily, the segregated sources of the collections, reflected in the balance sheet as unreimbursed expenditures, trade debtors, and uncollected progress payments. Further, if the ratio proves to be historically valid, approximately 56.4 per cent of the total collections may be assumed to represent current period invoices.

Developing progress payments and period payments

Model 8.3 displays the computerized process for developing progress payments and period payments. You can use this process for each contract, project, or combination of the two, providing you give consideration to the realistic averaging of the percentage involved (progress payments, funding, and period payments).

On a contract or project basis, the developed information can be readily consolidated through automated processes. Thus the detailed information can be reported for analysis and assessment, as well as for future planning.

When you use the consolidated contract approach, you lose the detail. When changes, additions, and deletions are required by contract, the percentages must be recalculated and reinput unless a computer program routine is developed to accomplish this task.

Let us look more closely at Model 8.3.

Processing progress payments

In this process, you combine work in progress costs with the changes in material and supply (M&S) costs, to obtain the total period's incurred costs. Apply a negotiated or planned progress payment percentage to the incurred costs to obtain the progress payment on period cost value. Combine period advances to supplier changes with the progress payments on costs to derive the progress payment potential. The period values are accumulated to obtain the cumulative progress payment potential. Collections depend on the constraints of negotiated available funding.

Calculating funding availability

Certain contracts – particularly government-negotiated contracts – have provisions specifying the funding percentage available to meet progress payment requirements. Model 8.3 displays the general process involved. A brief description of the procedure follows:

- Accumulate the period's incremental funding by contract to obtain the cumulative funding available to date.
- Apply the funding limit percentage or ratio to the cumulative funding value to ascertain the cumulative funding available in a specific period.

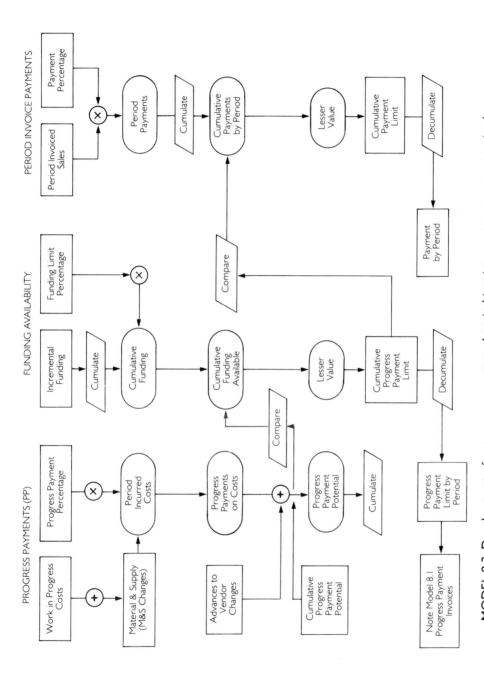

MODEL 8.3. Development of progress payments and period invoice payments: a computerized process

● At this point, compare the cumulative progress payment potential to the available cumulative funding. The *lesser value* represents the cumulative progress payment limit for collection. The resultant value is *decumulated* to obtain the progress payment limit for a given period. As shown in the model, this is the maximum value for collection as reflected at the top of Model 8.1 under the caption of 'Progress payment invoice limit'.

Step-by-step invoice collection procedure

The progress payment collection process is displayed at the extreme right of Model 8.3, as follows:

● Apply the *payment percentage to the period invoiced sales*. In so doing, you determine the amount that may be collected in a given period provided that the cumulative value at a point in time does not exceed the cumulative progress payment limit.

● Accumulate the period collections, as shown in the model, and compare the amounts to the cumulative progress payments. The *smaller value* of the two represents the cumulative collection limit. In other words, this value is the maximum that can be collected within the period.

● Decumulate the cumulative payment limit to obtain the potential payment by period. The period payment amount cannot exceed the established progress payment limit by period.

Assessing the ratio aspects of progress payments and period payments

Model 8.4 illustrates the data used in developing progress payments, funding, and period payment ratios. The computation procedure reflects the processing steps shown in the flowchart in Model 8.3.

How to determine progress payment ratios

An illustration

Apply the assumed progress payment of 50 per cent to the current period's total incurred costs of £100,000 to obtain the value lagged for collection in the following period. The difference between the £100,000 and the lagged payments of £50,000, plus the *advances to suppliers*, represents the current period's progress payment *collection potential*. Consolidate the potential amount with the prior period's progress payment total of £150,000 to obtain the cumulative progress payment potential of £210,000.

The following comments pertain to the ratio development.

MODEL 8.4. Ratios for progress payments and period payments: a computerized approach

Progress payments (PP): assumptions (in £000s)		*Ratio development*	*%*	*£*
Current period costs	100.0	PP on costs to incurred cost	50.0	(50 ÷ 100)
Progress payments on costs	50.0	Current PP potential to cum. PP	28.6	(60 ÷ 210)
Advances to suppliers	10.0	Prior period's PP to cum. PP	71.4	(150 ÷ 210)
		Period incurred costs to cum. PP	47.6	(100 ÷ 210)
Progress payment potential	60.0			
Prior period accumulation (PP)	150.0			
Cumulative PP potential	210.0			

Funding availability (FDG): assumptions (in £000s)				
Incremental funding	80.0	Incremental funding to cum. FDG	36.4	(80 ÷ 220)
Prior period cum. funding	140.0	Cum FDG limit to total cum. FDG	70.0	(154 ÷ 220)
Cumulative funding to date	220.0	Cum FDG to cum. PP limit	73.3	(154 ÷ 210)
Cum. funding limit – 70%	154.0	Lesser value (cum. represents cum. PP		
		limit)		154
Remaining funding lagged	66.0			

Payments assumptions (in £000s)				
Sales invoices	60.0	Period payments limit to invoiced		
		sales	60.0	(36 ÷ 60)
Period payments limit	36.0	Payments limit to total cum. payments	23.1	(36 ÷ 156)
Prior accumulated payments	120.0	Cum. payments to cum. FDG available	101.3	(156 ÷ 154)
Cumulative payments	156.0	Cum. payments to cum. PP limit	101.3	(156 ÷ 154)
		Lesser value (cum. FDG represents		
		cum. payments limit)		154

Summary of progress payments/period payments (note above)	
Progress payment potential	210.0
Cum. funding available	154.0
Cum. progress payment limit	154.0 (cum. FDG lesser than cum. PP potential)
Cum. payments to date	156.0
Cum. payments limit	154.0 (cum. PP limit lesser than cum. payments)

1. The *progress payments on costs to period incurred costs* is calculated to be 50 per cent, as shown in Model 8.4 (£50,000 ÷ £100,000). Use this ratio to determine the progress payment value to be lagged to the next period. The difference from incurred costs represents the potential collectable portion in the current period. A valid ratio can be useful in projecting future progress payment collections.

2. The *current progress payment potential to the cumulative progress payments* is calculated to be 28.6 per cent. Make use of this ratio in estimating current progress payments based on the cumulative total. Conversely, to estimate the current progress payments, if the factor proves to be consistent, multiply the cumulative progress payments (£210,000) by 28.6 per cent.

3. The *previous period's progress payment to cumulative progress payments* is represented by a ratio of 71.4 per cent (£150,000 ÷ £210,000). This statistic may be useful in estimating the previous period's accumulated progress payments. Subtracting this value from the cumulative payments to date results in the current period's payment potential. This calculation assumes, of course, that the ratio factors prove to be reliable historically and that the operating circumstances remain relatively consistent.

4. Comparing *period incurred costs to cumulative progress payments* results in a 47.6 per cent ratio. This factor can be used to project preliminary period incurred costs if the cumulative progress payments have been estimated initially. This can be useful in several ways in planning, but an organization must experiment with past data results to determine which approach most effectively meets its purposes.

Determining funding availability relationships

An illustration

The period's *incremental funding* is £80,000, as shown in Model 8.4. The previous period's accumulated funding is £140,000, which is combined with the current period's funding to obtain the *cumulative funding to date* of £220,000. To derive the cumulative funding limit of £154,000, apply a funding limit percentage of 70 per cent to the cumulative funding. This value represents the maximum funding available within a period. The difference between cumulative funding and the maximum available in the current period is £66,000, which is lagged to subsequent periods(s).

The following comments pertain to the development of these ratios:

1. The ratio of the *period's incremental funding to the total cumulative funding to date* is 36.4 per cent, as shown in Model 8.4. If the incremental funding is very sporadic and its amounts vary, this factor may not be reliable for future planning. Exercise care in its use for planning – but it does represent a possibility.

2. The *period's cumulative funding available (or limit) to total cumulative funding* is generally a customer-negotiated situation – in this instance, 70 per cent. A maximum of 70 per cent of the cumulative funding is available for collection. The funding available limit factor can vary among projects and contracts depending on customer negotiations. This ratio is very important in planning the availability of future funding, which is vital to realistic cash flow projections.

3. Comparing *the cumulative funding available to cumulative progress payment potential limit* yields a ratio of 73.3 per cent, as shown in Model 8.4. This factor indicates that the progress payment potential (£210,000) is greater than the available funding of £154,000. This means that the funding limit prevails as the basis for progress payment collections. This comparison enables you to plan the extent to which progress payments can be collected. The cumulative funding available (the lesser value) therefore represents the cumulative progress payment limit.

Calculating and using payment ratios

To determine the amount of payments, apply a limit percentage to the invoiced sales. Based on the data in Model 8.4, the payment amount for the period is £36,000. The difference between this value and the invoiced sales of £60,000 is deferred to the next period. To obtain the cumulative total to date, which is £156,000, combine the payment limit with the prior accumulated payments. Compare this value to the established cumulative payment limit to determine the cumulative collection payment limit of £154,000. This amount is the lesser of the cumulative payment limit and the cumulative payments (note the flowchart in Model 8.3).

The following comments pertain to these ratios:

1. The *current period payment limit to total cumulative payments* is calculated to be 23.1 per cent, as shown in Model 8.4. This factor is probably not valid for projection since it represents only a point in time. Its prime importance is in comparing and assessing period-to-period trends in the payment limit based on cumulative totals. This assessment indicates whether the limit is growing or decreasing. Either direction has an impact on customer collections, which are of vital concern in the cash flow process.

2. To determine the ratio of the *period payment limit to invoiced sales,* divide the payment limit by the invoiced sales value. The percentage is calculated to be 60 per cent, which is usually a negotiated limit.

3. The ratio of *cumulative payments to cumulative funding available* is calculated to be 101.3 per cent. Since the payments exceed the available funding, the funding limit of £154,000 prevails in establishing the cumulative payment limit. The ratio can be used to verify the relative size of payments versus funding availability. Determining its utilization is difficult depending on the reliability of historical experience and future expectations.

4. The ratio of *cumulative payments to cumulative progress payment limit* is the same as payment to funding (101.3 per cent). The funding is the lesser amount (£154,000) of progress payment potential (£210,000), and thus represents the maximum that can be collected within this time period.

At the bottom of Model 8.4 is a summary of the data included in the schedule. It presents the prime information used in developing the various ratios.

Automated cash flow process and reporting

Model 8.5 presents an overview of cash flow processing in the computerized environment.

Setting input and processing guidelines

- Product sales and service performance are the basis for *customer invoicing, debtors, and cash collection scheduling*. The invoices represent operating income.

- *Non-operating income* results from other cash flow items, such as cash from the sale of share capital, disposal of fixed assets, bank borrowings, interest income, and so on, as shown in Model 8.5.

- Operating and non-operating income are combined to obtain *total income*.

- The various types of classifications of cash expenditure are shown in the model, and their summary represents the *total cash expenditure*. The lag interval on expenditure will vary among the various items depending on the due dates of scheduled payments.

- The total income less the expenditure equals the *net cash increase (decrease)* for the period. To this is added the opening cash balance to obtain the *closing balance*.

- Compare pre-established period cash requirements to the period end balance, and calculate the difference as shown in Model 8.5. If the actual cash balance exceeds the cash balance requirements, you might emphasize short-term investment opportunities, loan repayments, and capital expenditure. If planned requirements exceed the actual cash balance, consider short-term bank borrowings, delaying certain expenditure, accelerating debtor collections, and so on.

- Income and expenditure items, as well as the closing cash balance, are compared automatically to the period budget to *determine variances* for possible corrective action and/or adjustments to future cash budget planning. This system is fairly common to most organizations. Item classifications may vary depending on the organization's operations, procedures, and accounting format.

Setting output requirements

Reports from this system include a period and year-to-date cash schedule, as well as a budget comparison report indicating line item variances.

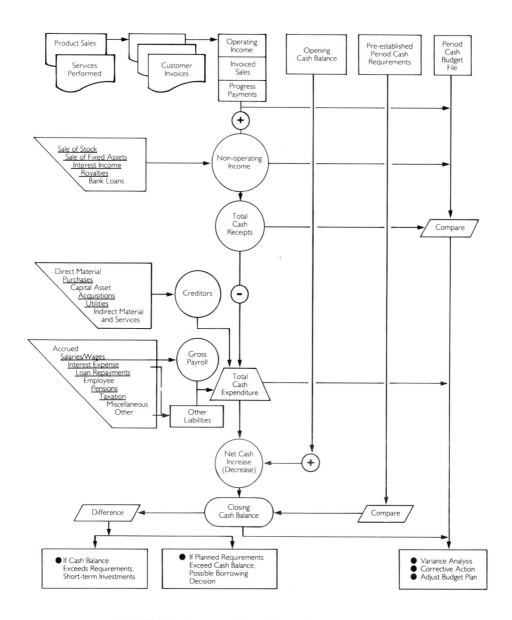

MODEL 8.5. Automated cash flow and reporting process

Preparing a cash income and expenditure schedule

Model 8.6 displays a typical internal cash flow schedule including ratios for assessment, performance measurement, and/or planning. The objective of meaningful ratios is to provide a basis for performance measurement, highlighting problem areas, and future planning – in this case, cash flow projections. The format and processing steps coincide basically with the flowchart in Model 8.5.

Let us analyse this schedule:

1. Major receipts represent *invoiced sales and progress payments*, which averaged about 88 per cent of the total collections for the year as reflected by their ratio to total receipts. Customer advances averaged 7 per cent and interest and bank loans accounted for the remaining 5 per cent.

2. The first-quarter receipts had the lowest quarterly collection ratio (21.5 per cent) during the year. This is attributed to the low receipts from sales invoices and progress payments (ratio of 77.3 per cent). The low receipts were partially offset by a bank loan of £20,000 or 14.6 per cent of the total receipts for the quarter.

3. Relative to expenditure, the ratio of *creditors and gross payroll* of total expenditure averaged 91.7 per cent. The first-quarter ratio of 22.8 per cent to the total expenditure for the year was the lowest in comparison to the other quarters. The primary cause is the relatively low sterling value of the creditors, and payroll paid in that quarter.

4. The various percentage ratios in Model 8.6 provide a rapid means to compare period results to the annual averages. With them, you can readily highlight deviations for further analyses and possibly corrective action.

5. As a result of the greater expenditure and lower income in the first quarter, there was a £7300 decrease in cash, which resulted in a closing balance of only £1600. This balance was 18 per cent below the average quarterly balance for the year. The situation was corrected in the second quarter due to an £8100 increase in income over expenditure. The third and fourth quarters also reflected modest increases over the average in the closing cash balances.

Comparing quarterly income ratios to annual collections

As displayed in Model 8.6, the quarterly collection ratios to the year's total ranged from 21.5 per cent in the first quarter to 27.0 per cent in the fourth quarter. This range indicates that an assessment of these major differences is in order. A review of the data reveals that the variances are attributed to the following:

MODEL 8.6. Cash flow schedule: cash income, payments, and balances

(in £000s)

Cash income	March	%	June	%	September	%	December	%	Total	%
Sales invoices	58.5	42.7	90.0	54.6	86.0	52.7	84.0	49.0	318.5	50.1
Progress payments	47.3	34.6	54.8	33.3	63.0	38.6	75.4	43.9	240.5	37.8
Customer advances	9.1	6.6	13.0	7.9	12.2	7.5	10.3	6.0	44.6	7.0
Interest income	2.0	1.5	2.0	1.2	1.9	1.2	1.9	1.1	7.8	1.2
Bank loans	20.0	14.6	5.0	3.0	—	—	—	—	25.0	3.9
Total cash receipts	136.9	100.0	164.8	100.0	163.1	100.0	171.6	100.0	636.4	100.0
Quarterly income ratios to total annual collections		21.5		25.9		25.6		27.0		100.0
Cash expenditure:										
Creditors	85.1	59.0	87.9	56.1	97.1	60.5	97.5	56.8	367.6	58.0
Payrolls, gross	51.1	35.5	53.9	34.4	54.4	33.9	53.7	31.3	213.1	33.7
Corporation tax	2.2	1.5	2.2	1.4	1.0	0.6	1.0	0.6	6.4	1.0
Other taxes	1.2	0.8	2.7	1.7	2.1	1.3	4.7	2.7	10.7	1.7
Pension fund	3.5	2.4	—	—	—	—	3.0	1.7	6.5	1.0
Loan repayment	—	—	8.0	5.1	5.0	3.1	10.0	5.8	23.0	3.6
Interest paid	1.1	0.8	2.0	1.3	1.0	0.6	1.92	1.1	6.02	1.0
Total cash expenditure	144.2	100.0	156.7	100.0	160.6	100.0	171.82	100.0	633.32	100.0
Quarterly expenditure ratio to total annual payouts		22.8		24.7		25.4		27.1		100.0
Net cash increase (decrease)	(7.3)		8.1		2.5		(0.22)		3.08	
Opening balance	8.9		1.6		9.7		12.20		8.90	
Closing balance	1.6		9.7		12.2		11.98		11.98	
Closing balance ratio to average annual balance (%)	(8.87)	18.0		109.0		138.0		135.0		

$$1.6 \div 8.87 = 18\%$$

1. The fourth-quarter *invoiced sales collections* are 6.3 per cent (49.0 per cent versus 42.7 per cent) greater than those of the first quarter. The annual average is 50.1 per cent. The differences require detailed analysis but the explanatory data are not available in Model 8.6.
2. The fourth-quarter progress payment collections exceed the first quarter receipts by 9.3 per cent (34.6 per cent versus 43.9 per cent). The annual average is 37.8 per cent.
3. The lower sales and progress payment receipts in the first quarter are primarily offset by a 14.6 per cent loan (versus zero in the fourth quarter).

Comparing quarterly expenditure to annual payout ratios

The *quarterly expenditure ratios to the year's total* ranged from 22.8 per cent in the first quarter to 27.1 per cent in the last quarter. Here are the following contributing causes:

The fourth quarter's combined creditors and gross payroll percentages are lower than the first quarter (88.1 per cent versus 94.5 per cent). The difference, however, is partially offset by the higher percentages in the fourth quarter for other taxes (2.7 per cent) *plus* loan repayments (5.8 per cent).

Comparing the quarterly closing balance to annual average

The quarterly closing balance average is calculated to be £8870. The ratio of the closing balance to the average balance is 18 per cent, 109 per cent, 138 per cent, and 135 per cent, respectively, for the four quarters. The first-quarter ratio was significantly below the other quarter ratios, which were all above 100 per cent. The problem in the first quarter requires detailed investigation as to specific causes.

To gauge a need to borrow funds to meet anticipated debt obligations with automated cash flow planning, compare the pre-established cash balance requirement to the resultant cash balance projection. In the actual environment reflected in Model 8.6, note that £20,000 was borrowed to finance the cash flow deficiency.

Analysing relationships among the sales, cash receipts, and debtors

Model 8.7 displays the development of various ratios concerned with the relationships among sales, cash receipts, and debtors. One or more ratios may be valid for use in some organizations but possibly not in others. Their validity and usefulness are predicated on an assessment of historical experience.

Developing the ratios

Cash receipts to sales invoices/progress payments. The annual ratio averaged 99.7 per cent (558.2 ÷ 560.0) as reflected in Model 8.7. The quarterly ratios range from 98 per cent to 103 per cent. These statistics indicate a reasonable consistency throughout the year. If future experience follows the same pattern, either the period ratio factors or the annual average can provide an acceptable means of projecting cash receipts based on sales/cost expectations.

The reciprocal of this ratio indicates the relationship of *invoiced sales/incurred costs to cash receipts*. Although this information is provided in the model, generally the procedure is to project cash receipts based on the sales/incurred cost forecast, which is the initial planning data in the organization's operating plan.

Closing debtor balance to invoiced sales/progress payments. The ratios range from 21.5 per cent to 28.9 per cent, with the largest figure of 28.9 per cent occurring in the first quarter. The principal cause for the high ratio is the below-average quarterly sales invoices/cost incurred. Note that *incurred cost values* are generally reflected in the cash receipt *progress payments*.

The *average ratio for the year* is calculated to be 23.8 per cent, as shown in the model. This percentage is based on an average quarterly sales-progress payment of £140,000 and an average closing debtor balance of £32,700.

Closing debtor balance to sales invoices/progress payments plus the opening balance. The developed ratios range from 17.8 per cent in the fourth quarter to 22.0 per cent in the first quarter, as shown in Model 8.7. The average quarterly ratio for the year is

MODEL 8.7. Sales, receipts, and debtor balances

(in £000s)

Debtors	March	June	September	December	Summary/ average
Opening balance	32.6	29.8	32.8	33.8	32.6
Sales invoices/cost incurred	103.0	147.0	150.0	160.0	560.0
Subtotal	135.6	176.8	182.8	193.8	592.6
Cash receipts	105.8	144.0	149.0	159.4	558.2
Closing balance	29.8	32.8	33.8	34.4	34.4
Ratio (%) development and analysis					
Receipts to sales/incurred costs	103.0	98.0	99.0	100.0	100.0*
Sales/incurred costs to receipts	97.0	102.0	101.0	100.0	100.0*
Closing balance to sales/incurred costs	28.9	22.3	22.5	21.5	23.8*
Closing balance to sales/incurred costs + opening balance	22.0	18.6	18.5	17.8	19.2*
Closing balance to receipts	28.2	22.8	22.7	21.6	23.8*
Receipts to closing balance	355.0	439.0	441.0	463.0	424.0*

*Quarterly ratio average was derived by adding the ratios for the four quarters and dividing by four.

calculated to be 19.2 per cent. The annual average is 5.8 per cent (34.4 ÷ 592.6). To develop the ratio, divide the closing debtor balance by the combined invoiced sales/progress payments plus the opening debtor balance. To obtain the quarterly average, divide the sum of the quarters by four in this instance.

The high ratio in the first quarter is attributed primarily to the relatively lower sales invoices/progress payments as compared to the other periods.

Applications

You can use this ratio as a planning factor to estimate the closing debtor balance based on projected invoiced sales/progress payments plus the opening balance. By deducting the estimated closing balance from the combined invoices plus the opening balance an *estimated cash collection* value can be obtained. The formula for the first quarter data is:

£135,600 × 22.0% = £29,832 (closing balance)
£135,600 − £29,832 = £105,768 (cash receipts)

As shown in the model, the closing debtor balance in one quarter becomes the opening balance in the following quarter or pertinent time period.

Closing debtor balance to cash receipts. The quarterly ratios are comparable to the sales/progress payment ratios because their values are practically on a one-to-one basis with cash receipts (£560,000 versus £558,200 of cash receipts). The figures in the model are annual totals. The quarterly ratios range from 21.6 per cent to 28.2 per cent, with an average of 23.8 per cent per quarter. The high ratio in the first quarter is attributed to the relatively lower cash collection results as compared to subsequent quarters.

Applications

This type of ratio can be useful not only for analysing differences among periods but also as a planning guideline and factor in projecting the closing debtor balance based on cash collection forecasts. Further, if proven to be relatively consistent, the ratio can be utilized to verify or confirm the validity or reasonableness of projected debtor balances that are developed by more detailed and conventional planning procedures.

Cash receipts to closing debtor balance. The quarterly ratios range from a low 355 per cent in the first quarter to a high 463 per cent in the fourth quarter, as shown in Model 8.7. The ratios are calculated by dividing the cash receipt values by the closing debtor balances. Note that, although *closing balances* are used in the discussion, the more precise method for quarterly periods is to use the *average* for the three-month periods within a quarter. A calculating formula for the first quarter is:

$$\frac{£105,800 \text{ (receipts)}}{£29,800 \text{ (debtors)}} = 355\%$$

The high ratio of 463 per cent in the fourth quarter is primarily due to the higher than average collections, as compared to the other quarterly periods. The debtor balance increased by only 15 per cent, as compared to the first quarter. On the other hand, cash receipts increased 50.7 per cent in the fourth quarter versus the first quarter. Note that the summary total of the quarterly ratios would provide the annual ratio factor.

If the developed ratios prove to be realistic over time and the organization's operations remain reasonably consistent in nature, you may use the factors to estimate cash receipts based on debtor closing balance projections or to check estimated receipts forecasted by other means. Further, the ratios may be utilized in a 'what if' process wherein cash receipts are manipulated by changes in closing debtor balances.

Caution in ratio usage

As useful as ratios are for analysis and planning, you must be aware of their possible shortcomings. As always, be sure that you are using comparable data when comparing one organization's results with those of another. You must also consistently analyse and assess historical experience to establish reliable and meaningful ratios.

Analysing costs, payments, and creditor ratios

Model 8.8 displays various ratios concerned with creditor costs, cash payments, and creditor balances. The ratios are predicated on the data provided in the upper part of the model. The reliability of the ratios depends on the consistency of the operational activity and a thorough assessment of historical experience.

Developing the ratios

Creditor payments to creditor costs. The quarterly ratios in Model 8.8 range from a high of 103.5 per cent in the first quarter to a low of 96.2 per cent in the fourth quarter. To develop the ratios, divide the quarterly payments by the quarterly costs. In the first quarter, for example, £85,100 was divided by £82,200 (costs) to obtain the 103.5 per cent factor.

You can use the ratios for assessment of the performance of actual period activity and for comparisons among periods to determine variations and their causes. Further, the ratios *may be valid* for use in projecting creditor payments based on creditor costs forecasts.

The principal cause for the relatively high ratio in the first quarter is that payments exceeded costs whereas the opposite occurred in the fourth quarter with a 96.2 per cent factor.

Creditor costs to payments ratios. The factors ranged from a low of 96.6 per cent in the

MODEL 8.8. Creditor costs, payments, and balances

(in £000s)

Creditors	March	June	September	December	Summary/ average
Opening balance	23.3	20.4	21.9	20.7	23.3
Incurred costs	82.2	89.4	95.9	101.4	368.9
Subtotal	105.5	109.8	117.8	122.1	392.2
Cash payments	85.1	87.9	97.1	97.5	367.6
Closing balance	20.4	21.9	20.7	24.6	24.6
Ratio (%) development and analysis					
Closing balance to payments	24.0	24.9	21.3	25.2	23.8*
Payments to closing balance	417.0	401.0	469.0	396.0	421.0*
Payments to costs	103.5	98.3	101.3	96.2	99.8*
Costs to payments	96.6	102.0	98.8	104.0	100.3*
Payments to BB + costs	80.7	80.1	82.4	79.9	80.8*
Closing balance to costs	24.8	24.5	21.6	24.3	23.8*
Costs to closing balance	403.0	408.0	463.0	412.0	421.0*

*Quarterly ratio average was derived by adding the ratios for the four quarters and dividing by four.

first quarter to 104 per cent in the fourth quarter. This type of ratio may not be much help since payments are generally predicated on costs incurred, rather than vice versa. The ratio is therefore presented only as a possible guide when planned payments are available and one is estimating a guideline cost figure.

Closing creditor balances to costs. The quarterly ratios range from a low of 21.6 per cent in the third quarter to a high of 24.8 per cent in the first quarter, with an annual quarterly average of 23.8 per cent. The primary reason for the low ratio in the third quarter is the high costs incurred, whereas the closing creditor balance remained fairly static compared to the first quarter.

The reason for the high ratio of 24.3 per cent in the fourth quarter is an 18.8 per cent (£20,700 to £24,600) increase in the creditor balance, as compared to the third quarter. There was only a 5.7 per cent increase in costs (£95,900 to £101,400) for the comparative periods.

Creditor balance to cost ratios can be used to compare actual results among periods and to provide a projection factor for estimating and planning creditor balances based on cost budgets and forecasts. Further, if historical experience is reliable, you can use the ratio to verify projected creditor balances that are developed in detail by more conventional planning procedures.

Creditor costs to creditor closing balance. The ratios are developed in reverse of the order for closing creditor balances to cost ratios: divide the costs by the creditor balances. As shown in Model 8.8, the ratios range from 403 per cent in the first quarter to 463 per cent in the third quarter, with an annual quarterly average of 421 per cent. The major cause for the low ratio in the third quarter is the below-average costs. The high ratio of 463 per cent in the third quarter resulted from a comparable closing creditor balance to the first quarter but the costs were 16.7 per cent greater (£82,200 to £95,900).

The value of the ratios as planning factors may be questionable, since creditor balances are more logically based on actual cost and projections than this reverse process.

Cash payments to closing creditor balance. The quarterly ratios range from a low of 396 per cent to a high of 496 per cent in the third quarter, as shown in Model 8.8. The primary cause for the low ratio in the fourth quarter is the high payable balance, whereas the payments are consistent with the third-quarter value with its low closing balance.

Use of this type of ratio in some organizations may be questionable. The closing creditor balance depends more on the payment activity than vice versa. In most organizations, cash payments are projected first and the closing creditor balance results from cost and payments calculations. The ratio factors, however, may be helpful in obtaining guideline payment values, but the information must be treated with caution.

Closing creditor balance to payment. The quarterly ratios range from a low of 21.3 per cent in the third quarter to a high of 25.2 per cent in the fourth quarter. To develop the ratios, divide the closing creditor balance by the payment values.

The low ratio of 21.3 per cent in the third quarter can be attributed to the low closing creditor balance of £20,700 and the higher than average payment activity. Conversely, the high ratio of 25.2 per cent in the fourth quarter resulted from the high creditor balance of £24,600 versus a payment value that was similar to the third quarter with its lower balance.

The ratios developed in Model 8.8 can be used to

- analyse the activity among time periods and assess major variations;
- estimate preliminary closing creditor balances based on payment values.

You have to review historical experience to determine the validity of these factors for use in your organization. Although the ratios demonstrate the relationship among the data, each organization must determine their value, their usefulness for analysis and planning, and possible reservations about their employment.

Creditor payments to opening creditor balance plus costs. The quarterly ratios vary from 79.9 per cent in the fourth quarter to a high of 82.4 per cent in the third quarter. The low ratio in the fourth quarter is due to high costs, while the payments remained relatively the same as in the third quarter. The high ratio of 82.4 per cent in the third quarter resulted from a combined increase of 7.3 per cent in the opening creditor balance and costs over the second period, whereas payments increased 10.5 per cent.

Application

The annual ratio average of 80.8 per cent appears to be fairly representative of the four quarters' financial activity. If the factor proves to be valid, you can project the creditor payments based on an estimated opening creditor balance plus costs.

If you obtain a consistent payments application factor and calculate reliable estimated payments, then you can approximate the projected closing creditor balances. As shown in Model 8.8, the opening balance of £23,300 for the first quarter, plus the creditor costs of £82,200 less the payments of £85,100, results in a closing balance of £20,400. This amount becomes the opening balance in the subsequent period, and so on thereafter for monthly and quarterly periods.

Caution

The ratios in Model 8.8 may serve as performance assessment and planning guidelines. As always, their usefulness in an organization depends on the reliability of historical experience and the assumption that future operations expectations will remain relatively consistent.

Assessing accrued salaries/wages, costs, and balances

In addition to creditor costs, assessing gross payroll costs is generally one of the significant costs in operating a business enterprise.

Developing the salaries/wages (S/W) closing balances

Calculation process

	Accrued (S/W) opening balance (previous period)
(+)	Current period accrued payroll costs

(=)	Subtotal (outstanding payroll costs)
(−)	Period cash payments

(=)	Accrued (S/W) closing balance (current period)

The following relationships can be employed for assessing financial performance based on historical analysis and planning guidelines.

1. Period cash *payments* versus current *period accrued* payroll costs.
2. Period *accrued payroll costs* as a percentage of payroll *payments*.
3. Accrued payroll *closing balance* as a percentage of *current period payroll* costs.

4. Period *payroll cost relationship* to accrued payroll *closing balance*.
5. Period payroll *payment relationship* to accrued payroll *closing balance*.
6. Period *closing payroll balance* as a percentage of payroll *payments*.
7. Period payroll *payments* as a percentage of *accrued salaries/wages opening balance* plus current *period accrued gross payroll costs*.

To calculate all these ratios, divide the first data element indicated by the following data identifier. For example, to obtain the first ratio, divide the *payments* by the *accrued payroll costs*.

As in the case of creditors, you must exercise discretion in the use of these ratios. To determine their reliability and validity in assessing performance and their usefulness as planning guidelines, a thorough analysis must be made of the ratio results.

9 Employing statistical techniques for effective planning and operations

Chapter highlights

How do ratios make operations and planning effective? This chapter demonstrates how statistical and graphic display techniques can help you to analyse and interpret financial data with an eye towards fixing operating policies and establishing realistic planning objectives. As always, however, remember that statistical tools provide only basic data assessment. You must supply the judgemental analysis and interpretation before reliably employing the methods for planning or assessment.

The *cost–volume–profit* relationships are concerned with profit optimizations, specifically with product sales price, production costs, and volume sold. Break-even analysis is illustrated with graphic display charts. The effects of plant expansion costs, production costs, sales increases, operating income, and plant capacity are all relevant to the break-even point. The advantages and disadvantages of each are explained.

The *profitgraph technique* is explained and its objectives described. You will familiarize yourself with the relevance of break-even analysis and the impact on profit goals. You will see the relationships of cost and operating income analysis, as well as investment assessment criteria and applications, to product line, performance measurement, pricing decisions, and facility expansion.

The *capitalgraph model* is illustrated by means of case data. A practical example demonstrates how the operating capital position results from the status of current assets and liabilities and net fixed assets versus the impact of fluctuating sales volumes.

Although illustrated throughout the chapter, the *least squares correlation* procedure is the focus of the last section of the chapter.

Various statistical techniques can be used not only in analysing results from operating events, but they can also provide a realistic basis for establishing and achieving financial goals and objectives. To use these techniques, however, you must thoroughly understand the procedures, their significance, and their applicability. You must also assess and interpret your organization's operational results, because some of the techniques in this chapter may not apply to *all* organizations. Yet a thorough screening through practical application will undoubtedly reveal the limitations of these techniques or their potential as a useful and effective tool for an organization's consideration.

The procedures described in this chapter are concerned with

- cost–volume–profit relationships;
- operating gearing ratios;
- break-even point usage and illustrations;
- profitgraph techniques;
- capitalgraph assessment;
- the principles of least squares correlation.

Making use of cost–volume–profit relationships

Influences on profitability

Of basic and sensitive concern in a business enterprise is *profit optimization* and how to accomplish it successfully. The three major influences on an organization's profitability are:

- product sales price;
- cost of producing and delivering the product;
- product demand and/or volume sold.

The product or service sales price is equal to the cost of production or of performing the service plus a reasonable profit. The sales price is generally a governing factor in the volume sold. In turn, the production volume influences the cost; hence, the interaction among price, volume, and cost. An organization must be able not only to measure and understand the impact of these factors, but also how to keep them in proper proportion.

Analysing the break-even point

The fundamental accounting concept is that sales income less costs equals profits. Assessing the break-even point is a common tool used in measuring the relationship among costs (variable and fixed), volume (sales revenue), and net income. The vertical axis *(y)* on a break-even chart represents costs in pounds and sales. The horizontal axis indicates volume, which can be expressed in terms of product units, machine hours, pounds weight, gallons, and so on.

To calculate the break-even analysis, use the following equation:

$$\text{Break-even sales} = \frac{\text{Fixed expenses}}{1 - \dfrac{\text{Variable expenses}}{\text{Sales}}}$$

EXAMPLE

Let us examine sales to produce a zero income from operations:

Sales	£300,000
Variable expenses	(234,000)
Fixed expenses	(36,000)
Profit from operations	£30,000

Calculation:

$$\text{Break-even sales} = \cfrac{36,000}{1 - \cfrac{234,000}{300,000}}$$

$$= \cfrac{36,000}{1 - 0.78}$$

$$= £163,636$$

The break-even sales are calculated to be £163,636. Let us go one step further and assume that the objective is to estimate sales on a zero pretax profit in which there was an additional expense for interest. In that case, add the interest to the fixed expenses, and recompute the equation to reflect the difference in the break-even point.

Variable expenses (utilities, repairs, supplies) fluctuate with production volume, whereas fixed expenses do not because of their usually constant nature (depreciation, leases, insurance). Some expenses can be semi-variable, that is, they may fluctuate to a degree but not in direct proportion to volume changes. At times, segregating semi-variable costs from the variable or fixed expenses is difficult, and very often the distinction is one of judgemental categorization.

How to calculate the operating gearing ratio

Fluctuations in sales price can have a decided effect on operating profits, particularly when fixed expenses are high. To measure the operating gearing, use the following equation.

The formula

$$\text{Operating gearing} = \frac{\text{Sales} - \text{Variable expenses}}{\text{Sales} - \text{Total expenses}}$$

EXAMPLE

Let us use the data from the previous example.

$$(1) \quad \frac{£300,000 - £234,000}{£300,000 - £270,000} = \frac{£66,000}{£30,000} = 2.2 \text{ times}$$

If the sales increase or decrease by 15 per cent the gearing results change as follows:

(2) £300,000 × 115% = £345,000

$$\frac{£345,000 - £234,000}{£345,000 - £270,000} = \frac{£111,000}{£75,000} = +1.48\,\text{times}$$

(3) £300,000 × 85% = £255,000

$$\frac{£255,000 - £234,000}{£255,000 - £270,000} = \frac{£21,000}{-£15,000} = -1.4\,\text{times}$$

Example (1) indicates that the operating gearing is 2.2 times sales of £300,000, with variable expenses of £234,000 and total expenses of £270,000. Under the gearing concept, profit from operations changes 2.2 times the percentage change in sales from the original base. For instance, if there is a 15 per cent change in sales, then the estimated operating profit would be approximately 33 per cent (15% × 2.2). In this example, the operating profit would change by £9900 (£30,000 × 33%).

Examples (2) and (3) show how the gearing changes when the sales base increases and decreases by 15 per cent – assuming there are no changes in the fixed and variable expenses (rarely possible). The results are +1.48 and −1.4 times the percentage change in the revised sales base.

Making use of the gearing factor

The operating gearing enables you to assess the profit risk resulting from a change in sales price. In Example (3), a 15 per cent decline in sales resulted in an *estimated negative factor* of 1.4 times the income from operations. The *operating risk* results from the level of fixed operating expenses. The *financial risk* in an organization, on the other hand, arises from the use of debt support by creditors – both short and long term. In the evaluation of financial gearing ratios, you can gain an informative insight as to the total operating risk resulting from sales price fluctuations and increased creditor debt. Fixed expenses have an important impact on an organization's total risk.

How to illustrate the break-even point

Typically, break-even charts display graphically the two types of expenses that influence operating profits based on a given sales level. Break-even analyses involve the segregation of costs into fixed and variable. The break-even chart is based on (1) estimated price levels and (2) fixed and variable cost trends. The *break-even point* is the volume at which sales and total costs are equal. Contribution margin represents the difference between sales and variable costs, which is used to absorb fixed costs, taxes, and profits. In essence, this type of analysis is concerned with volume, sales mix, and management operating efficiency in controlling costs and the use of investment resources.

Model 9.1 demonstrates different versions of break-even analysis.

MODEL 9.1. Cost–volume–profit relationships and break-even points

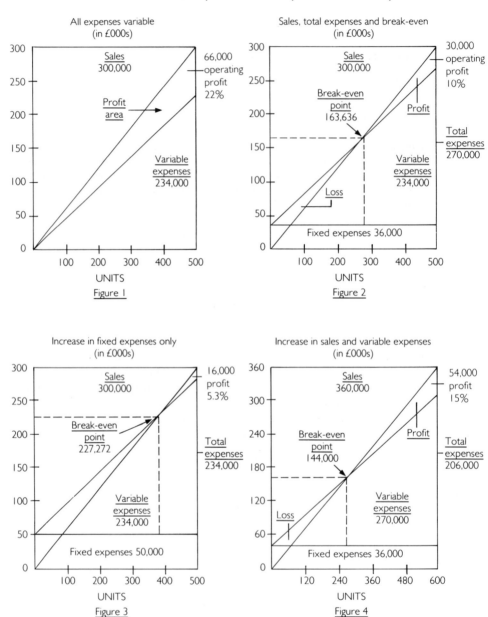

All expenses variable
(in £000s)

Sales
300,000

66,000
operating
profit
22%

Profit
area

Variable
expenses
234,000

UNITS

Figure 1

Sales, total expenses and break-even
(in £000s)

Sales
300,000

30,000
operating
profit
10%

Break-even
point
163,636

Profit

Total
expenses
270,000

Variable
expenses
234,000

Loss

Fixed expenses 36,000

UNITS

Figure 2

Increase in fixed expenses only
(in £000s)

Sales
300,000

16,000
profit
5.3%

Break-even
point
227,272

Total
expenses
234,000

Variable
expenses
234,000

Fixed expenses 50,000

UNITS

Figure 3

Increase in sales and variable expenses
(in £000s)

Sales
360,000

54,000
profit
15%

Break-even
point
144,000

Profit

Total
expenses
206,000

Variable
expenses
270,000

Loss

Fixed expenses 36,000

UNITS

Figure 4

Sales and variable expenses only

In Figure 1 of Model 9.1, all expenses are assumed to be variable (not a typical situation), and the operating income of £66,000 represents a 22 per cent ratio to sales. With no fixed expenses, the diagonal line is drawn from the '0' locations to a point on the total variable expense (the vertical axis) representing £234,000. The difference between the sales value and expenses represents the operating profit. The profit at varying sales unit volumes is reflected by the vertical distance between the lines representing sales and variable expenses.

The sales line rising at a 45-degree angle represents the increases in sales (on the vertical axis) and results from increases in unit volume (on the horizontal axis). The principal assumption in this instance is that the product mix and sales price remain constant.

Significance of fixed costs on break-even

The greater the fixed expenses, the higher will be the break-even point, as demonstrated in Model 9.1. An increase of £14,000 in fixed expenses resulted in the break-even point rising 38.9 per cent (from £163,636 to £227,272). In the short run, fixed costs cannot be immediately reduced to meet declining customer demand. Certain fixed costs remain fairly constant, such as taxes, insurance, rent or lease costs, depreciation, security and certain aspects of administration (accounting, supervision, marketing). Most of the fixed costs are essential in order to maintain the integrity and environment survival of the organization.

As sales revenue decreases and fixed costs remain fairly constant, the earnings will naturally decline accordingly because of the fixed cost impact. It is only logical to assume that an organization with greater fixed expenses must have larger sales revenue to break even.

If sales revenues increase, however, the organization can increase its earnings position because the increased profit will more than offset the fixed cost needs.

Sales, total expenses, and break-even

Figure 2 in Model 9.1 shows the break-even point to be at the intersection of sales and the total expenses line. Horizontal and vertical dash lines are drawn to the point of intersection. The vertical line indicates the number of product units to be sold at the break-even point, and the horizontal line represents the sales volume in thousands of pounds. As shown in Figure 2, the break-even point in pounds is calculated to be £163,636.

The addition of £36,000 in fixed expenses (shown at the bottom of Figure 2) led to a reduction of operating profit to 10 per cent of sales, as compared to the 22 per cent results in Figure 1.

Increase in fixed expenses only

Figure 3 in Model 9.1 demonstrates what happens when only fixed expenses are increased by £14,000 but the sales volume and variable expenses remain the same. The break-even point increases from £163,636 to £227,272. The break-even point is thus raised to a higher level on the chart. Conversely, the opposite effect (a downward trend) is experienced if the fixed expenses decrease.

Increasing sales and variable expenses

Figure 4 in the model shows the results of increasing sales by 20 per cent (£60,000) and increasing a mixture of price and volume and variable expenses by 15.4 per cent (£36,000). Fixed expenses remain at the original £36,000 level.

The ratio of operating profit to sales is calculated to be 15 per cent. The break-even point is reduced to £144,000, as plotted on the graph.

Analysing data by means of alternative methods

Model 9.2 demonstrates two alternative cost volume relationships that can be used for analysing and assessing data.

Method 1. In Figure 1, the scattergraph technique is used. The plotted points represent two years of historical experience; costs were measured against sales based on percentage of plant capacity. Fixed expenses are presumed to be constant in this illustration, but variable expenses fluctuate with production volume.

Using the least squares correlation approach, you can calculate a representative line (a pattern of cost behaviour) and fit it to the data, or you can just determine the line from visual observation. The regression line represents the average location of the plotted points. By extending the line slope, you can estimate costs based on past performance results.

Application
The break-even point formula can be used to determine the intersection between cost and volume, which indicates the sales break-even and the percentage of plant capacity.

Method 2. In Figure 2 in Model 9.2, the fixed expense line is drawn parallel and above the variable line slope. In other words, the fixed line represents the *contribution margin*, whereas the distance between the total expense line and sales is indicative of the *operating profit*. If the variable expenses maintain a constant pattern, then any change in the fixed expense results in *raising or lowering* the break-even point depending on whether fixed costs increase or decrease. You can draw fixed expense lines to reflect various situations and ascertain estimated break-even points for gaming and/or planning purposes.

MODEL 9.2. Cost–volume–profit relationships: alternative plotting techniques

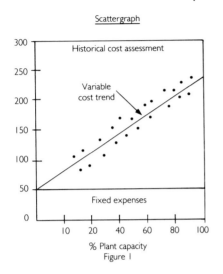

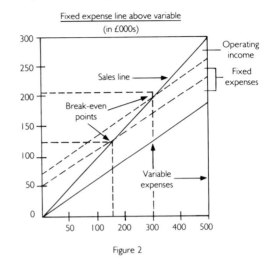

Putting break-even analysis to work

Break-even analysis enables you to highlight the factors relevant to expenses and sales. The practical applications will be illustrated through the use of equations.

EXAMPLE

		%
S = Net sales	£400,000	100.0
VE = Variable expense	(238,000)	(59.5)
FE = Fixed expense	(42,000)	(10.5)
Operating income	£120,000	30.0

1. Current break-even point:

$$\text{Break-even sales} = \frac{FE}{1 - \dfrac{VE}{S}} = \frac{£42,000}{1 - \dfrac{£238,000}{£400,000}} = \frac{£42,000}{0.405} = \begin{array}{c} £103,704 \\ \text{(break-even)} \end{array}$$

2. Plant expansion will create higher fixed expenses of £30,000:

$$\text{Break-even sales} = \frac{£72,000}{1 - \dfrac{£238,000}{£400,000}} = \frac{£72,000}{0.405} = \begin{array}{c} £177,778 \\ \text{(break-even)} \end{array}$$

3. Sales will have to increase by £74,074 (£177,778 − £103,704): Hence the difference in break-even points to achieve the current operating profit of £120,000:

   Current sales of £400,000 + £74,074 = £474,074

4. To verify the sales increase required to maintain current profit:

$$S = £72,000 + 0.595S + £120,000$$
$$S - 0.595S = £72,000 + £120,000$$
$$0.405S = £192,000$$
$$S = \underline{£474,074} \text{ (revised as shown above)}$$

5. Verifying current net profit results through increased sales needs:

		%
Revised net sales	£474,074	100.0
Less: Revised FE	(72,000)	(15.2)
Revised VE	(282,074)	(59.5)
Current operating profit	£120,000	25.3

6. Summary of calculations illustrated above:

   a. *Sales* have to increase by £74,074 to maintain current operating profit.
   b. *Fixed expenses* have to increase by £30,000 to meet plant expansion needs. *Variable expenses* increase to £282,074 (£474,074 × 59.5 per cent).
   c. *Current operating income* now represents 25.3 per cent of sales versus 30 per cent previously. The difference of 4.7 per cent is reflected in the increased fixed expense as a percentage of sales (from original 10.5 per cent to 15.2 per cent).
   d. If sales do not increase as required to maintain current income, then the higher fixed expense of £30,000 will reduce current income results to £90,000. Plant expansion is assumed to result in greater sales volume achievement.

These computations are merely approximations based on the assumption that all expenses are either fixed or variable.

Calculating the percentage of plant capacity at which an organization will break even

EXAMPLE
Let us make the following assumptions:

● Present level of production is 80 per cent of plant capacity.
● Fixed expense is established at £72,000.
● Sales are £474,074; variable expenses are £282,074.
● The relationship between plant capacity and sales proceeds is constant.
● *x* represents the percentage of plant capacity at break-even.

We use the following formula:

$$x = \frac{FE \times \% \text{ plant capacity}}{S - VE}$$

And here is the calculation:

$$x = \frac{£72,000 \times 80\%}{£474,074 - £282,074} = \frac{£57,600}{£192,000} = 30\%$$

Caution

These hypothetical data are used only to illustrate the computation process. This application can, however, be used to *approximate* an estimated percentage of plant capacity at the break-even point based on the realistic data available. The objective is to ascertain plant capacity requirements.

EXAMPLE

Let us make the following assumptions:

x = Sales volume required at present prices to produce an operating profit of £120,000.

OI = Income required to compensate for plant expansion costs.

FE = £42,000.

VE = £238,000.

S = £400,000.

A = Additional FE of £30,000.

Here is the formula with the calculations:

$$x = \frac{OI + FE + A}{1 - \dfrac{VE}{S}}$$

$$\frac{£120,000 + £42,000 + £30,000}{1 - \dfrac{£238,000}{£400,000}}$$

$$= \frac{£192,000}{1 - 0.595} = \frac{£192,000}{0.405}$$

$$= £474,074$$

This is another version of item 4 in the first example. If the organization's objective is to maintain the same operating profit level in spite of increased expenses, it needs a sales volume of £474,074.

Assumptions to remember in break-even assessment

1. If variable costs remain constant, the increases or decreases in fixed expenses change the break-even position (either higher or lower on the chart). This factor should not affect volume changes.
2. If the general price level changes significantly, you should review the break-even point and make revisions accordingly.
3. For more realistic results in the analysis, identify fixed and variable costs based on historical experience and your own judgement. Segregating semi-variable expenses into fixed and variable is highly desirable.
4. In the preceding discussion and analysis, only one product is assumed. If there is a varying number, however, the sales mix is presumed not to change, with its incorporated different sales mix gross margins.
5. Selling prices are generally assumed not to change with volume; hence, the sales line is straight. As price changes occur, supplemental sales lines can be drawn to reflect this situation.

Weighing the pros and cons of break-even analysis

Like most techniques, break-even analysis may have a degree of inaccuracy in its use and interpretation, and it has its advantages and disadvantages.

Advantages

1. Break-even analysis provides a forceful communication tool in demonstrating the relationship and interaction of cost, volume, and profit. If properly utilized and relevant, it aids in establishing realistic profit objectives and operating budgets.
2. It provides management with a distinctive insight into the economic characteristics of its business, not only in terms of the fixed and variable expenses at varying sales volumes, but also of the break-even relationship and its effect on the consequences of unearned income required to support the investors' return on both the preference and ordinary share equity. Through break-even chart presentations you can readily determine the effect of changes in these relationships.
3. You can advantageously employ 'what if' modelling to determine the anticipated results from contemplated managerial decisions. The break-even process may involve such planning questions as plant expansion, equipment modernization, change in product mix or sales prices, and the introduction of new product lines.
4. Management is often confronted with the decision to increase sales volume with an optimistic view towards enhancing profit. Profit enhancing is a

possibility, providing costs are controlled within prescribed limits. The break-even technique can be an important tool in establishing expenditure constraints and control by adequate supervision.

5. An important influence on profit is the product sales mix with variable gross margins. The break-even chart can highlight problem areas requiring corrective management action, but you must first be aware of the problem.

Disadvantages

1. Break-even analysis is not a panacea. It cannot be used unquestioningly without a thorough understanding of its concept and limitations.
2. The break-even chart generally reflects a number of estimates and judgements, and the resultant data developed and their implication may be misleading. For example, measuring costs and sales volume at a particular output level may be an inaccurate method of assessment, particularly when the volume approaches the break-even point, which can change depending on operating circumstances.
3. Usually, the break-even is developed at a point that represents a static position. Changes in relationship factors should be correctly and logically reflected in a revised chart or a series of charts.
4. The improper understanding and usage of the charts can lead to inadequate decision making, inaccurate planning assumptions, and possibly inhibited control actions.
5. Fixed and variable expenses may be inaccurately segregated with the resultant effect on the break-even position. Plotting sales as a function of production volume may be misleading; the assumption that sales equals production activity may not necessarily be true because of the buildup or reduction of stocks at varying business cycles. Exercise extreme care in compiling homogeneous and compatible data for the break-even analysis.

Using the profitgraph technique

Applications

The profitgraph technique is used principally for profit measurement and control. It is concerned with management decisions involving product and plant profitability, improvement and/or expansion of plant facilities, performance measurement and operational control. In our discussion, the emphasis is on determining the probable pattern of gross margin, net profit, and return on investment.

In constructing a profitgraph, you must understand the underlying principles of product price and costs and how, particularly, changing volume affects costs. Profitgraph construction and usage involve (1) break-even analysis and (2) the principles of variable budgeting.

Relating break-even assessment to the profitgraph technique

A break-even analysis reflects two separate measures of the relative profitability of varied product line: fixed and variable costs. In long-range planning, for example, fixed costs are generally flexible over longer time spans, and you can compare and assess product line profit potentials. In the immediate period(s), fixed costs are fairly stable; the contribution margin as a percentage of or ratio to sales provides a more realistic measure of individual product profitability and the effect resulting from the sales mix.

Applications

Relative to operating efficiency, you can use the break-even charts to compare alternative planning courses of action and their effect on proposed projects. In facilities planning, the cost for additions can be compared to lower cost production or increased capacity.

In reviewing cost-reduction projects as an analyst, you can compare the cost of new methods with the anticipated savings. Further, break-even analysis can be used as a budgetary control tool for measuring performance and the results from decision making.

EXAMPLE

How break-even principles are reflected in the break-even charts.

Sales volume	Variable expenses 70%	Contribution margin 30%	Fixed expenses	Pretax profit (loss) value	% of sales
£20,000	£14,000	£6000	£6500	£(500)	(2.5)
£22,000	£15,400	£6600	£6600	*Break-even	0
£25,000	£17,500	£7500	£6600	£900	3.6

*£6600 ÷ 30% = £22,000 sales. Sales under £22,000 result in a loss, but above that value there are anticipated profits.

Understanding the principles of variable budgeting

The variable budget is a management tool used primarily for monitoring and controlling production costs. Comparative analyses are made between budgeted and actual costs, and variances are assessed as part of the cost-control procedure.

In the production process, certain expenses are generally fixed and others are variable. When related to *unit costs*, fixed expenses actually become variable with volume changes, whereas variable expenses become fixed with volume changes. Generally, fixed costs remain constant regardless of sales volume changes (which is untrue for unit costs).

Examples of fixed costs include depreciation, property taxes, rentals, and so on. Variable costs fluctuate in direct proportion to product output or sales volume.

Typical examples include direct labour, material, maintenance, utilities, supplies, and so on. Semi-variable expenses may vary with production output but not in the same relative proportion; in other words, their increases are periodic or 'stepped' with volume.

Volume, representing the rate of activity, is measured in terms of production or sales units or pounds, direct labour hours or pounds, machine hours, weight, and so on. Product unit measures are probably more significant than monetary ones because they do not reflect the effect of changes in price and wage levels. For purposes of management presentation, however, unit volumes should be converted to pounds, which are more readily interpreted and understood.

The basic considerations in constructing the variable budget include the following.

- Generally, use at least five volume levels, with the range from 40 per cent to 100 per cent of plant capacity.
- For each account and selected volume level, develop budgeted expenses by cost centre and department – both production and service.
- Express the data in terms of the number of employees (as applicable) and of pounds by time period.
- The budget reflects the best judgement and experience of the individual supervisors and their management.
- Develop scattergraphs for each expense item that illustrates the principle of segregating fixed and variable expenses.

Model 9.3 illustrates a variable budget scattergraph chart for operating supplies. The horizontal line at the bottom of the chart represents units of production, and the vertical scale indicates the weekly expense allowance. The plotted points reflect the budgeted expense for the various volume levels. A trend line is drawn so that it either passes through the points or as close as possible to them, since it represents the median of the various points. At the intersection of the diagonal line on the left vertical axis, the point represents the fixed expense value, which is £875 in this case.

Establishing the ratio of variable expenses to production volume

Calculate the variable expenses by means of the following equation:

$$\text{Variable expense} = \frac{\text{Total expense allowance} - \text{Allowed fixed expense}}{\text{Production volume}}$$

EXAMPLE

$$
\begin{aligned}
\text{Variable expense} &= \frac{£2000 - £875}{9000} \\[2mm]
&= \frac{£1125}{9000} \\[2mm]
&= £0.125
\end{aligned}
$$

MODEL 9.3. Variable budget scattergraph chart: production department

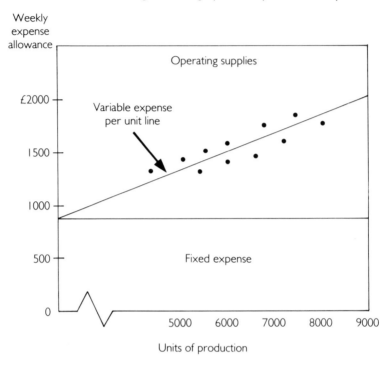

Units of production

Assessing the profitgraph technique

While break-even analysis displays the profit–volume relationship based on the segregation of fixed and variable expenses, the profitgraph presents a broader view of the business. To obtain more comprehensive information for management decisions, the technique makes use of both the break-even and investment analyses. These data relate primarily to profit measurements, such as gross margin, net profit, and return on investment. The profitgraph provides not only the sales break-even and the profit at any level of capacity, but also the trend patterns of gross margin, net profit, and return on investment *ratios* under a given set of conditions.

Model 9.4 summarizes the profitgraph principles. The terminology is commonly used in the accounting profession.

Analysing cost and operating income

Model 9.5 provides an overview of a profit and loss account to the point of gross margin from operations and its ratio to sales revenue. The statement is segregated into four volume levels (or capacities) – 40 per cent, 60 per cent, 80 per cent and 100 per cent. Pound values are shown for the various elements plus the estimated number

MODEL 9.4. Fundamentals of profitgraph analysis

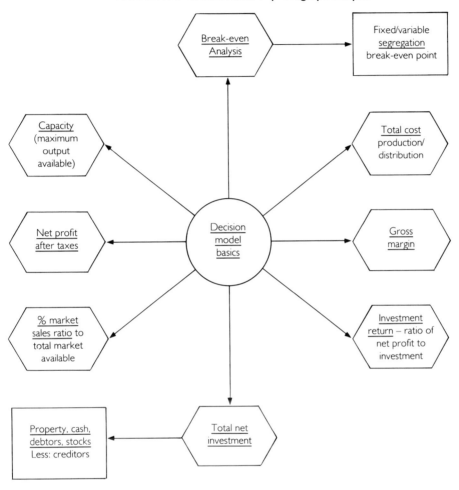

of employees (as applicable) for direct labour activities and indirect support based on volume levels. In a more detailed analysis, the overhead expenses are typically arranged by individual accounts and their associated headcounts. This information serves as a comparative control tool in analysing and planning performance results.

The expense information in Model 9.5 is similar to that in a break-even analysis except that it is segregated into fixed and variable costs. Under the variable caption are also reported the direct labour and material values representing percentages of *x* pounds of sales revenue. The fixed and variable costs of sales are developed for the break-even analysis presentation.

The *ratios* of gross profit to sales range from 6% at 40 per cent volume to 20% at the 100 per cent level. The principal cause for the increased gross profit

MODEL 9.5. Sales, cost of sales, and profit analysis at varying volume levels

(in £000s)

Profit statement data	Volume levels – % capacity							
	40%		60%		80%		100%	
	value	employed	value	employed	value	employed	value	employed
Net sales	20,000	—	30,000	—	40,000	—	50,000	—
Cost of sales								
Direct labour	4,700	313	6,900	445	9,000	560	11,200	710
Overhead*	7,500	234	11,200	290	14,400	360	17,600	440
Direct material/ODC	6,600	—	8,600	—	10,200	—	11,200	—
Totals	18,800	547	26,700	735	33,600	920	40,000	1150
Gross profit	1,200	—	3,300	—	6,400	—	10,000	—
Ratio to sales	6.0%		11.0%		16.0%		20.0%	

*As required, expense data can be developed by individual major expense account (segregated, fixed and variable) using the scattergraph technique. These overhead costs do not include distribution and administration.

is a *250* per cent higher sales volume at the 100 per cent capacity versus the 40 per cent level, whereas cost of sales increased by only *222* per cent.

Assessing investments

At this point in developing the profitgraph, you have to assess net investment. To do so, consolidate the gross current assets (including short-term marketable securities if existent) with the gross fixed assets to obtain a total as shown in Model 9.6. From this total, deduct the provision for doubtful debts and fixed assets (depreciation). Some organizations may have other provisions in this presentation. Combine short-term liabilities, such as creditors, with the provisions; this total represents a reduction to gross investment. The result is net investment by the categorized sales volumes.

> *EXAMPLE*
> Note, in Model 9.6, that *net* investment is estimated to increase by 35 per cent in the 50 million sales volume level, as compared to the £20 million level. This is due to an anticipated 31 per cent higher *gross* investment, which results from a greater current asset value with only a 17 per cent increase in reserves.

Net investment may be computed in other ways depending on an organization's policies and procedures, for example, total net assets less current liabilities equals owners' equity and creditor investment. In this case, long-term debt is recognized as a *creditor* investment.

Summarizing profitgraph data

Model 9.7 provides a summary of sales volume levels and net profit plus the *ratio* of net profit to net investment. The ratios range from 0.9 per cent at the £20 million sales volume level to 25.4 per cent at the £50 million level. The primary cause for the dramatic increase in the ratio is the rise in net profit from £100,000 to £3.75 million at the £50 million sales volume level. On the other hand, net investment is only 35 per cent greater at the £50 million volume.

Although not shown in the model, summary data are highly desirable in a profitgraph chart. They should display the break-even analysis (cost and sales lines) and a percentage scale on the *right vertical axis*, which indicates the percentage of return on net investment as well as the gross margin return on sales. The summary graphic numeric display in Model 9.7 provides an immediate visual view of the profit situation in relation to sales volume levels, associated cost and profit, as well as the return on investment.

How to apply the profitgraph

The profitgraph helps management to assess its planning actions/decisions relative to anticipated profits and performances at varying sales volume levels. This type of aid

MODEL 9.6. Capital investment assessment (profitgraph)

(in £000s)

Item description	Sales volume levels			
	20,000	*30,000*	*40,000*	*50,000*
Gross fixed assets	10,000	10,000	10,000	10,000
Current assets				
Stocks	1,070	1,300	1,500	1,600
Debtors	1,660	2,400	3,200	4,000
Cash	1,300	1,600	2,200	2,800
Subtotal	4,030	5,300	6,900	8,400
Total gross investment	14,030	15,300	16,900	18,400
Ratio to sales volume	0.715	0.510	0.423	0.368
Gross profit/gross investment	0.085	0.216	0.379	0.543
Provisions				
Bad debts	160	180	230	240
Depreciation	2,500	2,500	2,500	2,500
Subtotal	2,660	2,680	2,730	2,740
Creditors	430	600	720	870
Total reductions	3,090	3,280	3,450	3,610
Net investment	10,940	12,020	13,450	14,790
Ratio to sales volume	0.547	0.401	0.336	0.295
Gross profit/net investment*	0.110	0.275	0.476	0.676

*Pound values of gross profit are shown in Model 9.5.

is extremely important in achieving profit objectives, in attracting equity investments, and in providing a reasonable return on the investors' capital. Further, a sound profit position aids the organization in obtaining financial institution loans at favourable rates and in generating good working relationships with the current and anticipated creditors.

Applications
The profitgraph technique can be used in a number of ways. Some of the common areas of usage include:

- product line/product mix assessments;
- performance measurement;
- establishment or verification of pricing policies;
- facility expansion/modernization decisions.

MODEL 9.7. Profitgraph data summary

(in £000s)

Income statement	Values	% sales	Values	% sales	Values	% sales	Values	% sales
Sales volumes	20,000	100.0	30,000	100.0	40,000	100.0	50,000	100.0
Cost of sales	18,800	94.0	26,700	89.0	33,600	84.0	40,000	80.0
Gross profit	1,200	6.0	3,300	11.0	6,400	16.0	10,000	20.0
Less: D&A	1,000	5.0	1,500	5.0	2,000	5.0	2,500	5.0
Pretax profit	200	1.0	1,800	6.0	4,400	11.0	7,500	15.0
Less: Provision for taxes	100	0.5	900	3.0	2,200	5.5	3,750	7.5
Net profit	100	0.5	900	3.0	2,200	5.5	3,750	7.5
Net investment	10,940	54.7	12,020	40.1	13,450	33.6	14,790	29.6
Total costs (excluding taxes)	19,800	—	28,200	—	35,600	—	42,500	—
Ratio: Net profit to investment	0.9%		7.5%		16.4%		25.4%	
Total costs to investment	1.81%		2.35%		2.65%		2.87%	

Product line mix contribution. Profits must be measured by product line to 'weed out' the current or potential non-contributors so that you can concentrate on more promising or potential profit-makers. In reality, each product line is a separate entity. Supervision has direct responsibility for its profitability. Product line managers are generally notified in advance of the amounts to be charged against their products for the operation of each service section. The data are expressed in terms of fixed costs per week and of variable costs per output unit. This procedure may vary among organizations. Having knowledge of their activity units and requirements, supervisors can then approximate what their charges will be for service expenses (power, maintenance, production, and the like). Service expenses are often allocated on an accepted and equitable basis, such as direct labour hours, machine time, percentage of occupancy, number of personnel, units produced, and so on.

Scattergraph charts based on historical experience and break-even analysis play an important role in determining fixed and variable costs by direct element and expense account. Segregating the investment data by product line may require some arbitrary decisions and judgements, but there are some key considerations. Space occupied and property possession dictate fixed asset allocation. Material purchases and usage can be the keys to stock levels. Sales volume is a major consideration in debtors, and estimated cost expenditures are a basis for projecting creditors.

Profitgraphs have proven to be, in some organizations, most effective at the product line and productive cost centre levels. Similar product line profitgraphs for the total organization would be developed for the individual product line. A final plant summary from the detailed data would highlight specific overall problem areas and their causes.

Performance measurement. By segregating costs into finite detail such as labour (productive, setup, support), you gain an immediate insight as to variances in actual performance versus projected goals. Direct material basically follows units of production – planned versus actual. Variable expense deviations can indicate either inefficiencies or improvement on budgeted cost. Measuring performance and establishing controls in any operational area are essential in monitoring and evaluating an organization's progress. The profitgraph is a suitable procedure.

Decision making for pricing. Pricing policy decisions are never-ending, and the effect on the profit picture is inevitable. Management often faces the problem of deciding on appropriate product pricing. Their decisions can have either short- or long-range consequences. Long range, the question arises as to the alternatives for correcting the situation. Should they eliminate the product line, increase the sales price, reduce costs, seek new markets, accept less margin, or what? In introducing a new product, what is an acceptable customer sales price, while maintaining a reasonable profit margin? Suppose the product demand is greater than the productive capacity – or vice versa – what is the decision?

Applications

The profitgraph technique may provide a suitable answer. At least, it might assist management in evaluating the problem and possibly in assessing alternative courses of action.

Facility expansion/modernization. Another major decision facing management is whether to expand the facilities and/or modernize the plant in terms of automation and acquisition of highly advanced machinery/equipment. This action can be highly expensive, affecting profitability, and may not lead to the results anticipated. Before the decision is made, you should carry out investment-appraisal studies to ascertain the advantages and disadvantages, including the impact on the financial position.

What the profitgraph can do for you

Profitgraphs help you to assess and project varied profit patterns given alternative courses of management action. Variable profit factors result from changing sales volume and costs. The break-even point is influenced, as well as the return on investment. The anticipated savings in variable costs from facility expansion and/or modernization may, however, be more than offset by added fixed costs and investment. The profitgraph technique is a reasonable approach to determining potential results from a changing operational environment. It is an aid to management in making decisions before committing resources.

Making assessments by means of the capitalgraph technique

The capitalgraph technique assumes that fluctuations in sales volume influence current assets and liabilities, which, in turn, have an impact on working and operating capital. In this discussion, *operating capital* represents the combined working capital and net fixed assets. Basically, increases or decreases in sales volume result in higher or lower debtors, stocks, and cash balance requirements. Current liabilities are influenced because large cost commitments (labour, material, overhead, taxes payable, and the like) are involved in producing products or performing necessary services. Capital assets, in the form of expanded facilities or new machinery, may be necessary to support operations.

How to construct the capitalgraph model

Like the development of most analytical and planning models, the capitalgraph technique assumes that the data derived from historical experience are relevant to the current and future operating environment. In some instances, determining relevance may be difficult because of the constantly changing economic and business climate and/or rapidly moving events in the organization itself (such as accelerated sales volume growth, plant expansion or acquisition, increased manpower and costs, or possibly a reduction in operational activity). A realistic assessment of current and anticipated events is the key requisite for adopting and using the results from historical data analysis and interpretation.

The capitalgraph procedure includes the following steps:

1. Determine the relationship between sales (the independent variable) and other dependent variables (such as major current asset and liability elements). For this purpose, the regression analysis technique is employed.
2. Use scattergraphs to plot asset and liability balances by sales volume levels. (This is a common statistical process.) One or two years of monthly data should be represented in the graph depending on their particular relevance at a given point in time. Some organizations may find that monthly annualized sales are appropriate, and others may use monthly sales results. Annualized sales generally provide a smoother curve line than monthly sales.
3. Upon completion of the plotting, draw a regression line to represent the median location of all the plotted points. In developing the formula, eliminate points located in extreme locations, due to unusual circumstances, to avoid their influences on the data relationships.
4. Model 9.8 illustrates the scattergraph plotting for current assets, current liabiities and net fixed assets. Ordinarily, each major asset and liability element is plotted against sales, but for illustration and brevity only the totals were used in this model.
5. The following capitalgraph relationships were developed based on the least squares equations:

(1) $Y = Na + b\Sigma X$ (*Y* represents current assets, current liabilities and net fixed assets in Model 9.8)

(2) $XY = a\Sigma X + b\Sigma X^2$ (*X* represents sales volume)

Figure 1. *Current asset relationship to sales*

Developed formula: $Y = £203 + 0.257X$
Regression line locations:

Point *A*:	£203 + 0.257 × £36	Point *B*:	£203 + 0.257 × £45
A =	203 + 9 = 212	*B* =	203 + 12 = 215

To locate the slope of the regression line, Points A and B were calculated as shown; £36 million sales were used for Point A and £45 million for Point B. The results are shown above.

Figure 2. *Current liabilities relationship to sales*

Developed formula: $Y = £129.8 + 0.09X$
Regression line locations:

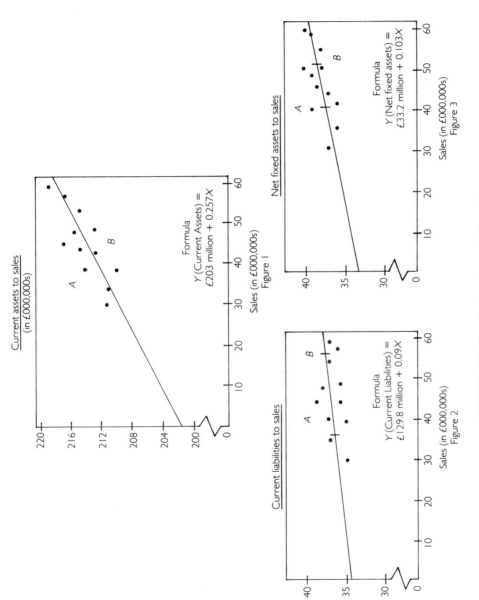

MODEL 9.8. Developing the capitalgraph

Point *A*:   £129.8 + 0.09 × £40   Point *B*:   £129.8 + 0.09 × £55
        A =   129.8 + 3.6 = 133.4   *B* =   129.8 + 5.0 = 134.8

The regression line was drawn as shown in Model 9.8 for sales volumes of £40 and £55 million.

Figure 3. *Net fixed assets relationship to sales*

Developed formula: $Y = £33.2 + 0.103X$
Regression line locations:
    Point *A*:   £33.2 + 0.103 × £40   Point *B*:   £33.2 + 0.103 × £50
        A =   33.2 + 4 = 37.2   *B* =   33.2 + 5.1 = 38.3

The regression trend line is displayed in Model 9.8.
        Develop points *A* and *B* as shown above. Based on the sales values, locations of points *A* and *B* were established as shown in Model 9.8.

Putting the capitalgraph method to work

The capitalgraph approach may be applied as follows:

1. It helps you rapidly to assess operating capital trends pertinent to current assets and liabilities, as well as net fixed assets based on past fluctuations in sales volume. The main assumption is that you may expect historical results to continue. If judgement and plans indicate major changes or deviations from the past, then you must revise the trend equations accordingly.
2. You can estimate the individual balances for current assets and liabilities based on projected sales volumes, at least on a preliminary basis, until more conventional and detailed planning method results are available. The process can also be used at the summary level for current assets, liabilities, and net fixed assets.
3. It gives you a modelling capability. You can assess 'what if' possibilities under varying sales volume projections to determine the effect on balance sheet items and to verify the reasonableness of the planning process objectives.
4. The correlation approach under the least squares method is simple to apply on an automated basis, and, further, it can be updated periodically as new actuals become available. The data can be readily manipulated to reflect any anticipated events not characterized by past actuals.
5. The working capital can be selectively calculated and assessed in terms of past and future requirements without detailed calculations. It can then be tested for reasonableness.

A practical application

EXAMPLE

Based on the relationship equations developed above, the following illustration is provided in connection with the projection process at varying sales volumes.

	Capitalgraph projection process				
	Developed average factors		*Monthly sales projections		
Summary balances	*Fixed	Variable	£45.0	£55.0	£65.0
Current assets	£203.0	0.257	†£214.6	£217.1	£219.7
Current liabilities	129.8	0.090	133.9	134.8	135.8
Working capital	£ 73.2	0.167	£ 80.7	£ 82.3	£ 83.9
Net fixed assets	33.2	0.103	37.8	38.9	39.9
Operating capital	£106.4	0.270	£118.5	£121.2	£123.8
Ratio current assets to current liabilities	1.56	—	1.60	1.61	1.62

*Millions of pounds.

†Equation calculations: £203 million + 0.257 (£45 million sales); £203 + £11.6 = £214.6 million

This example demonstrates the use of the capitalgraph to project summary balance sheet items at *three* varying sales volumes. This technique provides management with a tool to simulate anticipated balance sheet results using estimated sales volume levels and factors developed from historical experience.

Understanding the least squares correlation

The least squares procedure establishes a most probable relationship between two sets of variables based on historical experience. The x (horizontal) axis represents the independent variable, and the y (vertical) axis signifies the dependent variable. The primary assumption is that, if past conditions caused a particular *relationship or ratio* between or among variables, then similar conditions will create the same relationships in the future. The premise is that the relationships have been tested and verified.

Using the correlation method

Mathematical measures of correlation are proof only of covariation among two or more variables, not of functional or causal relationships. The scattergraph itself provides only a visual indication of the type and degree of association among variables. The basic concepts in correlation analyses are the regression line, the standard error of estimate, and the coefficient of correlation. You must exercise judgement in the use of the correlation technique as an absolute and valid means of making estimates or projections.

Historical experience has proved a definite relationship between:

- direct labour hour activity and overhead expenses;
- production and materials usage;
- sales volume and costs;
- sales/costs and net profit;
- sales/production and current assets and liabilities, and so on.

The least squares approach verifies the validity of the relationship among variable sets of data. Only adequate investigation can ensure that the results of this procedure can be used for measuring performance and planning future objectives.

10 Employing ratios to assess investments

Chapter highlights

This chapter looks at investment analysis from the standpoint of both the investor and the organization. First, capital structure is defined and its importance highlighted.

The following types of ratios are explained and demonstrated:

- *Debenture measurement ratios* – times interest charges earned, working capital to loan capital, fixed assets to loan capital.
- *Preference share measurements* – earnings per share and times preference dividend earned.
- *Ordinary share measurements* – earnings per share, price–earnings ratio, market to book value ratio, and so on.

The various aspects of dividend yield are described and its significance explained.

The important subject of increasing equity capital is presented, particularly with respect to the use of gearing. Subsidiary or supplemental gearing ratios are described in terms of source of funds and borrowing constraints, with the focus on liquidity ratios.

Finally, the use of discriminant analysis as a predictor of company failure is presented.

Defining capital structure

The term 'capital structure' may have different connotations to various users. Organizational accountants and analysts generally use the term 'capital' to identify the organization's proprietary/ownership equity. Investment analysts, concerned with a broader aspect of the capital structure, consider not only the owners' equity but also the long-term creditors' investment in the form of debentures or unsecured loans to financial institutions. In some instances, even current liabilities may be included.

In the following discussion, the term *capital structure* encompasses the total book value of all shares and loan capital, retained earnings, and other additions to the outstanding capital. Thus, the data and its relative assessment include the total equity investment of both the shareholders and long-term creditors.

Gauging the effect of the relative investment

The relative equity position of the shareholders (ordinary and preference) and loanholders is of major concern to the investment analyst. As the investment in loans becomes larger in proportion to that in shares, the shareholders' position becomes weaker due to the greater prior claims of the loanholders. Further, the position of the loanholders becomes less attractive because of the smaller margin of safety provided by the shareholders' investment. Generally, the capital structure of a business enterprise becomes unsatisfactory – or possibly even detrimental – at high proportions of debt to the total investment.

EXAMPLE

Three types of securities are proportioned as follows:

	Capital structure (£)	
Preference shares	600,000	23.1%
Ordinary shares and retained earnings	1,600,000	61.5
Bonds/long-term loans	400,000	15.4
Totals	2,600,000	100.0%

These proportions indicate that 84.6 per cent of the capital structure is contributed by the shareholders (ordinary and preference), whereas only 15.4 per cent is provided by the loanholders. In assessing the pound value contributions, note that the shareholders' equity provides £5.50 (£2,200,000 ÷ 400,000) for each pound by the loanholders.

Another variation of the contribution measure is to *price the shares at market value*. This reveals the extent to which the loan commitments are covered by the shareholders' equity on the basis of the investing public's opinion of the prevailing share values.

EXAMPLE

Based on share pricing at the annual average market quotation, the capital structure is as follows:

	Revised capital structure (£)	
Preference shares *at market prices*	540,000	27.3%
Ordinary shares and retained earnings	1,040,000	52.5
Bonds/long-term loans	400,000	20.2
Totals	1,980,000	100.0%

On this basis, the shareholders contributed £3.95 (£1,580,000 ÷ 400,000) for each pound provided by the loanholders, which is 28.2 per cent ((5.50 – 3.95)/5.50) less than the £5.50 calculated in the prior example. This difference can be of significance in the investment assessment.

Considerations in earnings per share assessment

Earnings or loss per ordinary share are commonly shown in the profit and loss statement by a number of organizations. The calculation is made on the basis of profit after tax *before* extraordinary items.

In the simplified capital structure, earnings per share are reported on outstanding ordinary shares or equivalent type of securities. If a company has securities that may rank for dividends in future, for example convertibles, warrants or options, then these may be taken into account to produce 'fully diluted earnings per share'. Financial standards require companies to show fully diluted eps if dilution reduces the basic eps by 5 per cent or more.

The rate of return on owners' capital can be obtained based on year-end data or using weighted averages during the year. In the latter process, data distortions are minimized in ratio results and assessment. It further provides the means to isolate specific changes and causes.

Putting loan measurement ratios to work

In analysing the safety of a loan investment, you must determine the asset protection of the principal, if secured, as well as the stability and adequacy of the organization's earnings to meet the loan interest payment schedule.

Four types of ratio analyses are common in the measurement process:

1. times interest charges earned;
2. ratio of working capital to loan capital;
3. ratio of fixed assets to loan capital;
4. disposition of loanholders' investment.

Calculating times interest charges earned

How adequately do earnings compare with the payment of loan interest? To answer this, determine the number of times the interest charges have been earned.

EXAMPLE

	£
Pretax profit before loan interest	200,000
Less: Loan interest	18,000
Pretax profit after interest	182,000
Less: Provision for taxes (50%)	91,000
Net profit	91,000

By dividing the pretax profit before interest (£200,000) by the loan interest (£18,000), you determine that the loan interest was earned 11.1 times. This factor is generally considered to be more than adequate to meet loan interest payments.

Calculating the ratio of working capital to loans

In this approach, you determine whether sufficient liquid capital is being maintained to meet loan (long-term debt) obligations. The ratio of working capital to loans indicates the information required.

EXAMPLE

Loans   £180,000
Working capital   £270,000

If you divide the working capital by the loans, you get the computed ratio of 150 per cent. This ratio indicates that there is £1.50 of liquid capital for each pound of loan capital, which is generally considered to be adequate.

Calculating the ratio of fixed assets to loans

Comparison of the loans with the fixed assets indicates the general degree of protection for the loanholders' investment, providing the loanholder has priority claims on the assets. To assess the results of this comparison, compute the ratio of fixed assets to loans.

EXAMPLE

Loans   £180,000
Fixed assets   £900,000

The resultant ratio is 500 per cent (£900,000 ÷ £180,000). The ratio indicates that, for every pound of loans, there is £5.00 in book value of fixed assets (tangible property, plant, and equipment). Historical experience and comparative industry averages would reveal the adequacy of this ratio.

Measuring the disposition of the loanholder's investment

An alternative approach in the analysis of the loan position is the measurement of the disposition of the loanholder's investment in the organization.

EXAMPLE

Distribution of the investment (£)			
Current assets	150,000	Current liabilities	80,000
Non-current assets	900,000	Long-term liabilities	180,000
		Equity capital	790,000
Totals	1,050,000		1,050,000

Another method for measuring the disposition relationship is to compare current assets with total liabilities. In this case, compare current assets of £150,000 to total liabilities of £260,000, with the difference of £110,000 being invested in non-current assets.

Other considerations

In addition to these data comparisons, the analyst or investor must consider other pertinent facts, such as the very important maturity date of the loans. If the redemption date is near, then a greater degree of liquidity is required.

Working with preference share measurements

Computing earnings per share

The earnings on preference shares are commonly expressed on a per-share basis. To obtain the data, divide the net profit by the number of shares outstanding.

EXAMPLE

Earnings per share (£)

Income before debenture interest	400,000
Less: Debenture interest	50,000
Pretax profit	350,000
Less: Provision for taxation (50%)	175,000
Net profit	175,000

The net earnings after taxes are calculated to be £35/share (£175,000 ÷ 5000 shares).

Calculating times preference dividend earned

Earnings per share does not consider the margin between earnings per share and the dividend requirement. The amount of the dividend has a decided influence on the *times earned factor*: the larger the margin, the greater the ordinary share equity. The situation results in a strong preference share position. A meaningful measure of preference share earnings would be the number of times the preference share dividend has been earned.

EXAMPLE

The preference share dividend is £5.00 per share, and there are 5000 shares outstanding. The dividend requirement is therefore £25,000 (5000 shares × £5.00). Dividing the net profit of, say, £175,000 by £25,000 shows that the preference dividend has been earned seven times.

Comparing times debenture interest and preference dividend earned

The times preference dividend earned is adequate if no debentures (long-term creditor debt) are outstanding. If debentures are outstanding, as in the prior example, the debenture interest represents a fixed lien on the income prior to that of the preference shares dividend. Investment analysts therefore compute the number of times the preference dividend has been earned on an aggregate basis.

To make the calculation, combine the debenture interest and the preference dividend. Then compute the number of times the *total of the two* has been earned.

> *EXAMPLE*
> Using the data from the previous example, divide the net income of £175,000 by £75,000 (£50,000 debenture interest plus £25,000). The result is 2.3 times.

Employing ordinary share measurements

To obtain the book value of an ordinary share with no preference shares outstanding, divide the total equity capital by the number of shares outstanding. The equity per share includes retained earnings and any other additions to capital. If preference shares are outstanding, deduct their value from the total owners' equity before dividing by the number of ordinary shares outstanding.

Computing earnings per share

Ordinary earnings per share is generally the most important single ratio for the investor. It is used by the investor to appraise the market price of the shares. To derive it, divide the net profit available for the ordinary shares by the number of shares outstanding.

> *EXAMPLE*
> If the available net income is £300,000 and 40,000 shares are outstanding, the earnings are £7.50 per share.

Computing price–earnings (P–E) ratio

To calculate the price–earnings ratio, divide the average market or selling price of the share by its earnings.

> *EXAMPLE*
> The market price of the share is £50.00, and the earnings per share are £5.00. The price–earnings ratio is therefore 10 to 1. If the ratio is inverted, it then represents the *earnings yield*, the rate at which the stock market is capitalizing the value of the earnings. Here are the two calculations:
>
> $$\frac{\text{Market price}}{\text{Earnings}} = \frac{50.00}{5.00} = 10 \text{ P–E}$$
>
> $$\frac{\text{Earnings per share}}{\text{Market price per share}} = \frac{5.00}{50.00} = 10\% \text{ earnings yield}$$

Influences on the P–E ratio

The price–earnings ratio is strongly influenced by how rapidly the organization is growing, the inherent operating risks, its financial stability, and its policy with respect to retained earnings. Increases in financial risks generally cause a downward trend in the price–earnings ratio; anticipated earnings have the opposite effect. To gauge the integrity and reasonableness of the price–earnings ratio, compare it to those of similar organizations and industry averages.

Applications

The ratio is also used to come up with a realistic value of an organization's ordinary shares. To do so, estimate the earnings per share for a given time period and the ratio that the investors will pay for the organization's earnings. Then multiply the price–earnings ratio by the earnings per share. The result represents a projected estimate of the ordinary share value. Based on this information an investor can judge whether to buy or sell off certain stocks.

Computing the ratio of market to book value

Another ratio sometimes employed to assess the risk in investing in an organization's ordinary shares is *market versus book value*. To calculate this ratio, divide the market price per share by the book value per share.

To obtain the book value, as already indicated, divide the owners' equity (excluding preference shares) by the number of ordinary shares outstanding.

EXAMPLE

Market price   £25.00/share
Book value   £20.00/share

$$\frac{£25.00}{£20.00} = 1.25 \ ratio$$

The 1.25 ratio indicates that the market price is greater than the organization's book value. This ratio represents an investment risk factor, particularly if the ratio becomes much greater than 1. Conversely, if the book value is substantially greater than the market price, then the stock is considered to be underpriced. The organization could come under scrutiny as a possible acquisition by other interested investing organizations.

Calculating the dividend return ratio

The *yield* of an ordinary share investment is the ratio of the dividend declared to the stock's market price.

EXAMPLE
If the market price is quoted at £25.00 per share and the grossed up dividend rate is £2.00, the yield ratio is 8 per cent.

Note that the *dividend yield* represents the actual gross current rate of return being earned by the shareholder on the investment.

The dividend yield differs from the rate of dividend declared in that the latter ratio represents the total gross dividend as a percentage of the value of the ordinary shares. However, when the market price per share equals the book value, then the dividend yield and dividend rate are equal; otherwise, the dividend rate is of minor importance.

Things to remember about the dividend yield

Here are some points about the dividend yield to keep in mind:

- The dividend yield result depends on the earnings yield (net profit divided by the market value of the ordinary shares). The advantage of using price–earnings ratios is that they represent an accepted measure of ordinary share results. Further, P–E ratios are commonly quoted in trade/financial publications (such as *Extel cards, Investor's Chronicle, Financial Times*).

- The equity earnings per share ratio is influenced by the net profit on owners' capital ratio. It is also affected by the net asset value per share ratio, which is derived by dividing the book value of the net assets by the number of shares outstanding.

- To a degree, the magnitude of the asset value per share provides a lower limit for the market price. If the asset value drops significantly below the market price, then the stock's marketability may be jeopardized. If the asset value measurably exceeds the market price, then its marketability is enhanced considerably and the organization may be subject to takeover attempts. If the assets are orientated to a specific use, the asset value provides very limited protection to the market price.

- The magnitude of an organization's net profit to owners' equity ratio poses such questions as:

    If the net profit on capital is extremely high, can it be maintained?

    Is the size of the net profit due to successful management, sole source product, or lack of competition?

    If the net profit on owners' equity decreases significantly, what are the consequences on market price and on the organization's financial stability? Will conditions improve on mediocre profitability or further deteriorate, with its ultimate effect on an organization's survival?

What to consider when increasing equity capital

Other than shareholders' investment, a primary source of capital acquisition is to increase the rate of return on the capital available.

EXAMPLE

An organization borrows funds that cost x per cent in interest and invests these funds in assets that yield y per cent. If the y per cent yield is greater than the x per cent cost, then the difference represents pure gain to the equity shareholder. This process is known as *gearing*.

Advantage

There is another advantage to the use of gearing. Although profits and asset values tend to increase in a period of inflation, the repayment liability on borrowed capital is fixed in money terms. So, in actual or real terms the borrowed capital represents a decreasing liability.

Risks

This type of activity entails inherent risks, particularly if the rate of interest paid increases and/or the rate of profit decreases. For example, if the interest rate paid is greater than the income earned, the difference represents a loss to the equity holder.

Disadvantage

Another possible disadvantage of *gearing* is that it magnifies any change in the asset profitability to the extent that the return on equity capital fluctuates more widely than the return on the assets.

EXAMPLE

Gearing ratios (£)		
	19X3	*19X4*
Profit/loss accounts		
Asset profitability	300	200
Interest on borrowed capital	(72)	(72)
Net profit	228	128
Balance sheet account		
Equity capital	1000	1000
Loan capital	1000	1000
Total capital and assets	2000	2000
Ratios		
Profit to total assets	0.15	0.10
Interest to loan capital	0.072	0.072
Profit to equity capital	0.228	0.128
Borrowed capital to equity capital	1	1

The ratio of profit to assets decreased by $(0.15 - 0.10)/0.15 = 33.3\%$. This decrease resulted in a decrease in return on equity of $(0.228 - 0.128)/0.228 = 43.9\%$. Note that the return to the equity shareholder for the two years is greater than it would have been if the organization had not financed part of its assets with borrowed capital. Debt, therefore, is used as a gearing to increase the owners' rate of return.

Calculating ordinary share gearing

Let us see how the *gearing of ordinary shares* is computed when the capital structure includes debentures and preference shares.

> *EXAMPLE*
>
> 1. £3,000,000 in 8% debentures.
> 2. £2,000,000 in £100 par value 6% preference shares.
> 3. 400,000 ordinary shares issued at £7 per share.

Capital structure		Ordinary share gearing
Debentures	3,000,000	$\dfrac{5,000,000}{2,800,000} = 1.79$ gearing
Preference shares	2,000,000	
Ordinary shares	2,800,000	
Total	£7,800,000	

The resultant gearing factor indicates that, for each pound invested by the ordinary shareholder, the debenture creditors and preference shareholders have invested £1.79. There is a heavy drain on the profit for debenture interest, and the claims of the preference shares take precedence over dividends available for the ordinary shares.

In successful trading periods (booms) this may be satisfactory as the return to ordinary shareholders may be high. However in recessions, falling margins and high interest could mean the return to shareholders is greatly reduced and may even threaten the dividend.

Computing earnings per share

Refer to the previous example and further assume £1 million earnings before deducting the debenture interest. The available amount for the ordinary shareholders is calculated as follows:

> *EXAMPLE*

Earnings per share (£)	
Income before interest	1,000,000
Less: Debenture interest (3 million × 8%)	240,000
Profit before taxation	760,000
Less: Corporation tax	380,000
Net profit	380,000
Less: Preference dividend needs (2 million × 6%)	120,000
Available net profit for ordinary shareholders	260,000
Earnings per share (400,000 shares)	0.65

Note that, to achieve a more conservative position in determining the available net profit for ordinary shares, investment analysts may include overdraft in the gearing calculations. In this situation, you must recognize the current creditors' claims against the assets.

Determining the actual cost of interest payments

The true cost of interest to an organization reflects the influence of the following factors:

1. a decrease in taxation if interest is an allowable deduction;
2. less the inflation trend factors;
3. issue expenses.

EXAMPLE
The assumptions are as follows:

    1. 8% debenture, par value £100.
    2. Provision for taxes, 50%.
    3. Inflation, 10%.
    4. Issue expenses, 2%.

Calculations:

1. To pay the 8% on the issued debentures, earnings must be:

$$\frac{8\% \times 100}{100\% - 2\%} = \frac{8}{98\%} = 8.16\%$$
$$\text{for issue expenses}$$

2. Allowance deduction for taxes:

$$8.16\% \times (100 - 50\%) = 4.08\% \text{ in pounds}$$

3. The cost of inflation to the organization is 10%:

$$\frac{100\% + 4.08\%}{110\%} = 94.6\% - 100\% \text{ or } -5.4\% \text{ in real terms}$$

Compare the interest rate with the return on the project only after making allowances for the effect on costs of both taxation and inflation *plus* debenture issue expenses. Since corporation tax, inflation, and issue expenses affect different sources of financing in varying degrees, use the real cost of raising funds in relevant management decisions and in planning activities.

Assessing the basic gearing ratios

Four basic ratios are generally associated with the gearing assessment:

$$A: \textit{Pretax profit to owners' equity} = \frac{\text{Pretax profit}}{\text{Equity capital}}$$

$$B: \textit{Asset profitability to total capital} = \frac{\text{Asset profitability}}{\text{Total capital}}$$

$$C: \textit{Interest paid to borrowed capital} = \frac{\text{Interest paid}}{\text{Borrowed capital}}$$

$$D: \textit{Gearing of borrowed capital to equity} = \frac{\text{Borrowed capital}}{\text{Equity capital}}$$

Calculate the pretax profit to owners' (equity) capital ratio as follows, using the above alphabetic designations:

$$A = B + (B - C) \times D$$

EXAMPLE

Assume the following calculated ratio data:

	19X3	19X4
B. Profit to equity (total assets)	15.0%	10.0%
C. Interest to borrowed capital	7.2%	7.2%
A. Pretax profit to equity capital	22.8%	12.8%

Using the formula:

19X3	19X4
$A = 15\% + (15\% - 7.2\%) \times 1$	$A = 10\% + (10\% - 7.2\%) \times 1$
$A = 22.8\% \times 1 = 22.8\%$	$A = 12.8\% \times 1 = 12.8\%$

The analysis indicates the results of reduced profits in 19X4 with the total equity capital remaining constant. When involved in gearing, you must consider the long-term movements of interest rates and their anticipated effect on an organization's financial stability and ability to meet its debt obligations.

Using subsidiary gearing ratios

In addition to gearing analysis, give some consideration to important subsidiary ratios. The two major category ratios to be considered are:

1. primary source of funds;
2. borrowing constraints.

Primary source of funds. Excluding shareholders' investment and retained earnings, the primary source of funds consists of debentures and bank loans. Other sources are less significant. In addition to the sources of borrowed capital, examine the rate of interest paid to each type of lender, to determine which capital source has the greatest or lowest rate of interest. Since the objective of management should be to borrow capital at minimal cost, it definitely has an interest in this comparison.

The formulae are as follows:

$$\text{Percentage ratio} = \text{a.} \ \frac{\text{Debenture interest}}{\text{Value of the debentures}}$$

$$\text{b.} \ \frac{\text{Interest on the bank loans}}{\text{Averaged value of the loans}}$$

Borrowed capital constraint ratios. These ratios enable you to measure the factors governing the amount of capital that can be borrowed. Potential investors and lenders use these ratios to assess an organization's financial strength. The ratios are:

1. asset coverage;
2. interest coverage;
3. liquidity factors.

1. To derive the *asset coverage ratio*, divide the total assets by the amount of borrowed capital. This ratio indicates the safety of the lender's capital – both the investor's and the creditor's.

2. Obtain the *interest coverage* ratio by dividing the total profit by the amount of interest paid. The objective of this ratio is to indicate the *vulnerability* of the lender's interest when the borrower's profits decline. In such a case, the interest payments reflect a greater portion of the profits. Note that interest coverage is considered to be more important in the constraint assessment than the asset coverage due to the more immediate need for payment.

3. An *adequate liquidity position* is a prime and positive constraint on the organization's borrowing action. Two major considerations, relative to liquidity, need mentioning and monitoring:

The *marketing (sales)* organization must select reliable customers to assure their liquidity status and their ability to meet their debt obligations. The *purchasing* organization must ensure the supplier's liquidity position to *preclude the possibility* of an interruption in the flow of material and supplies to support an organization's manufacturing process.

The primary ratios and their role in the data analysis are as follows:

$$\text{Current ratio} = \frac{\text{Current assets}}{\text{Current liabilities}}$$

This ratio provides an insight as to whether sufficient current assets are available to meet current debts outstanding.

$$\text{Quick ratio} = \frac{\text{Quick assets}}{\text{Current liabilities}}$$

This determines the status and value of the most liquid assets: cash, debtors, and short-term marketable securities. A generally accepted standard for this ratio is 2 to 1, but there may be other influencing factors, such as stock turnover, speed of collections, prospect of auxiliary capital acquisition, borrowing capacity and extension, and so on.

$$\text{Funded capital ratio} = \frac{\text{Long-term debt} + \text{Owners' equity}}{\text{Fixed assets}}$$

This ratio's objective is to determine the extent to which required fixed assets are financed by long-term commitments, both creditors' and investors'.

Assessing multi-discriminant analysis models

To date we have looked at calculating numerous individual ratios. However, researchers have shown a keen interest in trying to identify individual ratios that when used together can predict the likelihood of a company failing. The statistical technique used is called multi-discriminant analysis, MDA for short. The aim is to produce a 'Z score' for an individual company which indicates its likelihood of failure. This is calculated by multiplying the specified ratios by certain weights that the MDA model has computed and adding them together. The best-known MDA models are Altman's in the USA and Taffler's in the UK. In arriving at the model two sets of data are matched by size and industry. The sets are accounts for companies that have failed and those for going concerns. Of the numerous ratios taken from the accounts MDA identifies those that discriminate best by weighting them in order to locate an appropriate cut-off point where the chances of misclassifying a company are minimized. Altman's 1968 model contained five ratios weighted as follows.

$$Z = 1.2X_1 + 1.4X_2 + 3.3X_3 + 0.6X_4 + 1.0X_5$$

where Z is the sum or the ratios times the weights and the individual ratios are:

$$X_1 = \frac{\text{Working capital}}{\text{Total assets}}$$

$$X_2 = \frac{\text{Retained earnings}}{\text{Total assets}}$$

$$X_3 = \frac{\text{Profit before interest and tax}}{\text{Total assets}}$$

$$X_4 = \frac{\text{Market value of equity}}{\text{Book value of total debt}}$$

$$X_5 = \frac{\text{Sales}}{\text{Total assets}}$$

Altman arrived at a figure for the USA of 2.675 as being the appropriate 'cut-off' point.

Taffler's 1991 UK model for quoted companies has only four variables, which are:

$$Z = C_0 + C_1X_1 + C_2X_2 + C_3X_3 + C_4X_4$$

$$X_1 = \frac{\text{Profits before tax}}{\text{Current liabilities}} \ (53\%)$$

$$X_2 = \frac{\text{Current assets}}{\text{Total liabilities}} \ (13\%)$$

$$X_3 = \frac{\text{Current liabilities}}{\text{Total assets}} \ (18\%)$$

$$X_4 = \text{No credit interval} \ (18\%)$$

Defined as immediate assets − current liabilities/operating costs − depreciation.

C_0 to C_4 are the coefficients and the percentages in parentheses represents the ratios' contributions to the power of the model; X_1 measures profitability, X_2 working capital position, X_3 financial risk and X_4 liquidity. A Z score above 0.3 indicates a company with good long-term survival prospects while a Z score below 0.2 shows characteristics of companies that have failed in the past.

A model not restricted to certain industries is that of Robertson (1983). The five ratios and their weights are:

1. $\dfrac{\text{Sales − total assets}}{\text{Sales}} \times 0.3$

2. $\dfrac{\text{Profit before tax}}{\text{Total assets}} \times 3.0$

3. $\dfrac{\text{Current assets − total debt}}{\text{Current liabilities}} \times 0.6$

4. $\dfrac{\text{Equity − total borrowings}}{\text{Total debt}} \times 0.3$

5. $$\frac{\text{Liquid assets} - \text{bank overdraft}}{\text{Creditors}} \times 0.3$$

A low score (year on year) predicts failure.

It is important to note that the models (excluding Robertson's) are developed to operate on a single year's data, are for specific industries and that the mathematical analysis is strict.

Despite the lack of a suitable theoretical base these models, used correctly, do appear to work very well. However, behavioural factors also need to be taken into account in predicting failure and therefore a full appreciation of the wider environment is a necessary accompaniment to ratio analysis.

References

Altman, E. I. (1968) 'Financial ratios, discriminant analysis and the prediction of corporate bankruptcy' *Journal of Finance* September, pp. 589–609.

Robertson, J. (1984) 'Laker Airways: Could the collapse have been foreseen?' *Management Accounting* June, pp. 28–31.

Taffler, R. J. (1991) 'Z-scores: An approach to the recession' *Accountancy* July, pp. 95–7.

Index